Piano Freedom
for
Frustrated Pianists

Play by note, chord or ear

by
Linda Schoenfeld Spangler, M.Mus.

with
illustrations and cover art by James Cloutier

WHOLE BRAIN PIANO INSTITUTE
Eugene, Oregon

First edition, 2018
Deluxe first edition, 2019
Second edition, 2021
Deluxe second edition, 2021

Previously printed as
Chording: The Key to the Keys © 1992, Linda Spangler,
and as *Piano Freedom* (with a variety of subtitles), 1994–2016.

Whole Brain Piano Institute
2441 Emerald Street
Eugene, Oregon 97403
www.pianofreedom.com

James Cloutier drew the covers and all of the illustrations, except:
"One Man Band" (on the facing page) and "**face**" (page 6-6) by Elva Nevar
"Jim and Linda Jamming" (page xiii) by Barbara Weinstein
"Smiling Upright" (page T-2) by Dahna Solar

This book was typset using Goudy Sans, Times and Sonata fonts on the inside and Florentine and Baskerville on the covers.

Library of Congress Catalog Number: 2020915680

ISBN: 978-1-7354565-1-5

This book is dedicated to the memory of:

My friend Elva Nevar (1941–1997), who shared fine laughter, deep conversation,
and the wonderful whimsical illustrations that she drew for this book.

My father, Jack Schoenfeld (1910–1999), who gave me his gifts
of awe, reverence, diligence, kindness and love.

My mother, Lee Schoenfeld (1912–2009), who gave me her gifts
of loving people, music and teaching,
and took my Piano Freedom class in her nineties.

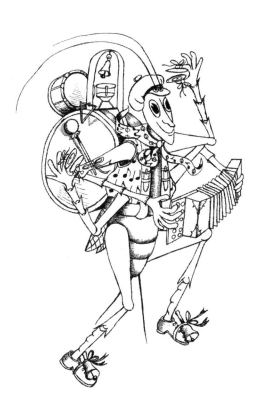

TABLE OF CONTENTS

PERSONAL PRELUDE

The inspiration for this book came after attending a fourteen-day silent meditation retreat in Northern California in the summer of 1991. Ajahn Sumedho (then the American abbot of a Buddhist monastery in England) and Ajahn Amaro (soon to be the British abbot of a Buddhist monastery in California) suggested that we meditate on the "sound of silence." Unlike the previous meditation practices I had tried, listening to the ever-present, high-pitched inner sound felt easy, joyful and profound. Finally, I had found a style of meditation that worked for me!

Driving home from the retreat on July 6, 1991, I visited Joseph, a piano teacher who gave chord-style piano workshops. As director of the University of Oregon Senior Citizens Piano Program for almost a decade, I'd just completed a National Institutes of Health research grant and was looking for a new project. Both Joseph and I were thrilled with the possibility of collaborating, but I knew that his introductory seventeen-page book would not work for every student's learning style. I offered to write my own introductory book and send it to him. Driving back to Oregon, I began thinking about how to organize the book. A week later, camped out by the Deschutes River in 100°F heat, I wrote the outline for *Piano Freedom*. Although Joseph decided to stick with his book, I continued passionately writing, testing and revising my book in the hope that frustrated pianists around the world would benefit from my labor of love.

May you enjoy ever-unfolding piano freedom.

Linda Schoenfeld Spangler
Eugene, Oregon
April 2021

INTRODUCTION

Welcome, piano pilgrim. There are many paths to piano freedom—that musical reality where you can confidently play the music you love. Which path(s) you take, will depend on your particular learning style and musical taste. Have you already visited the lovely black and white landscape enough to know that you will be returning often? If so, do what any reasonable traveler would do in order to get around easily, feel secure and communicate with fellow travelers: start learning to speak the language of music in whatever "dialect(s)" work for your learning style.

Learn the Language

Everyone intuitively understands music, but to speak the language fluently, you'll need to learn music's alphabet (notes), its vocabulary (scales, chords and progressions), and its grammar rules (harmony). Once you know the alphabet of notes, learn how those notes relate to one another to create meaningful units of melody (phrases, like phrases in prose) and harmony (chords, three or more simultaneous notes) that together form progressions (like the choir singing "amen" at the end of a phrase).

When a child learns to read, a breakthrough happens when the child stops sounding out every word letter by letter and begins to recognize words. You'll experience a similar breakthrough when you start recognizing scales, chords and progressions.

Once you've learned a scale, chord, progression or harmony rule, you can use it as a memory peg for holding onto the notes of new songs. Without these memory pegs, you're like someone trying to learn the words to a song in a foreign language. When you speak the language of music, you have a ready-made set of memory pegs for holding onto familiar chords and phrases. If a song makes sense, you can learn it efficiently, need less practice time, and delight in playing it ever after.

The language of music is vast. In this book, I've assumed that you can read notes (at least on the treble clef) well enough to strike the corresponding keys most of the time. How much of the language you need to learn, and whether you'll speak it, read it and/or write it, will depend on you. What type(s) of music do you want to learn? Which way(s) will you play? And, which learning strategies work for your learning style?

Which Way(s) Will You Play?

At the piano, you'll want to learn the necessary vocabulary to play folk, popular, jazz, classical or whatever you like. You get to choose not only the type of music that you want to learn, but also the approach you'll use to learn each new song. Notice that each of the following ways of playing uses different elements of the language.

• Play by note

 Like a classical pianist, read multiple notes on treble and bass clefs while paying attention to any musical markings—dynamics, phrasing, etc. You may already be able to happily recreate sumptuous Chopin nocturnes, sacred soul-lifting hymns and luscious Gershwin tunes. Or, you may feel frustrated because it takes so much concentration to read all the notes that you're unable to play freely and expressively.

When you understand chords and musical grammar, your intuition can assist your intellect by supplying the overview of how all the interlocking puzzle pieces fit together. Like a speed reader who sees groups of words and sentences, you'll read music faster by seeing groups of notes as chords and progressions. As you become familiar with the rules of harmony, you'll know what to expect as you read in difficult keys or confusing ledger-line territory. Learning songs will be easier once you use chordal and melodic concepts as memory pegs to hold on to the specific notes. Moreover, as your reading becomes less labor intensive, you'll have more energy to devote to interpretation and expression.

• Play by chord

 Like a jazz pianist, read a lead sheet—a treble clef melody with chord symbols above it and lyrics below. Flesh out the melody and harmony, adding fills, frills and whatever else suits your fancy. Does reading multiple notes on treble and bass clefs seem tedious or overwhelming? If so, you may prefer reading uncluttered lead sheets.

Playing by chord may feel like the perfect blend of intellect and intuition. Reading the melody uses your intellect, while interpreting the chord symbols uses your intuitive, patterning expertise. In this book, you'll learn enough chords to try out this potentially liberating way to play.

• Play by ear

 Like many folk pianists, start with an aural memory of something you've heard, seen or imagined. Play whatever sounds good to you. When asked why he never learned to read music, jazz great Erroll Garner replied, "Hell, man, nobody can hear you read." At the other end of the spectrum from playing by note, playing by ear can be totally intuitive. Or, if you learn chords and the rules of harmony, playing by ear can be a collaboration between your intellect and intuition.

Contrary to popular opinion, you can learn to play by ear, even if you're not an Erroll Garner or a Ray Charles. With the desire and enough tinkering time, you can develop your intuition's innate ability to pick out melodies, just as some people develop their intellect's ability to read melodies. If you've been blessed at birth with a great ear, please nourish your gift by learning some chords and concepts.

When you play by note, chord or ear, you may also want to improvise and/or play with people.

• Improvise

 Like jazz, blues, country, rock and New Age pianists (or classical pianists who get lost), start with something you've read, discovered or imagined, then improvise your own version of it. When you improvise, you rely primarily on your intuition, perhaps with some help from your intellect. You can embroider familiar melodies, create new melodies over a given chord progression or make up entirely new songs. If you already enjoy doodling at the keyboard, you've probably found some things that sound good. Hopefully, each musical shape, pattern and concept you learn will kick-start your creativity in new and exciting ways.

• Play with people

 Like members of ensembles, bands and orchestras, start in any of the above ways to make music with friends and family. Accompany singers, play duets with fellow pianists, or jam with other musicians who share your musical interests. After all your practice in isolation, treat yourself to the thrill of being in harmony with people to create something that's more than the sum of its parts.

If you play by note, find a friend who also reads music and dive into the vast duet repertoire. If you play by chord or ear, seek out people who enjoy the same kinds of music as you do. Start out simply, then gradually tackle more complicated songs. Last but not least, invite your friends and family to sing along while you play. While performing *for* people can be stressful, playing *with* people is usually just plain fun.

Finding Your Learning Style

Imagine the instructions for learning a piece are being broadcast on a number of channels. On which channels do you usually get the best reception—aural, visual, kinesthetic and/or analytic channels?

Aural

How does the music sound?

Develop your ear to identify intervals, chords & progressions.

Major triads sound happy and bright, like singing **Michael, Row** *the boat ashore...*

Visual

How does the music look on the staff and/or keyboard?

Develop the ability to recognize notes, intervals, chords & progressions on the staff and/or keyboard.

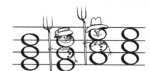

Triads look like snow people standing on the staff.

Kinesthetic

How does the music feel in your fingers and body?

Practice playing scales, intervals, chords & progressions with eyes open, then with eyes closed.

For each new piece, pencil in the fingerings you'll use and helpful choreographic reminders.

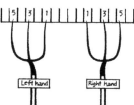

Shaping your hand like a pitch-fork, grab every other white key.

Analytic

How do the melody & harmony together create a coherent structure?

Learn music's underlying concepts and patterns.

Analyze a new piece and make a cheat sheet showing the structure and whatever information you find helpful.

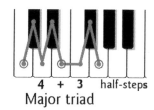

4 + 3 half-steps
Major triad

Experiment to find the combination of learning channels that works best for you.

♪ *Debbie, a bright, caring pediatrician, reads classical music (visual), pencils in the fingerings (kinesthetic) and labels the chords (analytic). Debbie finds reading relaxing and absorbing.*

♪ *Dale, a successful businessman and avid ballroom dancer, only learns familiar songs (aural), because he doesn't read music. Instead, he pencils in fingerings on a lead sheet, uses a keyboard diagram to map chord changes and practices a lot (kinesthetic). Dale looks at his lead sheet (visual) until he can play the song by heart. His repertoire includes about twenty songs.*

♪ *Rick, a tango teacher, guitarist and retired programmer, has learned to read music by using a music notation software (analytic). For each new song, he notates and fingers it (kinesthetic), looks at his arrangement on the staff (visual), then hits the play button to hear it (aural). After cycling through this procedure for some time, he can play the song by memory.*

The Structure of this Book

Think of *Piano Freedom* as a travel guide. Its itinerary will efficiently route you from one musical concept or learning strategy to another. Its drills and chapter reviews will help you to teach the language of music to your fingers, ears, eyes and mind. Its optional excursions will give you opportunities to play by note, play by chord, play by ear, improvise and play with people. Choose the thrills that suit your interests (classical, popular, hymns, jazz and/or blues) and learning style (aural, visual, kinesthetic and/or analytic).

ITINERARY

1. Visit the black keys, where any combination of notes will sound good.

2. Move down to the white keys, play scales, and find out what to do in case of a clash.

3. Try out triads and discover the acoustic magic of their overtones.

4. (Re)learn the fine art of fingering and start collecting chord voicings.

5. Measure distance in intervals to improve your sight-reading and ear-playing.

6. Meet the cast of chords, investigate inversions and say, "Viva closest position voicings!"

7. Learn about chord recycling, musical relativity, the blues and seventh chords.

8. Discover how it's the same, but different, in any key.

DRILLS

Install memory pegs for holding on to groups of notes by drilling music's basic shapes and patterns. The more memory pegs you have, the easier learning new pieces will be.

CHAPTER REVIEWS

Make sure you understand each new concept by doing the chapter reviews. Then, check your answers in the Appendix to decide whether to continue on or go back and review.

THRILLS
Play what excites and delights you!

Improvise   *By ear*   *By chord*   *By note*   *With people*

How to Use this Book

"Follow your bliss."

Joseph Campbell

Some travelers enjoy following step-by-step itineraries, while others prefer to passionately plunge into whatever adventures beckon them. To live out your piano dreams, you'll need to learn the language of music step by step *and* passionately plunge into songs. How you combine the two will depend on your innate temperament and your commitment to living out your piano dreams.

Are you a step-by-stepper?

Do you enjoy making step-by-step progress? Do you want to be an efficient learner? Do you want to understand why a certain scale, chord or song sounds the way it does? If so, gradually learn the underlying elements of music while learning songs that are at (or slightly above) your level of facility. When you drill scales, chords and progressions, you're installing memory pegs that will serve as a scaffolding on which to "build" songs. The more memory pegs you have, the easier learning new songs will be and the fewer time-consuming workarounds you'll need. If you just play pieces, but never work on the underlying skills, each new piece will take a very long time.

♪ *Pam, fascinated with learning the language of music, studied each new concept, then did every drill and exercise. Often, at the beginning of class, she'd ask a question which turned out to be the subject of that day's lesson. Although she played lots of* Piano Freedom's *songs, she didn't go deeply into any one song until six months later. Then, having laid a strong foundation, Pam started passionately plunging into songs that excited her.*

♪ *Peter is a guitarist and singer/songwriter who played tuba in his high school band. He wanted to pick up some piano skills so he could accompany himself singing blues, folk and Irish songs. By drilling all the chords in all the keys and taking all the fast lanes, Peter was performing on keyboard within two years. A few years later, he bought a baby grand piano and started learning pieces by Mozart and other beloved classical masters.*

Building a Dog House

A little boy was building a doghouse out of two-by-fours. When his grandmother noticed that he'd started with the roof, she asked,

"Shouldn't you be putting down the foundation first?"

"I'll worry about that when I get to it," he replied.

An hour later, the little boy walked into the house saying,

"I've gotten there and now I'm worried."

Are you a passionate plunger?

Do you often long to play some particularly fabulous song? Do you find it boring to work on something unless you really love it? While step-by-steppers find the learning process fascinating, passionate plungers don't care how they learn a song, as long as it's the right song. They want to memorize the song and play it passionately ever after, each time savoring the richness of their aural, kinesthetic, emotional experience.

If you are a passionate plunger, feel free to nourish your musical hunger by occasionally jumping into songs that are not on the itinerary. Before tackling each song, ask yourself whether the amount of time needed to learn it now would be worth it. While an occasional super-effort may be stimulating, one huge super-effort after another will probably lead to burnout.

♪ *Mark's concert pianist mother taught him to read music and his opera singer father taught him to play jazz tunes by ear. He never liked reading music, but played beautifully by ear in the key of F. After six weeks of step-by-step lessons, Mark told me he had a gig—would I help him learn to play and sing three Ray Charles songs? I put all the songs in the key of F, briefly explained the underlying concepts and showed him how to play the songs with smooth-sounding voicings. Six weeks later, after successfully performing the songs, Mark went back to learning chords and concepts until going off on his next musical binge—the blues. A few years later, he started singing with the chorus in the local opera company*

♪ *My mother skipped the drills entirely. At 90, Mom wasn't going to spend time doing drills to help her future piano life! A retired math teacher, Mom learned the formulas and used them to figure out whatever chords she needed. Three years later, after playing fake book songs and classical pieces (but no drills), she knew the basic chords in most positions. She stopped taking my class and announced that she would no longer practice—she would only play. Mom played (and sang with her choral group) until the week that she died at 96 ½.*

Are you a committed musician?

Treat yourself as you would a talented child. Nourish your passion for music by mastering pieces you love and teaching the language of music to your fingers, ears, eyes and brain. To become the best musician you can be, develop your strengths and work on your weaknesses!

♪ *My husband is a passionate plunger, and I'm a step-by-stepper. Before we met, Jim had played lead guitar in rock 'n' roll bands; I'd performed in classical and jazz trios. Early in our marriage, I was amazed that he could fluently play with other musicians, learn songs off the radio and remember the bass lines of old rock tunes. He was amazed that I could sight read songs I'd never heard, but couldn't play my own compositions without reading the music. He vowed to learn to read music and chord symbols; I vowed to memorize songs, especially my own. Now, we can both play by chord, note and ear. Still, when we start learning a new song, I look at the music, pencil in fingerings and figure out the structure. Jim often says, "Linda, will you play it for me, so I can hear how it goes?"*

Bon Voyage!

Remember, you're in the driver's seat. Personalize your piano journey to suit your needs and interests. Tune in to the channels that suit your learning style. If you'd like to chronicle your journey, keep a journal. If you want company, invite a friend along. If you want to see and hear a piece of music, visit the Internet or use a smart phone to record someone playing it. To learn the language of music step by step, follow the itinerary—tour the basic concepts, answer the chapter review questions, do the drills and take whichever optional excursions appeal to you. Go at your own pace. (To speed up your learning, take some of the "fast lanes." To slow down the pace, spend more time on each chapter.) When you feel like passionately plunging into a song, ask yourself, "Would learning this song now be a good investment of my time and energy?" If the song seems too difficult for now, set it aside. If you decide to tackle the song, learn it as efficiently as possible by following the suggestions in this book.

Most importantly, before setting out on your *Piano Freedom* journey, make a commitment to practice. Rather than wildly hoping that this will be a lifetime commitment, vow to practice regularly for just one month. At the end of the month (or whenever you fall off the practice bandwagon), renew your commitment to reflect what's going on in your life. Rather than frustrating yourself and eventually quitting because you can't squeeze in your ultimate dream of an hour a day, make a realistic commitment that you can fulfill—perhaps twenty minutes a day for five days a week, or five minutes a day every day. The hardest part will be getting yourself to the piano. Once you're there, that old piano magic will take over and you'll probably play longer. Like my mother in her nineties, if you sit down to play for twenty minutes before dinner, an hour later you may find that you're late for dinner. This book will teach you how to learn efficiently. Practice regularly and you'll be on your way to living out your piano dreams.

*"Until one is committed, there is hesitancy, the chance to draw back, always ineffectiveness ...
There is one elementary truth the ignorance of which kills countless ideas and splendid plans:
that the moment one definitely commits oneself, then Providence moves too ...
Whatever you can do or dream you can, begin it.
Boldness has genius, power and magic in it. Begin it now."*
Johann Wolfgang von Goethe

ACKNOWLEDGMENTS

Blessings to my meditation teachers—Ajahn Sumedho, who taught me to tune into the sound of silence, out of which this book emerged, and Ajahn Amaro, who guided me to let go and let the book unfold. My god-daughter, flutist and music teacher Terese Wagner, M.Ed., gave me editorial advice and moral support throughout. Suzanne Griffin, Elizabeth Lyons, Karen Deora, Nancy "Sam" Arnold, Dr. Cin Chubb, Lisa Marie DiVincent and Dr. Susan Hardwick edited early drafts. My colleagues at the Oregon Music Teachers Association—Dr. Claire Wachter, Eularee Smith, Ellen McQuilkin and Jane Young—edited later drafts. Copy editors Beth Kodama (in 2003) and Adele Berlinski (in 2005) fastidiously checked the details. Many students offered corrections, feedback and quotable quips. Cindy Armstrong, my marketing consultant, listened to the ongoing saga of the book; Jean Names, my business coach, helped me organize my priorities; and Grace Given, my secretary/angel, typed many drafts, cheering me on with jokes and wise words.

Thanks to my pedagogy mentor, Doris Allen (and vicariously, her mentor Frances Clark) and my piano teachers—Rodd Raffell, Jerome Diamond, Emily Van der Poole, Betty Phillips, Dr. Matthew Cooper, Ed Kammerer, W. A. Matthieu, Joan Benson, Dr. Dean Kramer, Victor Steinhardt, Art Lande, Monte Tubb, Bill Sabol and Gary Versace. My gratitude to my students, who gave me the pleasure of sharing so much great music and the motivation to keep finding new ways to teach.

Carol Lindstrom, a graphic artist in Portland, heard about *Piano Freedom* on our kayak trips in Eastern Oregon. She provided expert design advice and created the two-page "Twelve Major and Twelve Minor Triads" chart. Barbara Weinstein sketched many portraits of Jim and I jamming with our friends. Elva Nevar drew wonderfully whimsical illustrations until she died of cancer in 1997. James Cloutier stepped in as illustrator in 2002. He kept Elva's radiant "*fac*e" self-portrait and "one-man band," as well as Dahna Solar's "smiling upright." James gradually added an updated cast of chords and many new drawings. In 2007, graphic artist Tara Kemp, a talented guitarist, accordionist, and singer-songwriter, began laying out the book. She designed the drills pages and the "note finder."

In 2009, my mother died, my husband suffered a stroke and my own health deteriorated. Work on the book came to a standstill until 2012, when Carole Carlson, a fellow perfectionist teacher and kindred spirit, offered to be my editor—helping me save the good parts and throw out the unnecessary. To make the correction process more efficient, Carole urged me to learn the layout program. My computer consultant, Katsu Shibata, and Alexis Garrett, a graphic designer, began teaching me *InDesign*. My friend Lynn Sabol, an experienced graphic artist with a great eye, fixed and beautified what I couldn't. When Lynn got a demanding new job, she recommended a friend. Christine West, a graphic artist, frustrated pianist and beloved collaborator, created the coda's "wheels," "brad" & "paper clips," proofread and helped me bring this book to completion.

While vacationing in San Luis Obispo, California in 2013, I met Barbara Lees, a cello and piano teacher who loved my book. Barbara's enthusiasm, keen pedagogical sense and joyful musicality have made her a fabulous editor and soul sister. In 2014, James Cloutier envisioned and drew the "flying piano" cover. Finally, my editors—Dr. George Jones, Dr. Betsy Parker, Tracy Ilene Miller, Nancy Hopps and Terese Wagner—helped send *Piano Freedom* out into the world. Yay, team!

A special thanks to my husband and bass player, Jim Christian, who kept me grounded with his earthy wisdom, lightened me up with his adorable silliness and made beautiful music with me for all these years.

PART I

WELCOME TO PIANOLAND

THE BLACK KEY PENTATONIC PLAYGROUND

Long, long ago, people began to sing songs and play instruments. They celebrated their joys, grieved their losses, soothed their babies and praised their gods with music. Intuitively, all over the world, in every ancient civilization, people began with the same five-tone *pentatonic scale*.

The ancient Chinese believed that the sacred power of music influences people's bodies, emotions and morals. Emperors of new dynasties sent inspectors across the land to make sure that all the instruments were tuned the same way! While most cultures eventually adopted bigger and more dissonant scales, the Chinese still primarily use the pentatonic scale. To hear a pentatonic scale, simply play up five consecutive black keys with either hand's five fingers. (In piano lingo, the thumbs are *1*'s.) For instance:

Left hand

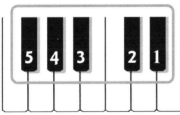

Right hand

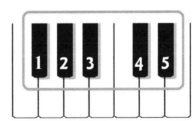

The often-shunned black keys are actually a safe pentatonic playground.

Play freely without fear of ugly clashes. You can slide down the black keys, see-saw between groups of two's and three's, swing back and forth between high and low black keys, or do whatever you want to do. Whether you scramble the notes to make *melodies*, or play them simultaneously to create *harmonies*, you'll never hit a wrong note when you use the no-fail pentatonic scale.

Pentatonic à la Mode

> *"One of the most striking phenomena of music is the fact that, throughout its evolution—in non-Western cultures, in Gregorian chant, and in harmonized music—practically every single piece gives preference to one tone ... making this the tonal center to which all other tones are related."*
>
> Harvard Dictionary of Music

Any of the pentatonic scale's five tones can serve as the main tone—the *tonal center* (✱)—the home base where a melody sometimes starts, often returns and always ends. Consequently, there are five *modes* of the pentatonic scale, each with its own distinctive mood, feel and look.

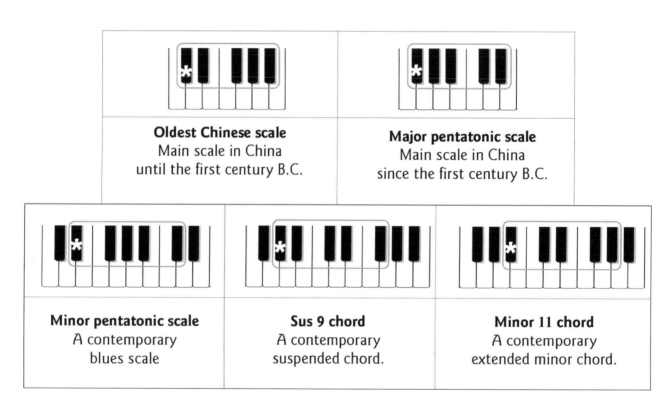

Oldest Chinese scale
Main scale in China
until the first century B.C.

Major pentatonic scale
Main scale in China
since the first century B.C.

Minor pentatonic scale
A contemporary
blues scale

Sus 9 chord
A contemporary
suspended chord.

Minor 11 chord
A contemporary
extended minor chord.

To sample each five-note pentatonic position:

- **Scale**

  Play up and down the pattern starting on the starred (✱) tonal center.

- **Melody**

  Play the notes in any order, returning often and eventually ending on the tonal center.

- **Harmony**

  Play a *chord*—three or more simultaneous notes—that starts on the tonal center.

Black Key Beauty

To experience a sense of freedom at the piano, play just on the black keys.
Pick any of the five tones to be the tonal center on which you begin and end.

• **With one hand at a time, have a conversation between your hands.**

1. Say something with one hand, then echo or respond with the other.

2. As you "talk," move your hands closer together or further apart.

3. Express contrasting moods in each hand:

Happy — Sad
Fast — Slow
Walking — Waltzing
High — Low
Lost — Found

• **With both hands together, experiment with different musical textures.**

4. Play the same melody (or just the same rhythm) in each hand.

5. While repeating a note (or a short pattern) in one hand, play a melody in the other.

6. Play two or more notes at a time in one hand, and one note at a time in the other.

7. Play two or more notes at a time in each hand.

8. As you play, hold down the right pedal for a long or short series of notes.

9. Play along with a metronome, drum machine or grandfather's clock.

DRILL 1: PENTATONIC CROSSOVERS

Play pentatonic scales, crossing hand over hand up the black keys. Like a blind piano player, learn to "read" black-key Braille with your eyes closed and ears open. Experiment with all five modes, starting with the most common—major pentatonic.

- **Play up the black keys starting on the lowest tonal center (✱).**

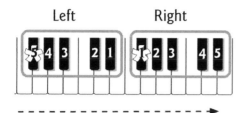

"There's a somebody" (... Someone to watch over me.)
"In a sentimen-" (tal mood ...)
The opening guitar riff for *My Girl*

- **Cross hand over hand up the keyboard.**

Crossing left over right, continue on for two or more *octaves*. To end, cross your left pointer *(2)* over to land on a tonal center (✱). Enjoy the ancient scale as it passes through time and space.

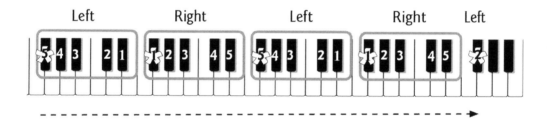

Basic Technique Guidelines

1. **Posture.** Center yourself at middle *c*, and sit upright with your arms level.
2. **Wrists.** Keep your wrists level and relaxed.
3. **Fingers curved.** Keep your fingers curved at every joint and your thumbs loosely curved towards the fingers.
4. **Pads.** Play the keys with the fleshy pads of your fingers and the sides of your thumbs.
5. **Poised.** Keep your fingers poised over the keys, not letting them fly up.
6. **Firm.** Keep your fingers firm, not allowing them to collapse.
7. **Be prepared.** For smooth crossovers, as one hand plays the last note of its group, start crossing it over (or under) while the other hand begins to play.

Each time you do a drill, turn it into a thrill.

Thrills with All-Black Pentatonic Scales

Choose the thrills that suit your interests and skill level.

1. **Crossover Your Own Way.** Anything goes on the black keys! Experiment with two notes at a time, two hands at a time, melodic curlicues or whatever sounds good to you.

2. **Black Key Blues**, page 1-6. Imagine that you're the piano player in a smoky bar room, wailing on the minor pentatonic blues scale. Start and end on the tonal center (✳), first in this position, then out of any of the other positions.

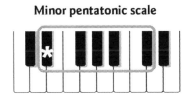

Minor pentatonic scale

3. *Short'nin' Bread.* Starting on the tonal center (✳), play the verse of this peppy major pentatonic song (*"Mammy's little baby loves short'nin' ..."*). For sound advice on working out ear tunes, see page 1-7.

Major pentatonic scale

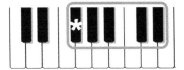

4. **Add Pentatonic Endings.** As a fancy final flourish or fill-in, play a pentatonic crossover that starts and ends on the song's tonal center. End *Short'nin' Bread* (#3) with a sweet major pentatonic crossover and *Black Key Blues* (#2) with a slinky minor pentatonic crossover.

5. **Black Key Jam**, page 1-8. Get together with a friend and play on just the black keys.

Black Key Blues

With your imaginary dark glasses and a bluesy attitude, use the top of the two blacks as the tonal center (✱). Stay cool!

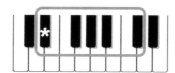

- **Left hand**

  With a slow, steady pulse, keep repeating the tonal center. Hear and feel the *beat*, the musical "heart beat" of your song. In blues songs, the *quarter note* usually gets the beat:

  ♩   ♩   ♩   ♩   ♩   ♩   ♩   ♩

- **Right hand**

  Play an all-black melody that starts, often returns, and eventually ends on the tonal center (✱). Think of a blues song you know and adapt its rhythm and attitude

Black Key Melodies

If you've always wished you could play by ear, now's your chance. You can play each of the pentatonic songs listed below on just the black keys.

To ear out a melody:

1. Sing and play the circled first note (○).

2. Sing the next note, listening for whether it goes up, goes down, or stays the same; then find that note on the piano. (Remember, this is the trial-and-error method. If at first you don't succeed, trial, trial again.)

3. Keep repeating step 2 for a manageable learning chunk—a few notes, a few measures or a whole phrase. Next, decide how you'll finger the chunk and what memory pegs you'll use to remember trouble spots. Finally, practice the chunk until you can play it correctly with consistent fingering and no pauses.

4. Follow the same procedure for the remaining chunks, linking each newly learned chunk to the previously learned chunk(s) until you've worked out the entire song.

Song	First Note
Oh, Susannah (Verse only: "Oh, I come from Alabama ... ") *Old MacDonald* *Rain, Rain* ("It's raining, it's pouring ...") *Short'nin' Bread*	
Canoe Song ("My paddle's clean and bright ...") *Do You Know the Way to San Jose* (first two phrases) *Merrily We Roll Along* *Nobody Knows the Trouble I've Seen* *Swing Low*	
Amazing Grace *Auld Lang Syne* *Farmer in the Dell* *Jesus Loves Me, This I Know* *Riddle Song* ("I gave my love a cherry ...") *Ring Around the Rosy* *Tom Dooley*	
Wayfaring Stranger	

Unless Amadeus is your middle name, it will probably take some time to find the right notes, and even more time to remember what you've already worked out. Fortunately, with patience and persistence, your ear playing will steadily improve.

Black Key Jam

When I meet someone who wants to improvise, I usually invite them to play along with me on the black keys. As the music takes us where it wants to go, we're soon grinning with pleasure, communicating non-verbally and making beautiful music together. Next time someone is interested in your improvising, invite him or her to play on the black keys with you.

- **Beginning**

  The person on the left starts by setting up a strongly rhythmic musical texture. The persoerson on the right improvises a melody that keeps in the rhythmic groove.

- **Middle**

  Play around with melody and musical texture. Like any relationship, you'll undoubtedly go in and out of sync. Just stay anchored on the beat and keep listening to each other.

- **End**

  Find a good place to end. Stay alert so you notice the energy winding down or hear a potentially dramatic climax. Then, either end together without saying anything, or say, "Let's bring it to a close," and quickly find a stopping point.

My Clock Chimed Nine

When I teach Piano Freedom *classes, I end the first session with Black Key Jam. First, I ask the students to select a sound on their electric keyboard. "I will start playing, then each of you can decide when to come in and what to contribute to the continually changing musical tapestry. By listening carefully to one another, we will know when it's time to end."*

One evening, I lit candles and turned off the lights. As our playing began, the connection among us seemed magical. The blend of sounds kept shifting, with a guitar, horn or choir occasionally emerging from the thick, multi-layered texture. Just when we were winding down, my grandfather's clock chimed nine. We all stopped playing and laughed at the perfect timing. Someone asked, "What note is that chime?" We all scrambled to find the note on our keyboards. Having never believed that I have a good ear, I was happily surprised to be the first to identify the note (e flat), the tonal center of my favorite key (E♭ major).

Is it time to revisit the black keys?

After a tiring day, relax with some intuitive meandering. The possibilities, like your own potential, are unlimited. Get yourself in the mood, perhaps closing your eyes, sipping your favorite beverage or lighting some candles. Finally, luxuriate in the feeling of freedom as you create your own black key beauty.

CHAPTER 1 REVIEW

To make sure that you've understood the material in this chapter, answer the following questions. (To check your answers, see the Appendix, page T-33.)

1. When you travel straight up the black keys, you're playing a
   _____ scale.

2. A chord is: (Circle the correct answer.)

   a. What you cut when you left your first piano teacher.

   b. Three or more notes played together.

   c. The bass "strings" of the piano, when made out of twine.

3. The tonal center is the: (Circle all correct answers.)

   a. Place where tones hang out.

   b. Main tone in a song.

   c. Tone that plays out in center field.

   d. Place where a tune almost always ends.

   e. Middle of the scale.

4. Modes are: (Circle the correct answer.)

   a. Means of transportation.

   b. Types of musical ice cream.

   c. Rearrangements of scales that use any of the notes as home base.

   d. Parts of a commode.

5. The word pentatonic could describe: (Circle all correct answers.)

   a. A five-note scale.

   b. A five-ingredient gin and tonic.

   c. China's most ancient scale.

   d. The Pentagon worker who sets the tone for the day.

   e. The scale played on just black keys.

When you feel comfortable
with this chapter,
go on to **Chapter 2.**

CHAPTER 2
SCALE THE HIGHS AND LOWS

When you come down from the black keys to play on the white keys, beware of a clash landing. Anyone can play freely on the black keys without understanding why the magic works. However, to play freely on the white keys, you need to avoid clashes by understanding the underlying *scale* (Greek *skala*, "steps") and/or know how to recover from a sudden clash.

First used by the ancient Greeks, the seven-tone *diatonic* (Greek *diatonikos*, "through the tones") scale cycles through all seven letters of the musical alphabet (*a b c d e f g*). When you step up the white keys from *c* to shining *c*, you are hearing the western world's most popular scale. The C major scale starts on the tonal center *c* (✱), uses two different size steps (*half-steps* and *whole-steps*), and ends on the tonal center an octave higher.

- **Half-step**

  Go from a note to its nearest white or black neighbor, like *e* to *f*. Simultaneously playing two notes a half-step apart sounds piercingly dissonant, like the buzzing of an obnoxious mosquito. (When you step up the black keys to play pentatonic scales, there are always intervening white keys; hence, no spicy half-steps.)

- **Whole-step**

  Bypass the nearest neighbor to land two half-steps away, like *f* to *g*. Simultaneously playing notes a whole-step apart sounds mildly dissonant, like the beginning of *Chopsticks*.

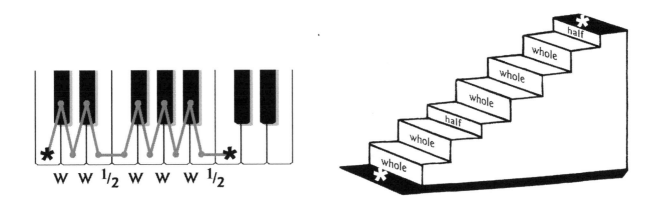

The major scale uses whole-steps (W) and half-steps (1/2)

The Sound of Major

In eleventh century Italy, a Benedictine choir director wanted to help his singers learn songs easily. First, Guido d'Arezzo invented the *staff* to help singers see the pattern of melodies. Then, noticing that the first six lines of a familiar hymn stepped up the major scale, Guido taught singers to use the first syllable of each line *(ut re mi fa so la)* as memory pegs for holding on to the sound of the scale tones. By the time Rodger's and Hammerstein's *The Sound of Music* came out in 1965, *ut* had become *do*, and *ti* had been added. Julie Andrews did a great job of teaching the *solfege* syllables to new generations of singers. To remember the sound of a major scale, just sing *do re mi fa sol la ti do*, as in "Doe, a deer, a female deer, ray, a drop of golden sun …"

Here's how the C major scale looks and sounds on the *treble clef*, as it steps up from *do*, the tonal center (✱) on *middle c* (ⓜ) to *do*, the tonal center on the next *c*.

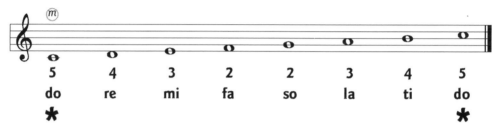

The question we need to ask as pianists is, "How will I finger this scale?"

The Thumbless, Two-handed Scale Fingering

Tetrachords

For a fascinating, physically easy option, split the eight-note scale between your hands. The ancient Greeks called each four-note pattern a *tetrachord*, literally meaning "four strings." In the case of a major scale, both tetrachords are tuned to the same whole-whole-half pattern.

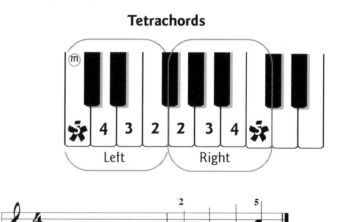

Putting your pinkies (5's) on octave apart *c*'s, play the major scale using your fingers, but not your thumbs.

The *time signature* tells you the *meter*, the recurring pattern of accents that invites you to walk, waltz or whatever.

- In (**4**/4), expect 4 beats in each box-like *measure*.
- Give the *quarter note* (♩ = 1/**4**) one beat.
- Accent the first beat of every measure.

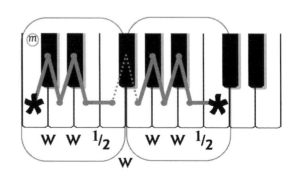

Look, Ma, Both Hands!

- **Parallel motion**

    Go in the same direction with each hand, starting with each hand's bottom finger (LH 5, RH 2). How does *parallel* motion sound, feel and look?

- **Contrary motion**

    Go in opposite directions, starting on your pinkies (5's) and using the same fingers throughout (5's, 4's, 3's, 2's, 1's). How does *contrary* motion sound, feel and look?

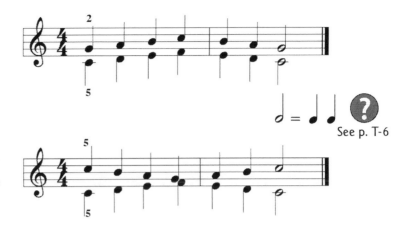

See p. T-6

Chopsticks

While experimenting with the C major scale, the sixteen-year-old sister of a music publisher came up with a delightfully clashy composition. In 1887, Euphemia Allen's *The Celebrated Chop Waltz*, published under the pseudonymn Arthur de Lulli, quickly became an international favorite. To learn what we now call *Chopsticks*:

- Use the two-handed fingering, starting with your left hand stepping down: 2's, 3's, 4's, 5's.

- Play in contrary motion, except the circled measures: 2's, (3-2), 4's, 5's ...

- Accent the first beat of each three-beat measure (**oom**-pah-pah) for this **3**/4 time waltz.

- Play through to the *first ending* ([1.). Heeding the *repeat sign* (:||), repeat the song from the beginning, but this time, skip the first ending and jump to the *second ending* ([2.).

- Give the *dotted quarter note* (♩.) three beats.

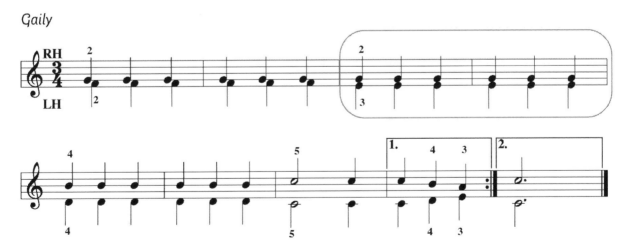

Euphemia suggests you imitate the chopping from which this waltz gets its name by turning both hands sideways (little fingers lowest). Does it seem harder without the contrary motion finger memory?

The Acoustics of Consonance

As he walked by a blacksmith's shop in sixth century B.C. Greece, Pythagoras heard the sounds of hammers striking anvils. The mathematician wondered why some combinations of tones sounded *consonant* (pleasing) together. To investigate the consonant *intervals*, he started experimenting with a monochord, an ancient one-stringed instrument with a moveable bridge.

Pythagoras discovered that he could produce consonant intervals by dividing the vibrating string into small integer ratios. For instance, fretting (holding down) a string halfway up, an *octave* will sound (first to *eighth* scale tone); fretting a string one-third of the way up, a *fifth* will sound (first to *fifth*). Historically, the earliest Gregorian chants (circa 600 A.D.) only used unisons and octaves. Centuries later, choirs started harmonizing with fifths and *fourths*. Sometime around the Renaissance (1450-1600), musicians began their long love affair with the *third*.

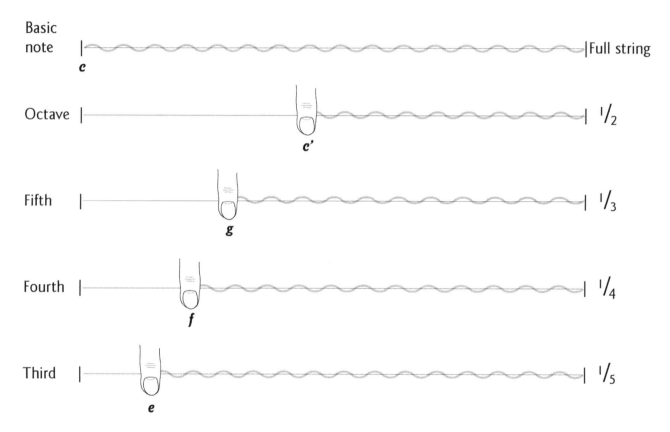

Though not a musician himself, Pythagoras was awed by the mathematics of music. He founded a mystical school, where he taught the "Pythagoreans" that the audible tones are a reflection of the inaudible music of the spheres. His research into acoustics and the overtone series created a scientific basis for tuning instruments. Mystics and math geeks will want to Google this guy.

Harmonizing with Consonant Intervals in the Key of C Major

Like painters using palettes of colors, pianists use palettes of notes. In the *key of C major*, the basic palette contains the seven tones of the C major scale in any octave, with *c* the tonal center (✱). For this *grand staff* arrangement of *Frère Jacques:* play the treble clef (𝄞) melody with your right hand and the *bass clef* (𝄢) accompaniment with your left hand.

See p. T-20

See p. T-6

Frère Jacques

Moderately

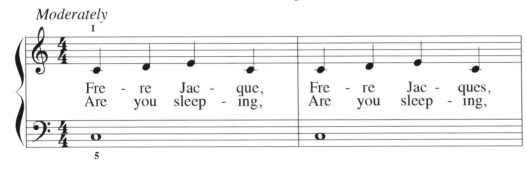

Fre - re   Jac - que,   Fre - re   Jac - ques,
Are   you   sleep - ing,   Are   you   sleep - ing,

Basic note *(c)*

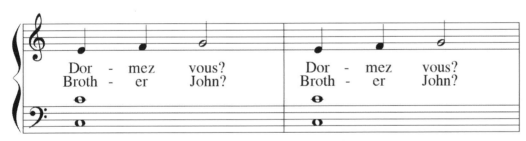

Dor - mez   vous?   Dor - mez   vous?
Broth - er   John?   Broth - er   John?

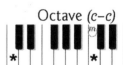

Octave *(c–c)*

Son -ne -les ma - ti - nes!   Son -ne les ma - ti - nes!
Morn -ing bells are ring - ing!   Morn- ing bells are ring - ing!

Fifth *(c–g)*

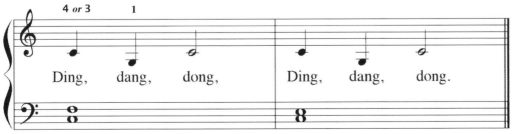

Ding,   dang,   dong,   Ding,   dang,   dong.

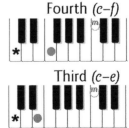

Fourth *(c–f)*

Third *(c–e)*

How to Avoid Clash

While playing *e* & *f* or *b* & *c* together (notes a half-step apart) sounds spicy, playing *f* & *b* together sounds downright ugly. Medieval theorists called the combination of the fourth and seventh scale tones the *diabolus in musica* ("devil in music") and banned its use! To find a major scale's pretty pentatonic notes, just omit the *diabolus*: the fourth and seventh.

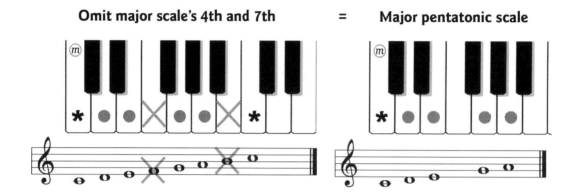

Pretty C Major Pentatonic

To avoid a clash, play only pentatonic notes. Here, your left hand repeatedly plays a consonant *c*–*g* fifth.

In Case of a Clash

Toward the end of the Renaissance, Western musicians discovered that a little bit of dissonance could be very exciting. Since then, the principle of tension/resolution has dominated our harmony. If clash happens, just do what *Chopsticks* does:

- Repeat the offending notes, making them part of the musical tapestry; and/or
- Move by steps until the tension resolves.

Salvation's just a step away.

How to Add a Dash of Clash

Artists can pep up their palettes by adding a dash of neon blue or glittery gold. Similarly, pianists can add pizzazz to C's basic all-white palette by including one or more black keys. When the palette is extended to include a more exotic note color, you'll see an *accidental* posted in front of that note on the staff. The *flat* (♭) or *sharp* (♯) affects that particular note throughout that particular measure, unless it is cancelled by a natural (♮). (You see "♭*d*," but you say "*d*♭.") For instance:

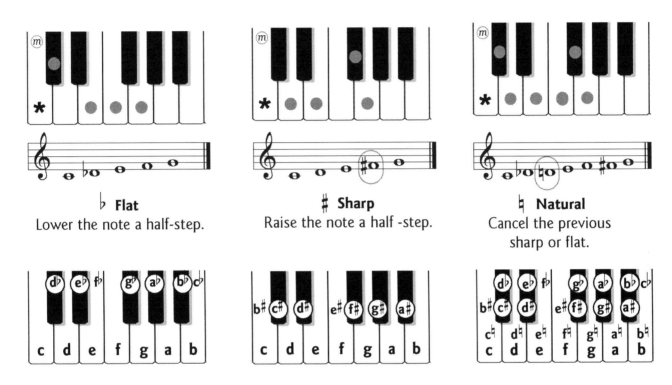

♭ Flat
Lower the note a half-step.

♯ Sharp
Raise the note a half-step.

♮ Natural
Cancel the previous
sharp or flat.

Accidentals Are Just a Step Away

Using *c* as the tonal center, make up melodies that include both white and black keys. In your left hand, repeat *c-g* fifths and relish the spicy *non-diatonic* (accidentals-added) sound.

Brashly

To avoid musical accidents, pay attention to the accidentals.

DRILL 2: C MAJOR SCALE

2

Play the C major scale *(c d e f g a b c)* until it sounds smooth and feels automatic.

• Play the left hand ascending.

Go up the C major *five-finger pattern* (5 4 3 2 1 on *c d e f g*), then cross over to finger the remaining three notes (3 2 1 on *a b c*). To make these fingering groups more visually obvious, highlight them with two different colors here and elsewhere.

LH

Fingers cross over. As the thumb plays *g*, cross 3 and 2 over as a unit, so each finger lands poised in readiness over its note.

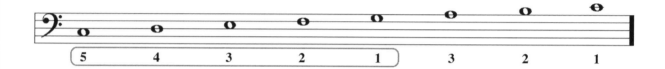

• Play hands in contrary motion toward one another.

The right hand descending mirrors the left hand ascending. You're using the same fingers, but playing different notes.

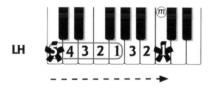

LH

do re mi fa sol la ti do

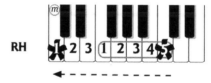

RH

"Joy to the world, the Lord is come."

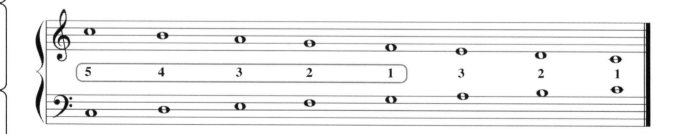

• Play the right hand ascending.

After learning the right hand descending, (5 4 3 2 1 3 2 1), reverse the fingering to ascend (1 2 3 1 2 3 4 5). Go up the group of three (1 2 3 on *c d e*), then cross the thumb under to play 1 2 3 4 5 on *f g a b c*.

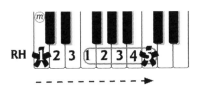

Thumb crosses under. After the thumb plays *c*, start gradually crossing it under 2 and 3 until it lands gracefully on *f*. As the thumb plays *f*, cross 2, 3, 4 and 5 over as a unit, with each finger landing poised in readiness over its note.

• Play hands in contrary motion away from one another.

The left hand descending mirrors the right hand ascending. Alternate between contrary motion toward and away.

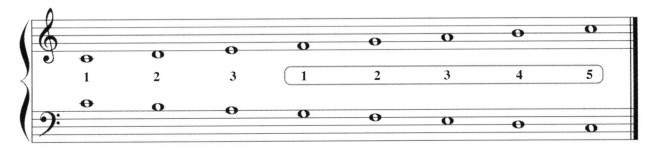

• Play hands together in parallel motion.

With your hands moving in the same direction, you play the same notes, but use different fingers. To master this two-handed trick, remember that in every octave, the right hand only uses finger *4* on *b*, while the left hand only uses *4* on *d*. Play this scale going up, then reverse the fingering to come back down.

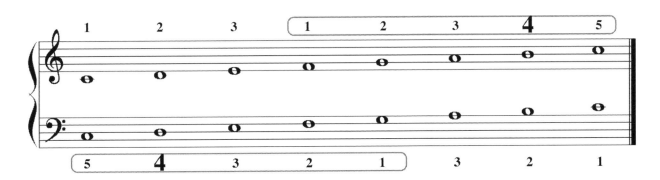

Thrills with Scales

Choose the thrills that suit your interests and skill level.

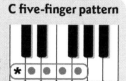

C five-finger pattern

Develop Your Technique with Scale Practice

Using the C major scale, or playing just its first five notes with your five fingers:

1. **Close your eyes.** Play scales with your eyes closed, listening for a beautiful, singing tone.

2. **Change the tempo and/or rhythm.** Playing along with a metronome or drum machine, gradually increase the tempo and experiment with different rhythms.

3. **Change the dynamics.** Begin the scale softly and gradually get louder. When you get to the top, start back down and gradually get softer. (*Imagine you're gradually adjusting the volume control knob of your stereo.*)

4. **Use contrasting dynamics.** Play a scale with one hand loud and the other soft. (*Imagine that you're adjusting separate volume control knobs for treble and bass.*)

5. **Use different types of touch.** Make the scale sound smooth and connected (*legato*), then short and detached (*staccato*). Finally, put your hands together—one hand staccato, the other legato. (*Imagine Mr. Staccato bouncing on a pogo stick while Ms. Legato glides by on skates.*)

6. **Play other major scales.** To find the notes, use your ear and/or the major scale's formula: whole-whole-half-whole-whole-whole-half. For fingerings, see *The Virtuoso Pianist in 60 Exercises* by C. L. Hanon or any scale book.

7. **Play one-handed pentatonic scales.** With either fingering, use as a fancy fill-in or ending.

8. **Pretty Pentatonic**, page 2-6. Play melodies that use the notes of the C major pentatonic scale over left-hand fifths (*c - g*). Then, experiment with other musical textures as suggested on page 1-3.

C major pentatonic scale

9. **In Case of a Clash**, page 2-6. Improvise fearlessly on the white keys. If clash happens, repeat the offending notes and/or move by steps until the tension resolves. To feel secure, remember that salvation's just a step away!

10. **The First Noel.** Start with 3 on *e* (○ = first note), and use the C major scale  fingering throughout. While the melody mostly steps or repeats, it sometimes jumps between *c* and *g* or vice versa. For the music, see page 2-12.

11. **A Dozen Chopsticks, Please.** To play any major scale, put your pinkies an octave apart. Sound out that major scale using your fingers, but not your thumbs. Then, play *Chopsticks* in that position. To understand how the twelve major scales relate to one another (and play all twelve *Chopsticks*), see page T-22.

$g^\flat \rightarrow c$
$a^\flat \rightarrow d$
$b^\flat \rightarrow e$
$d^\flat \rightarrow g$
$e^\flat \rightarrow a$

12. **Pentatonic Ear Tunes,** To move the black key pentatonic ear tunes on page 1-7 to the white keys, change the starting notes as follows:

13. **Joy to the World.** Starting with RH 5, play the descending C major scale.  At *"Let earth receive,"* stretch RH 2 up to *g*, and at *"Let heaven and nature sing,"* play out of the C major five finger position. Enjoy your *Joy!*

14. **Frère Jacques**, page 2-5. In the nineteenth century, impudent lyrics were set to an eighteenth century French tune. Play it with consonant intervals in your left hand.

15. **First Noel or Short'nin' Bread**, page 2-12 or 2-14. Play either song, then as an ending, tack on a one-handed C major pentatonic scale (page 2-10, #7).

16. **Chopsticks**, pages 2-3 and 2-15. Play the whole piece—the clashy first section and the sweet-sounding second section.

17. **Chopsticks for Two**, page 2-15. Teach someone the treble clef part. When your student feels confident, play (and perhaps embroider) the bass clef part. For inspiration, remember the fun Tom Hanks had playing *Chopsticks* with his feet in the movie *Big* (1988).

18. **Play a Round with Frère Jacques**, page 2-5. Decide on the order of entrances and how many times you'll each play the song. The first person begins at the first line. When he or she reaches the second line, the next person begins at the first line. The others enter in a similar manner. (At multiple keyboards: play both hands, but only use thirds on the last line. At one keyboard: each person starts two octaves apart and plays just the melody, leaving out notes if necessary.)

The First Noel

Traditional English carol, orginally from 17th century France

- **Melody**

  Start on the 3rd note (*e*) of the C major scale and use the standard scale fingering throughout. Expect a few repeated notes and some *c - g* or *g - c* jumps. Circle the jumps if it helps you.

- **Meter:** $\frac{3}{4}$

  Accent the first beat of each **three**-beat measure (**oom**-pah-pah) for this **3**/4 time waltz.

- **Harmony**

  The song begins with the left hand silent at the quarter rest sign (𝄽 = one beat of silence). Play the *first* harmony note on the *first* accented beat of the song, the word *first*. Play the root *(c)*, octave *(c')* and/or 5th *(g)* on the first beat of each complete measure, or create your own version.

- **Rhythm**

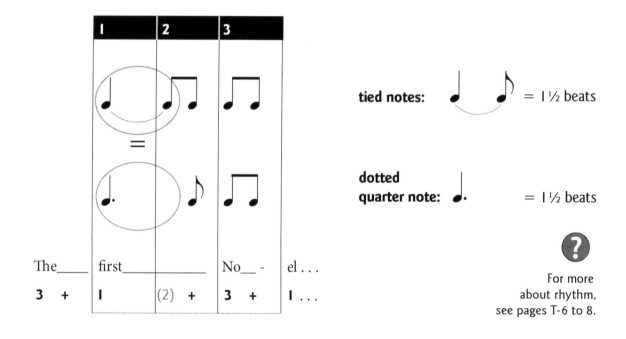

For more about rhythm, see pages T-6 to 8.

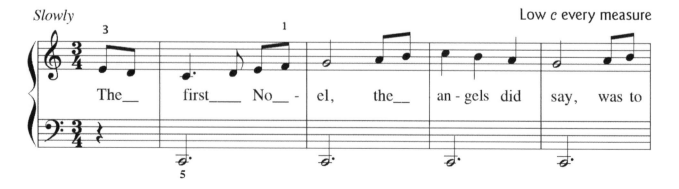

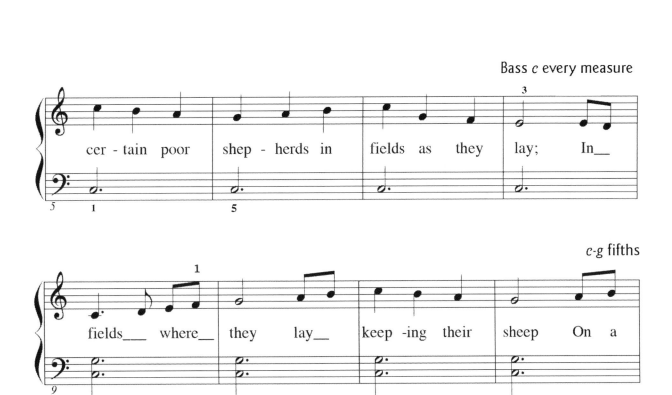

Bass *c* every measure

cer - tain poor | shep - herds in | fields as they | lay; In__

c-g fifths

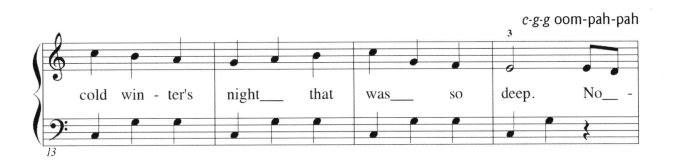

fields___ where___ they lay__ | keep -ing their | sheep On a

c-g-g oom-pah-pah

cold win - ter's | night___ that | was___ so | deep. No__ -

c-g fifths, then *c-c'* octaves

el,____ No___ -el, | No__ - el, | No - el;

c-c' octaves

Born is the | King___ of | Is___ - ra - el.

Short'nin' Bread

Traditional folk song of East Tennessee

Short'nin' bread is a fried batter bread made from corn meal, flour, water, eggs, baking powder, milk and shortening. First published in 1915, the song comes from the mountain folk of East Tennessee.

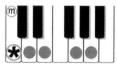

Happily

Parallel motion

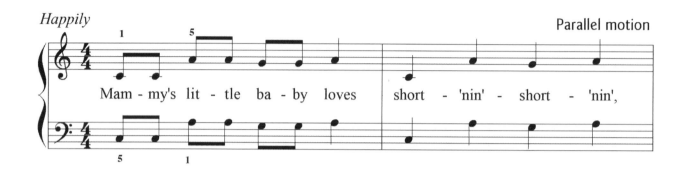

Parallel and contrary motion

Ostinato (left hand repeated pattern)

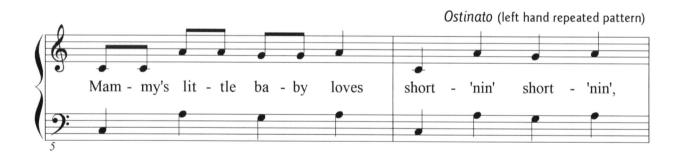

Ostinato and contrary motion

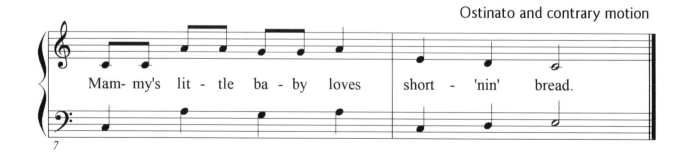

More Chopsticks

Euphemia Allen (1861–1949)

Over the years, people have made up countless versions of *Chopsticks*. Rimsky-Korsakov, Alexander Borodin and other classical composers published sets of variations. Generations of kids worldwide have developed their own unique duet versions. Now it's your turn to tinker with *Chopsticks*.

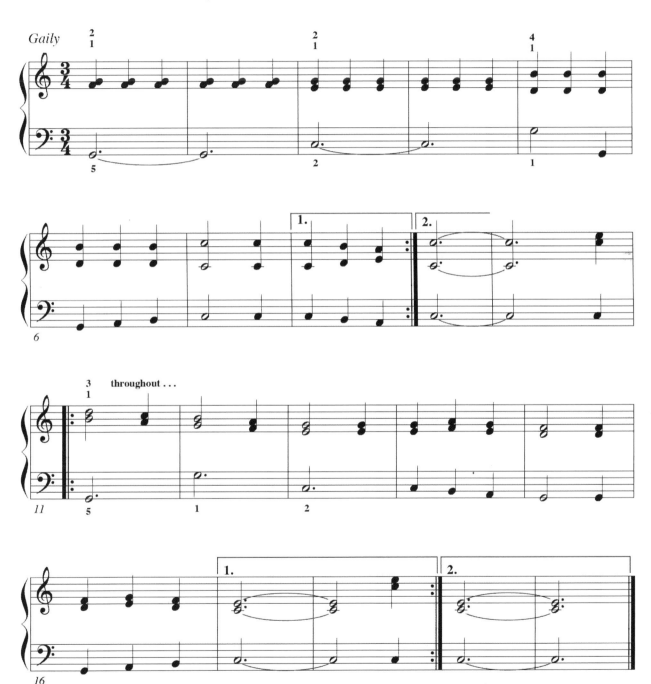

On page 2-3, the form of *Chopsticks* is AA—one repeated section; here, the form is AABB—two repeated sections. At ms.11, play through to the **left-facing repeat sign** 𝄇 (ms.18), jump back to the **right-facing repeat sign** 𝄆 (ms.11), then repeat this section, but jump to the second ending (ms.19).

CHAPTER 2 REVIEW

1. A diatonic scale is: (Circle all correct answers.)

    a. A scale used by the ancient Greeks.

    b. A scale sung while sipping diet tonic water.

    c. What you hear when you step up the black keys of the piano.

    d. What you hear when you step up the white keys of the piano.

    e. A scale that uses all seven letters of the music alphabet.

    f. A dieting device that weighs the ingredients for a gin and diet tonic.

2. Label the whole-steps (W) and half-steps (1/2) below.

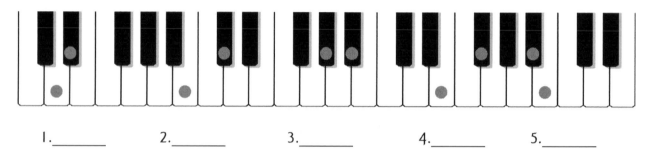

  1._____   2._____   3._____   4._____   5._____

3. The C major scale's pattern of whole-steps (W) and half-steps (1/2) is:

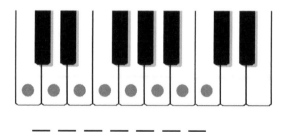

  — — — — — — —

4. *Solfege* is: (Circle all correct answers)

    a. An Italian perfume.

    b. A way for singers to learn melodies.

    c. A piece by Carl Philipp Emanuel Bach.

    d. Something that Guido d'Arrezo taught his choirs.

    e. The syllables *do re mi fa so la ti do.*

5. A time signature tells you: (Circle all correct answers.)

    a. What gets the beat.

    b. How much time it takes to play the piece.

    c. What time it is.

    d. How many beats per measure.

    e. The way time signs its name.

6. To find the pentatonic scale embedded within a major scale,

    omit the _____ and _____ scale tones.

7. The notes of the C major pentatonic scale are: _____ _____ _____ ____ ____ .

8. For the C major scale, you usually use the *1 2 3 1 2 3 4 5* fingering with the:

    a. Right hand descending.   d. Left hand descending.

    b. Right hand ascending.   e. Left hand ascending.

    c. Right hand condescending.   f. Left hand condescending.

9. The *diabolus in musica* is:

    a. The *enfant terrible* of rock.

    b. The second and sixth scale tones played together.

    c. The fourth and seventh scale tones played together.

    d. The ugly error that keeps popping up in the song you're learning.

When you feel comfortable
with this chapter,
go on to **Chapter 3.**

CHAPTER 3
TRY OUT TRIADS

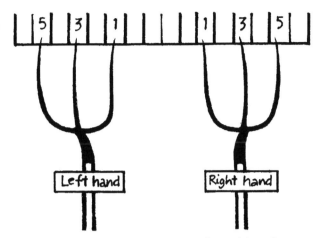

Play triads with pitchfork-shaped hands.

During the Renaissance (1450 – 1600), western composers discovered the acoustic magic of three-note chords. Ever since, the *triad* (German, *Dreiklang,* "three tones") has been the basic building block of harmony. To create this chord whose sum (song?) is greater than its parts, simply shape your hand like a three-prong pitchfork and grab every other note.

To generate many all-white triads:

1. Place the five fingers of either hand over five neighboring white keys.
2. Shape your thumb, middle finger and pinkie like prongs of a pitchfork.
3. Strike the keys under your pitchfork-shaped hand.
4. Move your "pitchfork" to grab other triads all around the keyboard.
5. Listen to the richly resonant sound as you grab each sonic treat.

On the staff, triads look like stacks of either three line-notes or three space-notes. If you use your imagination, you can see them as snowpeople standing on the staff.

Triads look like snowpeople standing on the staff.

Just as there are many ways to cook an egg, there are many ways to play a chord. To become an experienced cook, you'd experiment with boiling, frying, scrambling and making omelettes. To become a versatile pianist, experiment with these clef-less recipes for *blocking, breaking* and *arpeggiating* chords. Or better yet, dream up your own chordal concoctions.

STYLES MENU

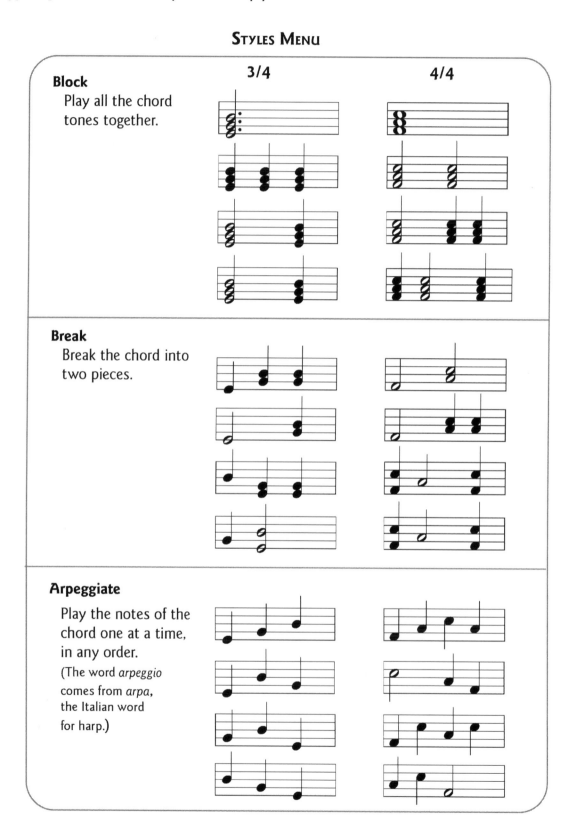

Progressions in the Key of C

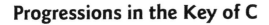

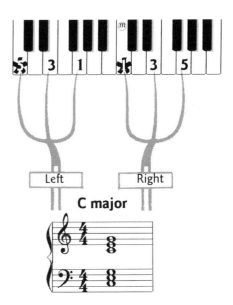

In the key of C major, the harmony usually starts, often returns and always ends on the *C major triad*—the *tonic* triad built on the *tonal* center. To play a C major triad, pluck the first, third and fifth notes from the C major scale with your pitchfork-shaped hand.

c d **e** f **g** a b c

To make up your own key-of-C songs, string some triads together into a *chord progression* that starts and eventually ends on C major. Change the rhythms, add melodies and/or make up your own progressions.

I. Starting on C major, play a series of neighboring white-key triads with both hands together.

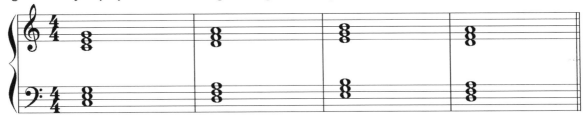

2. Play one hand at a time or both hands together. Give the half rest (—) two beats of silence.

3. Block, break or arpeggiate the chords using the same or different styles in each hand.

4. Play rhythmically, as if you were listening or dancing to an exciting band.

5. Play chords that skip or leap to one another, like the popular progression of *Heart and Soul*.

6. Experiment with progressions that start and end on white-key triads other than the C major. Give the quarter rest (𝄽) one beat of silence and the eighth rest (𝄾) a half a beat of silence.

7. As your left hand plays triads, make up white-key melodies with your right hand. If you hit a note that sounds bad to you, remember that "salvation is a step away" and move quickly to a neighboring note.

8. Same as above, but only play pretty pentatonic notes by avoiding *b* and *f*.

Give yourself permission to break the rules!

Improvisation instructions are meant to kick-start your creativity. If you find yourself intuitively knowing what to play, feel free to disregard the instructions and go wherever your intuition takes you.

The Acoustic Magic of the Triad

In the 1850s, a German scientist invented a resonator that could measure the rate of vibration, or *frequency*, of any note. Hermann Helmholtz discovered that when a string vibrates, it produces a basic tone, the *fundamental*, as well as a series of higher, softer *overtones*. Choosing *c* as the fundamental, you can see that the first five overtones are chord tones of a C major triad—*c g c e g*. The notes of a triad sound pleasant and consonant together because their overtones emphasize one another. Pleasing harmony literally and scientifically means "good vibrations."

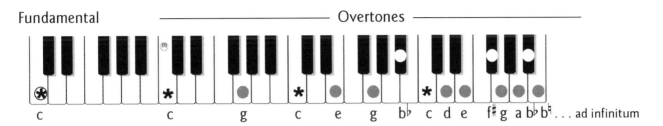

Fundamental ——————————— Overtones ———————————

c   c   g   c   e   g   b♭ c   d   e   f♯ g   a b♭ b♮ ... ad infinitum

To hear a C major triad's overtones on the piano:

1. Silently depress middle *c*, which raises its damper and allows its three strings to vibrate.
2. Forcefully strike the *c* an octave lower and immediately release it.
3. Listen for the higher *c* (the first overtone) resonating on the freely vibrating strings.
4. Continue by silently depressing the next overtones: *g* (the fifth), *c* (another octave) and then *e* (the third). Listen and enjoy this acoustic magic.

Anatomy of a Triad

Every triad consists of three notes—the first, third and fifth notes of the underlying scale. The first note of the scale, the all-important note from which the chord grows, is the *root*. To refer to the triad's notes by their generic names, call them the root, the third and the fifth.

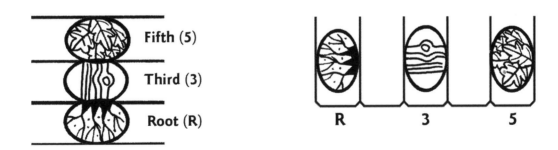

Fifth (5)

Third (3)

Root (R)

R   3   5

Acoustically, the root's fundamental generates the fifth as its second overtone and the third as its fourth overtone. No wonder the major triad sounds so magical! From the holy trinity of the triad, the entire history of western harmony unfolds. When you listen to Bach, Beethoven, the Beatles or your favorite band, you're hearing lots of triads.

> *"The history of harmony has followed the series of natural overtones."*
>
> Henry Cowell

DRILL 3: TRIAD CROSSOVERS

Shaping each hand like a pitchfork, play triads, crossing hand over hand up the white keys. Start with C major, then explore the sound and feel of other all-white triads.

• Build a triad from a scale.

Play the scale's first, third and fifth notes, and call them the triad's *root, third* and *fifth.*

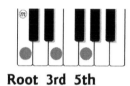

Root 3rd 5th

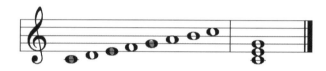

• Arpeggiate the C major triad with each hand.

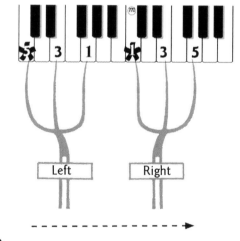

Sing: *do-mi-so*
 "Michael row" (the boat ashore...)
 "Morning has" (broken...)

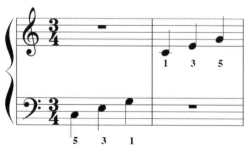

= A whole measure of silence when the rest appears centered in the measure.

See p. T-6 & T-46

• Cross hand over hand up the keyboard.

Start on *low c,* cross left over right at middle *c* and keep going. To end at *high c* (or higher), cross with your left pointer *(2).* Finally, put your right foot on the *damper pedal* and savor the sweetness of C major and all its ringing overtones.

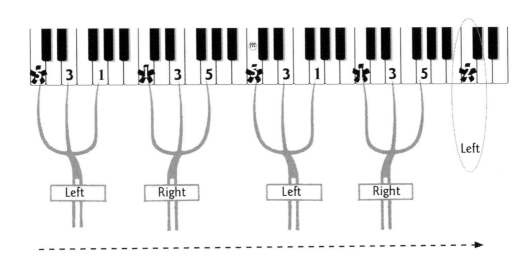

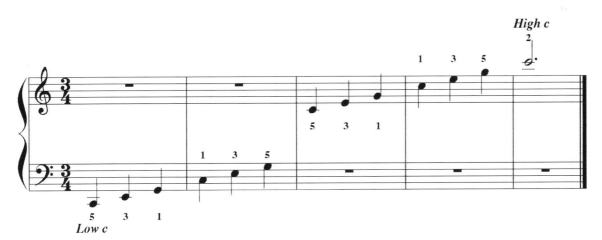

Continuous motion/continuous sound. Gently pass arpeggios between the hands, like a sigh rippling up the keyboard.

Thrills with Triads

Develop Your Technique

I. **Prepare to pivot.** When your arms start reaching past your body's center of gravity, rotate your weight toward your arms. To pivot effectively, keep your butt toward the front of your bench.

2. **Mismatched Crossovers.** In each hand, arpeggiate a different triad. For instance, play left hand *c e g* along with right hand *a c e*. If a clash happens, just move by steps until the tension resolves.

3. **Progress to Progressions**, page 3-3. Make up songs by starting with a chord progression, then experimenting with different styles, rhythms and melodies.

4. **Sing the solfege syllables as you play.** Teach your ear to hear the C major triad by singing: *do-mi-so* and *so-mi-do*.

5. *Lean on Me*, page 3-9. Play the melody starting on middle *c* (the tonal center). Add your left hand, first playing the melody an octave below the right hand, then playing triads on every melody note.

6. *The First Noel* **with Triads**, page 3-10. End with a C major crossover arpeggio.

7. *Short'nin' Bread* **with Stepwise Triads**, page 3-12. Play the song as is, or add your own fancy crossover arpeggio ending.

8. **Identify Triads** on the grand staff. For a rousing romp with triads, see the beginning of Wolfgang Amadeus Mozart's *Viennese Sonatina No. 1* on page 3-14.

9. **Progressions for Two in C**, page 3-3. To turn these improvs into a duet:

   • <u>Person on the left</u>: Play and vary these two-handed progressions an octave lower, omitting the left hand's 3rds (the middle notes). End on a C major triad.

   • <u>Person on the right</u>: Listen and feel the groove. When you're ready, begin to play out of the C major pentatonic scale in this (or any) position. End on *c*.

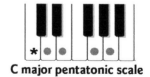

C major pentatonic scale

Lean on Me

Words and Music by Bill Withers

"Sometimes in our lives we all have pain we all have sorrow.

But if we are wise we know that there's always tomorrow."

This 1972 mega-hit reached number one on both the soul singles and the *Billboard* Hot 100. As you sound out the melody, you might jot down note names or other memory pegs above the lyrics. To hear the song, search for *Lean on Me* on YouTube. If you'd like to play along, click the gearshift icon (⚙) at the bottom right of the screen and select a slower tempo.

- **Starting Position**

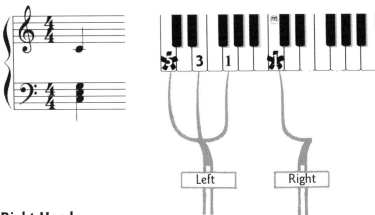

- **Right Hand**

  Starting with your thumb on middle *c*, sound out the melody. Expect mostly stepwise motion, a few repeated notes and one big stretch down to *b*.

- **Left Hand**

  First, play the melody in parallel motion, an octave below the right hand. Then, instead of all single notes, play triads on every melody note.

- **Big Ending**

  When your right hand stretches down to *b*, with your left hand:

  a. Play the triad on *b (b d f)*;

  b. Play the triad on *g (g b d)*;

  c. Play a combination of these two triads *(g b d f)*;

  d. Play any of these with a note omitted *(g _ d* or *g _ d f)*;

  e. Play any of these with a note *doubled (g b d g* or *g _ d g)*; or

  f. Play whatever sounds good to you.

The First Noel with Stepwise Triads

Traditional English carol, originally from 17th century France

Slowly

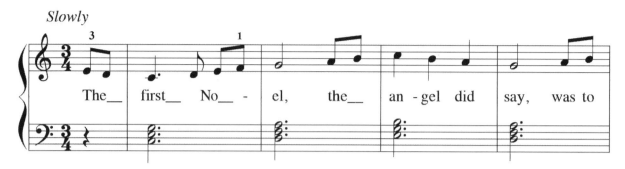

The__ first__ No__ - el, the__ an - gel did say, was to

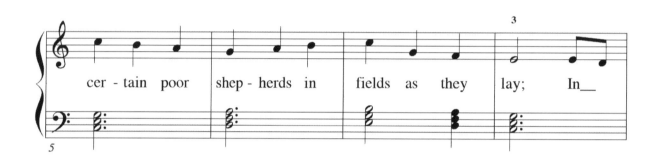

cer - tain poor shep - herds in fields as they lay; In__

fields___ where__ they lay__ keep - ing their sheep On a

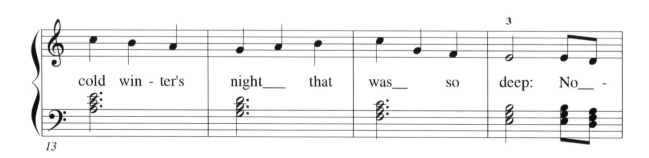

cold win - ter's night___ that was__ so deep: No__ -

Piano Freedom for Frustrated Pianists

Is reading bass clef difficult for you? If so, identify C major, then notice how the chords step up or down from it; and/or label the lowest note of the chords.

See p. T-20

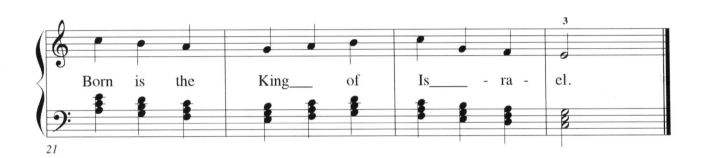

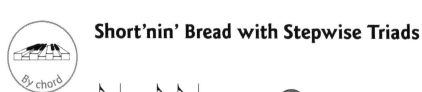

Short'nin' Bread with Stepwise Triads

Put on   the skil-let

See p. T-6 & T-7

Happily

Put   on   the   skil - let,   Put   on   the   lead,

Mam - my's   gon - na   make   a   lit - tle   short - nin'   bread.

That's   not   all   she's   gon - na   do,____

Mam - my's   gon - na   make   a   lit - tle   cof - fee   too.____

Is reading bass clef difficult for you? If so, identify C major, then notice how the chords step up or down from it; and/or label the lowest note of the chords.

See p. T-20

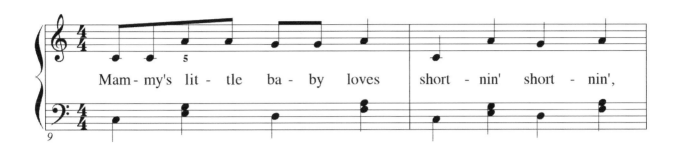

Mam - my's lit - tle ba - by loves   short - nin' short - nin',

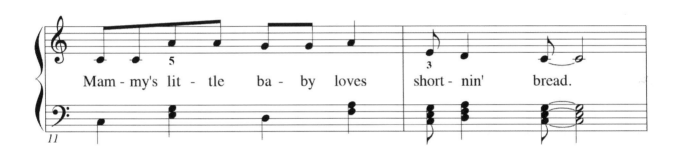

Mam - my's lit - tle ba - by loves   short - nin'   bread.

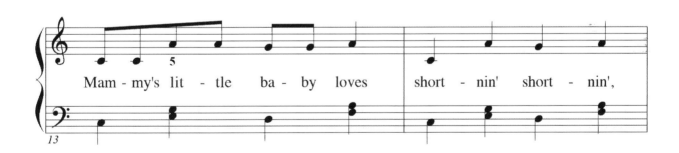

Mam - my's lit - tle ba - by loves   short - nin' short - nin',

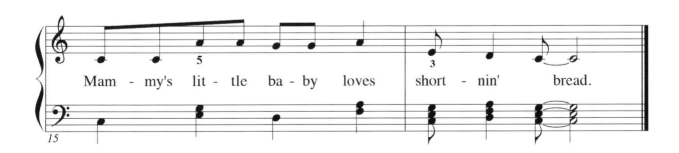

Mam - my's lit - tle ba - by loves   short - nin'   bread.

Viennese Sonatina No. 1

Wolfgang Amadeus Mozart (1756–1791)

When you arpeggiate the C major triad with octaves in both hands, reinforced overtones ring out to create a powerful, exciting sound. To fully enjoy this four-measure *phrase*, pay attention to the meter, tempo, dynamics, articulation and harmony.

- **Meter:** *Common time* (𝄴 = 4/4)

- **Tempo:** *Allegro* (fast, cheerful) *brilliante* (brilliant)

- **Articulation :** *Accent* (ͤ)= emphasize and *staccato* ( ) = shorten and detach)

- **Dynamics:** *Forte* (**f** =loud), then *mezzoforte* (**mf** = medium loud)

- **Harmony:** Up C major → down D minor → down C major.
  Once you've learned these chords, you may find it helpful to label them on the music.

Allegro brillante

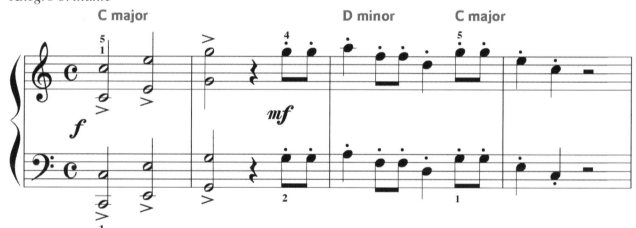

To meet the seven all-white
triads, see Chapter 6.

CHAPTER 3 REVIEW

1. A triad is: (Circle all correct answers.)
   a. Something that, once you try it, you'll like it.
   b. An ad that gives you three for the price of one.
   c. A three-note chord popular since the Renaissance.
   d. A poker term for three of a kind.
   e. The basic chord type in rock and roll.

2. To build a triad from a major scale, play the scale's _____ , _____ and _____ tones.

3. On the staff, a triad looks like a stack of _____ line notes or _____ space notes.

4. An arpeggio is: (Circle all correct answers.)
   a. A harp-like run.
   b. A way to play a chord.
   c. A type of perfume.
   d. A chord played one note at a time, in any order.
   e. A type of piano that has lots of fancy scrollwork.

5. The standard default fingering for a triad is:

6. Identify the generic names for each note of these triads.

When you feel comfortable with this chapter, go on to **Chapter 4**, where you'll learn the underlying principles of fingering and chording.

Or, if reading music still feels like an overwhelming, labor intensive ordeal and/or playing by ear seems way beyond you, go directly to **Chapter 5**, where you'll learn about intervals.

If you can't wait to meet the Cast of Chords and start drilling the all-white majors and minors, go directly to **Chapter 6.**

HAVE FAITH AND YOU'LL FINGER IT OUT!

Like rowing a boat, fingering and chording are learned skills that improve with experience. To begin, let's look at *Row, Row Row Your Boat*, the profound, quintessentially American nineteenth-century round.

To jump in and start "rowing:"

* With your right hand, play the melody starting on middle *c*.

* With your left hand, add the C major triad whenever and however it sounds good.

If life is but a dream, you might as well row your boat your own way!

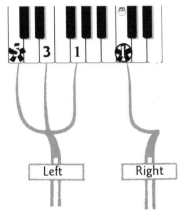

Don't worry about doing it the "right way." Just do it your own right-brained, intuitive way, then meet me on the next page.

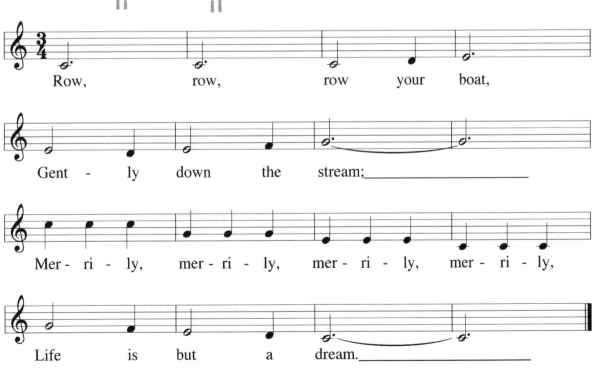

Row, row, row your boat,

Gent - ly down the stream;

Mer - ri - ly, mer - ri - ly, mer - ri - ly, mer - ri - ly,

Life is but a dream.

The Fine Art of Fingering

Was the third line a bit awkward to play? Until there, you could keep your right hand in a five-finger position, where the five fingers of your hand are playing five neighboring scale tones.

Five-finger position

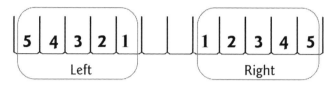

But on line 3, unless you have an eight-fingered hand, you'll need to perform some sort of finger gymnastics. Learning to choose elegant, efficient fingerings instead of cumbersome, clunky fingerings will make a huge difference in your piano life. The chart below shows how you could use all five fingering stunts to play *Row Your Boat*. Try each of them out, then pencil in your favorite fingerings on page 4-1.

FINGERING STUNTS

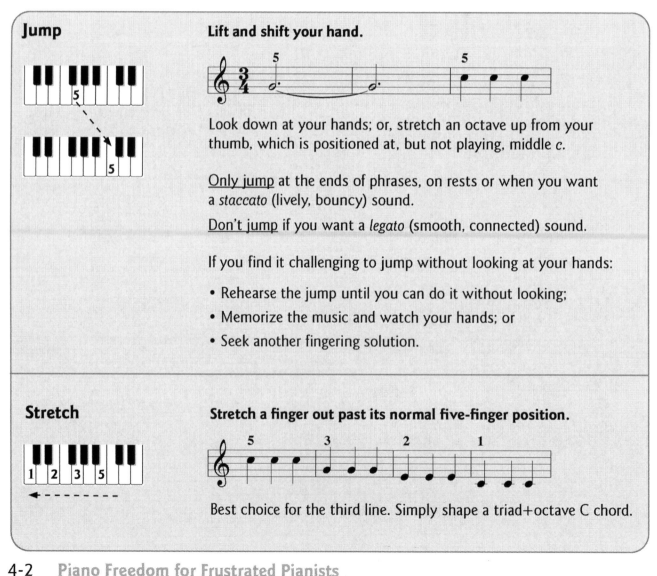

Cross

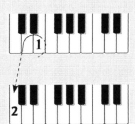

As you pivot on your thumb, cross a finger over it.

Awkward. You stretch to *e*, cross to *c*, and then need to do another fingering stunt to find the next note (*g*) with finger 5.

As you pivot on a finger, cross your thumb under it.

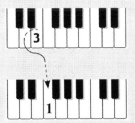

A clever way to avoid jumping on the third line.

Switch

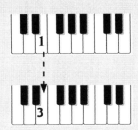

Change fingers when you replay a note.

Another good choice for line 3. Or, how about *1-2-3* or *1-1-3* switches on the *e*'s?

Change fingers while you're holding down a note.

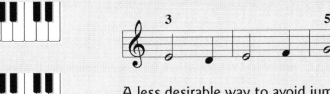

A less desirable way to avoid jumping on line 3, because repeatedly scrunching your hand could lead to injury.

Shrink

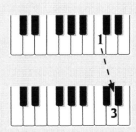

Pull a finger in closer than its normal five-finger position.

To shrink right now, "row" a bit further and tack on this ending.

If you like this shrink, add it to *Row*.

Figure Out Your Fingering

Consistent, efficient fingering is the secret ingredient of fluent playing. If you've been using the haphazard, whatever-finger-gets-there-first approach, you probably already know the frustrations of stumbling and fumbling at the same trouble spot every time. But as any efficiency expert will tell you, taking a little time to plan ahead will save a lot of time and aggravation in the long run. Especially at fast tempos, there won't be time to make conscious decisions about every movement. If you work out the details of each movement in advance, your fingers can execute the mechanical details on automatic pilot, and you can concentrate on your ultimate objective—making the music sing.

Good fingering is simple and logical. Unless you have a reason to do otherwise:

- Use the finger that naturally falls over each note.
- Use standard chord and scale fingerings.
- Minimize the number of jumps, stretches, crosses, switches and shrinks.
- Look ahead to see where you're going and what finger(s) you'll need when you get there.
- Pencil in finger numbers whenever you leave a five-finger position.

When there are no fingerings or you don't like the editor's suggestions, use a pencil, an eraser and/or some Wite-Out to neatly notate *your* fingering. Many overly zealous novices litter the page with excessive finger numbers, then ignore them. Since more is not better, only write in fingerings when they aren't obvious. That way, each number will be a "red flag" alerting you to perform a tricky maneuver.

Working out fingering is like solving a puzzle that has multiple solutions. If you've never paid much attention to fingering before, you may at first feel inept at finding elegant solutions. Fortunately, as puzzle enthusiasts know, it gets easier with experience.

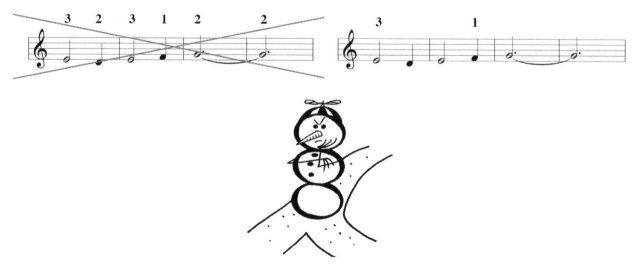

Have faith and you'll finger it out.

Get Me to the Chords on Time

Like fingering, arranging is a puzzle with multiple solutions. When you listen to a Chopin nocturne or a Ray Charles ballad, you can hear the many subtle nuances of elegant chording. To become more fluent at reading and/or arranging, first ask, "Which chords will I play?" and "How will I play them?" Then, keep practicing until your fingers can get to the chords on time every time.

Chording Finesse in 3/4

To accompany a song, the arranger first determines its meter and tempo, then chooses a style. Meter has to do with how you feel the beat and which beats feel louder than others. To determine *Row's* meter, start by looking at the time signature:

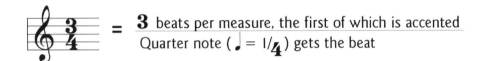

If you watched someone conduct this song, you'd see the baton trace a three-beat pattern. On the *downbeat* of every measure, you'd watch the baton go *down* to emphasize that the first beat of each measure is accented. To emphasize the accented first beat at the piano, you normally play a chord on every downbeat. But how you feel the downbeat depends on tempo and personal preference.

Row at a slow tempo

At a slow tempo, *Row Your Boat* feels like a waltz. If you waltz around the room singing "Merrily, merrily ...," you'll feel the downbeat every three beats (as you'd expect in 3/4). You might block the chord on the downbeat of every measure (#1), or arpeggiate the chord as three quarter notes per measure (#2).

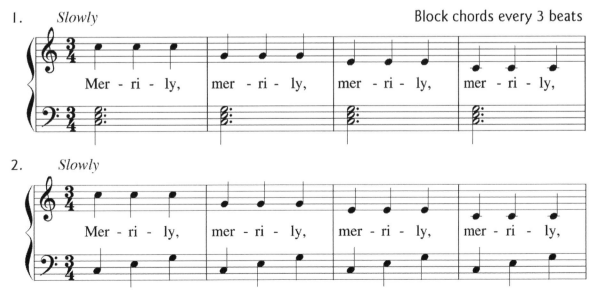

Row at a moderate tempo

At moderate tempos, you could skip around the room singing "Merrily, merrily... " and feel the downbeat every six beats. Play block chords every six beats (#3), or break the chord into two dotted half notes every six beats (#4). (Do you understand compound meters? If so, see page T-33.)

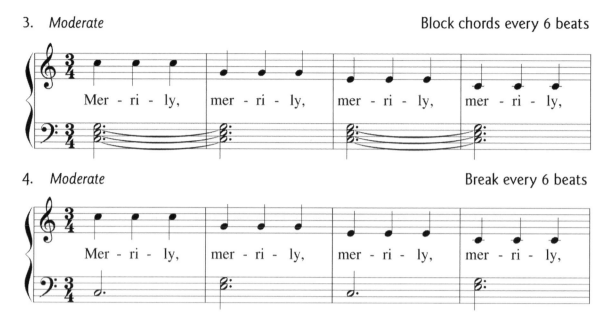

Row at a fast tempo

At fast tempos, you could boogie around the room singing "Merrily, merrily... " and feel the downbeat every twelve beats. Play block chords every twelve beats (#5), or "walk" the bass as four dotted half notes every twelve beats (#6). (Do you understand compound meters? If so, see page T-33.)

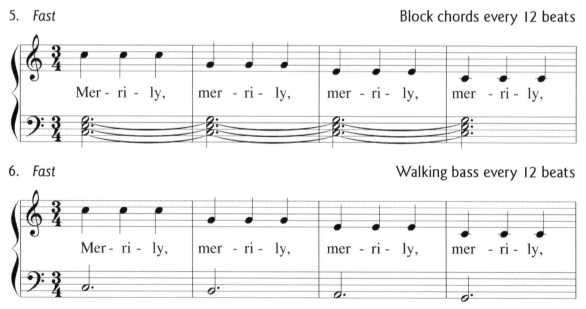

Imagine your left hand is a bass player. Start on *c*, and walk down the scale to another note in the chord (*g*).

Does this contradict the "chord on every downbeat" dictum? Well, that depends on whether your ultimate authority is what you see or what you hear. Although you *see* 3/4 meter, if you *hear* the downbeat every six beats or twelve beats, you're hearing the song in a different meter.

What's Amazing about *Amazing Grace?*

Lyrics by John Newton (1725-1807)

Traditional melody

During a fierce storm, the captain of a British slave ship called out for God's mercy. In 1773, John Newton, a slaver turned preacher, described the *amazing grace* of that night in his New Year's sermon. Although the hymn remained fairly obscure in England, churches in the United States soon began singing it

In nineteenth century America, shape-note singing communities and worshippers at camp meetings sang this powerful pentatonic melody. In the twentieth century, Civil Rights marchers and Vietnam War protestors sang it in the streets; Bill Moyers created a video documentary of it; and Mahalia Jackson, Judy Collins, Elvis Presley, Willie Nelson, Aretha Franklin and many others recorded it. By 2011, there were over 7,000 recorded versions of it. Now, it's your turn to play *Amazing Grace.*

Fingering the Powerful Pentatonic Melody

You can play this hymn out of just two hand positions. Compare your initial fingering with the options on the facing page, then practice your preferred fingering. Finally, close your eyes and let your ears guide you, as you play with *Amazing Grace*.

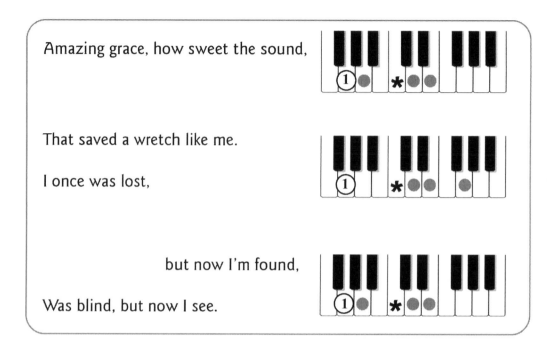

Amazing grace, how sweet the sound,

That saved a wretch like me.

I once was lost,

but now I'm found,

Was blind, but now I see.

Chording the Rousing Upbeat Rhythm

Amazing Grace starts on an unaccented *upbeat*, when the conductor's baton would be going *up* to prepare for the downbeat. Instead of chording on the first note *(g)*, play your first chord on the downbeat of the first complete measure *(c)*.

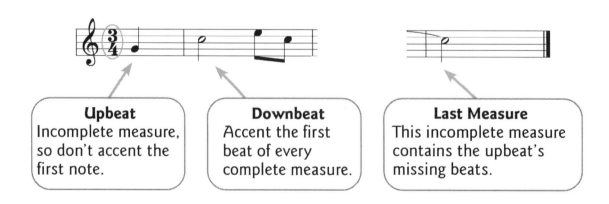

Upbeat
Incomplete measure, so don't accent the first note.

Downbeat
Accent the first beat of every complete measure.

Last Measure
This incomplete measure contains the upbeat's missing beats.

Don't chord on an upbeat!
Play the first chord on the downbeat of the first complete measure.

Fingering and Chording with *Amazing Grace*

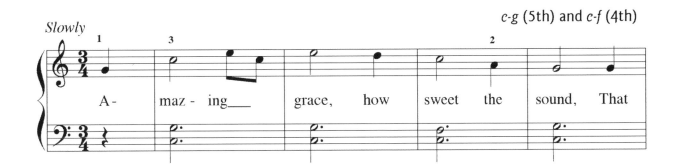

c-g (5th) and c-f (4th)

A - maz - ing___ grace, how sweet the sound, That

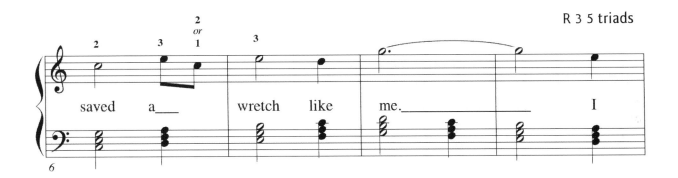

R 3 5 triads

saved a___ wretch like me.___ I

R 5 8 and R 3 5 arpeggios

once___ was___ lost, but now___ I'm___ found, Was

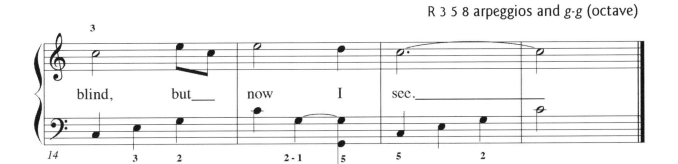

R 3 5 8 arpeggios and g-g (octave)

blind, but___ now I see.___

DRILL 4: TRIAD+OCTAVE VOICINGS

When singers harmonize, they decide which *voice* will sing which chord tone. When pianists play chords, we decide which finger(s) will play which chord tone(s). Whether sung or played, each chord *voicing* has its own unique sound and default fingering. Like a jeweler collecting gems, get to know each one's characteristic beauty and appropriate settings.

A. TRIAD+OCTAVE (R 3 5 8)

To the C major triad (root - 3rd - 5th), add the octave.

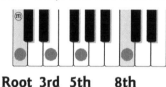

Root 3rd 5th 8th

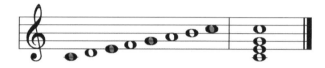

• **Arpeggiate the right hand going up.**

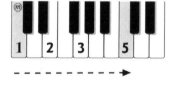

Rotate your wrist laterally as you transfer the weight of your hand toward your pinkie *(1-2-3-5)*.

Sing: *do-mi-so-do*
"*I could have danced*"   (all night)
(On) "*top of old Smo*"   (-key)
(On) "*top of Spagghet*"   (-ti)

• **Arpeggiate the right hand going down.**

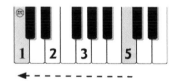

Trace a half circle with your wrist as you transfer the weight toward your thumb *(5-3-2-1)*.

Sing: *do-so-mi-do*
"*Merrily, merrily, merrily*"

- **Arpeggiate both hands in contrary motion.**

  Use the same fingering and wrist rotation in each hand.

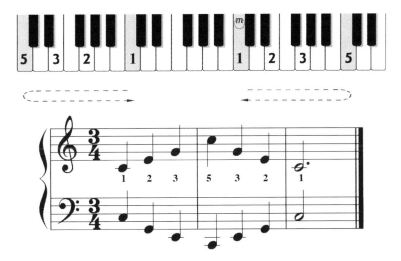

B. POWER CHORD (R 5 8)

If you omit the R 3 5 8's third, you're left with a spacious *open voicing*: root-5th-8th. The stable R 5 8 voicing makes a versatile left hand accompaniment that sounds great in low registers. Electric guitarists adore the overtone-rich *power chord*, because it sounds good (in a bad boy kind of way) when distorted.

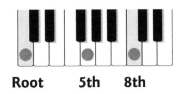

Root   5th   8th

- **Arpeggiate the left hand going up and down.**

  When C feels comfortable, move the power chord shape stepwise up the white keys.

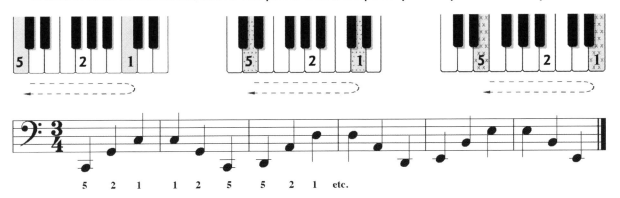

C. FIFTH+TRIAD (5 R 3 5)

Instead of adding the note an octave up from the triad's root (R 3 5 8), add the note an octave down from the triad's fifth (5 R 3 5).

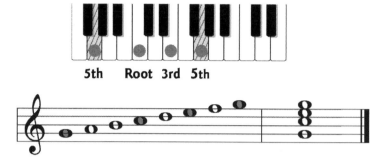

5th   Root 3rd 5th

- **Arpeggiate the right hand going up and down.**

    Going up, rotate your wrist laterally; going down, trace a half circle with your wrist

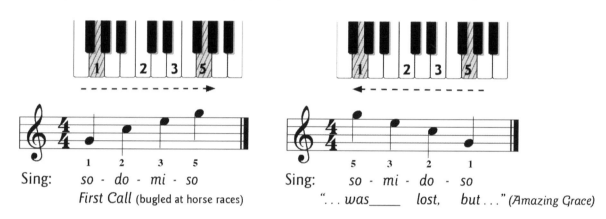

Sing: so - do - mi - so
First Call (bugled at horse races)

Sing: so - mi - do - so
"... was____ lost,   but ..." *(Amazing Grace)*

- **Arpeggiate 5 R 3 5 C and R 3 5 8 C in contrary motion.**

    Mirror the same fingering, wrist rotation and spacing! Play as shown, then vice versa.

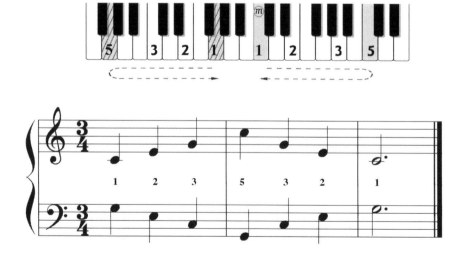

Thrills with Triad+Octave Voicings

Develop Your Technique and Ear

1. **Rotate your wrist when you arpeggiate R 3 5 8 power chord voicings.** Going away from the thumb, rotate laterally; going towards the thumb, trace a half circle. To make each tone sound equally full and rich, move further into (or out from) the black keys.

2. **Sing solfege syllables as you play.** Teach your ear to hear each new voicing by singing: R 3 5 8 as *do-mi-so-do*, R 5 8 as *do-so-do* and 5 R 3 5 as *so-do-mi-so*.

3. **Waltzing with R 5 8 C power chord.** While your left hand repeatedly arpeggiates R 5 8 C, play all-white melodies with your right hand.

4. ***On Top of Old Smokey*** (a.k.a. *On Top of Spaghetti*). Begin the melody by going up R R 3 5 8 C: *c c e g c ...*

5. ***Row, Row, Row Your Boat***, pages 4-1 to 6. Decide how you'll play the song.

6. ***Amazing Grace***, pages 4-7 to 9, 14, 15. Accompany this hymn with whatever sounds good to you, for instance, low R 5 8 power chord arpeggios throughout.

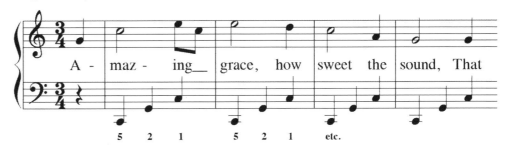

A - maz - ing__ grace, how sweet the sound, That

7. ***Jugglers, Acrobats and Jumpers with Bears and Monkeys*** by Francois Couperin (1668 – 1733), pages 4-17 to 19. Identify the two types of R 5 8 voicings.

8. ***Row Your Boat Around.*** To play this song as a round, see page 4-16.

The Amazing Grace of Stepwise Triads

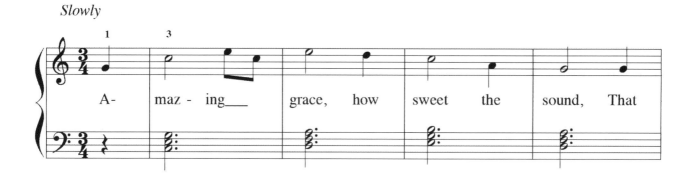

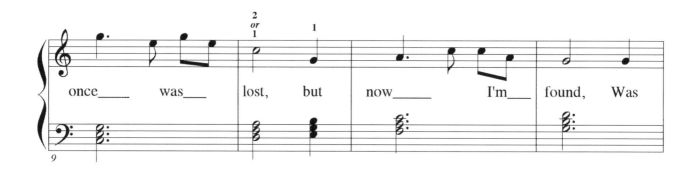

Your Amazing Grace

When you read an arrangement of a song, it may differ from the way you're used to hearing it. If it's not written the way you learned it from your Aunt Tillie or the record, feel free to play what you hear, not what you see. To create your own arrangement, play around with the notes and chords until you come up with something that sounds good to you. Then, learn your arrangement using some of the following strategies:

- Write note names, descriptive words and other reminders on the song's treble clef.
- Make a "cheat sheet," by writing down helpful reminders on a separate page.
- Notate your arrangement on the grand staff.
- Record your arrangement on a CD, DVD, cell phone or the latest technology.
- Practice your arrangement using consistent fingering and appropriate memory pegs.

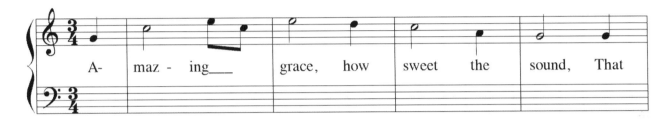

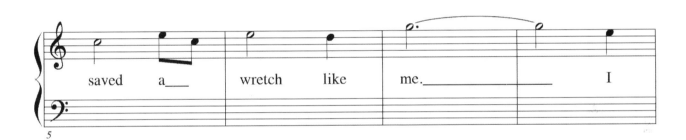

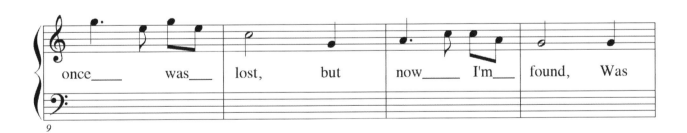

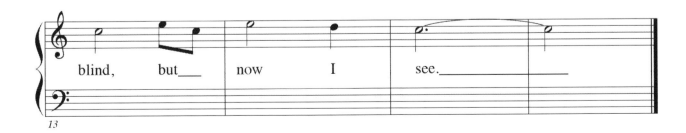

Row Your Boat Around

To play this song as a four-part round, decide on the order of entrances and how many times you'll each play the song. The first persons starts at ①. When he or she reaches the second line ②, the next person begins at ①. The others enter in a similar manner.

- At multiple keyboards: each person starts at middle *c*.
- At one keyboard: each person starts two octaves apart.

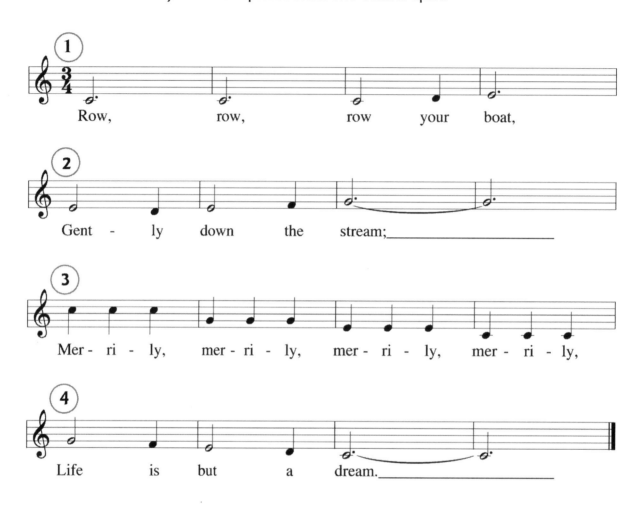

① Row, row, row your boat,

② Gent - ly down the stream;

③ Mer - ri - ly, mer - ri - ly, mer - ri - ly, mer - ri - ly,

④ Life is but a dream.

Play merrily, sing along and heed the message.

If life is but a dream, it certainly doesn't matter if you make a few mistakes.

The Jugglers, Acrobats & Jumpers with Bears & Monkeys

Les Jongleurs, Sauteurs & Saltimbanques avec les Ours et les Singes

by Francois Couperin (1668 – 1733)

At seventeen, Francois Couperin inherited his father's post as organist of a large church in Paris. In 1717, he became court organist and composer to King Louis XIV. Imagine "Couperin le Grande" performing this piece on a gilt harpsichord at the royal palace.

- **Form.** Two repeated sixteen-measure sections, each containing an eight-measure phrase accompanied first by quarter notes (R 5 8 C) and then by eighth notes (R 5 8 5 8 5 C).

A	A'	:|
|: B	B'	:|

- **Right hand.** Look for five-finger patterns, the C major scale fingering, and a rearranged *root-on-top* C triad (*e g **c***) at the end.

- **Left hand double stems.**

Imagine a bass and tenor singing together. The bass sings a *c* on the downbeat of every measure, then holds it for three beats. Meanwhile, the tenor arpeggiates an R 5 8 C major chord. To execute these two *voices*, keep holding the low *c* while you play the other notes and enjoy the ringing out of *c*'s overtones.

- **Signs and symbols.**

f	**forte**: Loud.
legerement	Lightly, briskly.
mf	**mezzo forte**: Moderately loud.
p	**piano**: Soft.
⌒	**slur**: Play the notes legato (smooth and connected).
♩ ♪	**staccato**: Play the note in a very short, bouncy, detached manner.
♩ ♪	**tenuto**: Hold the note for its full time value.

For other unfamiliar signs and symbols, see Wiggles & Squiggles (T-46) or the Glossary (T-39).

The Jugglers, Acrobats & Jumpers with Bears & Monkeys

by Francois Couperin (1668–1733)

CHAPTER 4 REVIEW

1. The right time to pencil in fingerings is: (Circle all correct answers here and throughout.)

    a. After sight-reading a piece no more than three times.

    b. At the beginning of the learning process

    c. A few weeks into learning a piece, once you almost know it.

    d. Once you're tired of making awkward errors.

    e. When the performance is the next day.

2. Upbeats are:

    a. Cool guys and gals playing the piano.

    b. Notes in an incomplete first measure of a song.

    c. An incomplete last measure of a song.

    d. Unaccented notes before the first downbeat of a song.

    e. Notes whose stems go up.

3. You could describe a R 3 5 8 voicing as:

    a. A triad plus the octave.

    b. An octave plus a fifth.

    c. A triad plus an octopus.

    d. A triad played by eight sets of triplets.

    e. The root, third, fifth and eighth notes of a scale.

4. You could describe a R 5 8 voicing as:

    a. A triad plus the octave.

    b. An octave with the fifth inside it.

    c. A root, a fifth of gin and an octopus.

    d. The first, fifth and eighth notes of a scale.

    e. A rutabaga, a fifth of gin and an octegenarian.

5. Which songs start on upbeats?

    a. *Take Me Out to the Ballgame*

    b. *St. James Infirmary*

    c. *Yesterday*

    d. *Farmer in the Dell*

    e. *Auld Lang Syne*

Does reading music feel like an overwhelming, labor intensive ordeal?
Do you wish you could play by ear? If so, go on to **Chapter 5**, where you'll
improve your sight-reading and ear-playing by learning about intervals.

 If you can't wait to meet the Cast of Chords and start
drilling the all-white triads, go directly to **Chapter 6**.

CHAPTER 5
BECOME INTIMATE WITH INTERVALS

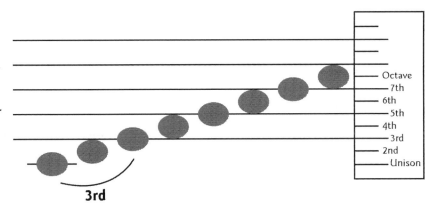

Intervals are music's inches and feet. To measure the distance between any two notes, count the number of scale tones you'd play to climb from one note to the other. (For instance, from the first note to the third note of a scale is a 3rd.) However, while all 3rds look and feel the same (note, skip-a-note, note), much to our aural delight, all 3rds don't sound the same. (Without a clef sign, you can't predict the sound.) To improve your sight-reading, learn the look, feel and sound of the major scale's common intervals. Then, go on to Chapter 6, where you'll discover what a difference a half-step makes.

- **Melodic interval** = Play two notes, one note at a time.

- **Harmonic interval** = Play two notes together.

COMMON INTERVALS

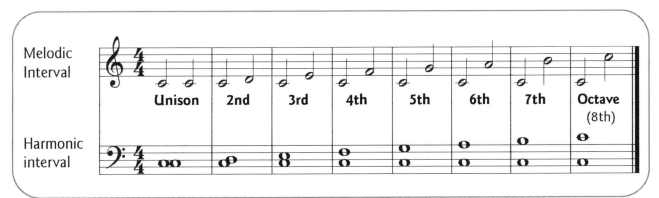

See and Feel Intervals

When you read music relatively, you don't have to keep glancing down at the keyboard to find notes. Instead, you efficiently keep your eyes on the music and feel your way around. Moreover, seeing patterns of intervals will make it easier to learn and memorize songs. To gain the dual perspective of reading by note *and* by interval, learn the look and feel of the common intervals.

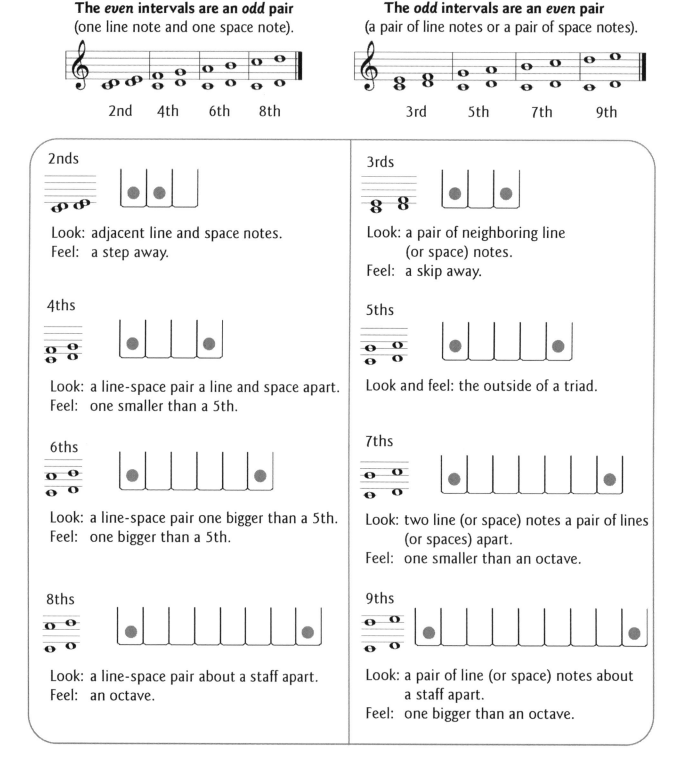

The *even* intervals are an *odd* pair (one line note and one space note).

2nd   4th   6th   8th

The *odd* intervals are an *even* pair (a pair of line notes or a pair of space notes).

3rd   5th   7th   9th

2nds

Look: adjacent line and space notes.
Feel: a step away.

4ths

Look: a line-space pair a line and space apart.
Feel: one smaller than a 5th.

6ths

Look: a line-space pair one bigger than a 5th.
Feel: one bigger than a 5th.

8ths

Look: a line-space pair about a staff apart.
Feel: an octave.

3rds

Look: a pair of neighboring line (or space) notes.
Feel: a skip away.

5ths

Look and feel: the outside of a triad.

7ths

Look: two line (or space) notes a pair of lines (or spaces) apart.
Feel: one smaller than an octave.

9ths

Look: a pair of line (or space) notes about a staff apart.
Feel: one bigger than an octave.

Doubles

Play pairs of white keys at the same time in either hand.

- **Right hand intervals**

  With your left hand, rhythmically repeat one note *(c)*. After a while, change to another note *(g)*. Finally, when you feel ready, return to the first note *(c)*.

Tonal center *(c)* or its 5th *(g)*

- **Left hand intervals**

  In your left hand, play this *boogie bass*, which alternates 5ths and 6ths. With your right hand, play a melody using notes from the C pentatonic scale *(c d e g a c)*.

Boogie bass (alternating 5ths and 6ths)

Motor Music

Walking past a loud lawn motor, I grimace at the ugly sonic intrusion, then start singing along. Using the noisy motor as a drone, I can feel the resonance—the overtones of the motor (the lower the better!) and my voice in unison. Next, I jump to the 3rd and savor the sweetness of the interval, the triad's magical ingredient. If the intruding noise persists, I'll leap to the 5th and experience some perfect stability. Eventually, the motor finishes its job and silence returns. Sometimes, after the sound's gone, I feel a little disappointed that my interval fun is done.

Read Relatively and Absolutely

Recognizing intervals will revolutionize your sight reading, especially above or below the staff in ledger-line territory. You'll read a few strategic notes by absolute name ("c") and the rest by relative position ("c up a 3rd"). To name the tunes shown below, use relative-reading starting on one of the outer c's (two ledger lines up from the treble clef or down from the bass clef).

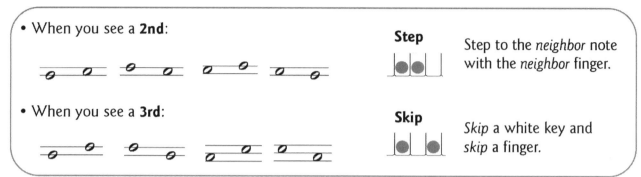

Can you name these tunes? (To check your answers, see page T-34.)

Big Bonus

Ends: _____

To read octaves in ledger-line territory:

1. Recognize line-space pairs as even intervals.

2. If they are about a staff apart, they are octaves (8ths)—not 6ths (too small) or 10ths (too big).

3. Read the easier note, then add the octave.

4. Grab an octave with your thumb and pinkie stretched about as far as you can reach.

For more practice reading and recognizing intervals, see page 5-16.

Snake Dance with 2nds, 3rds and 4ths

Traditional 19th century melody

For generations, mischievous children have delighted in singing silly lyrics to the tune of the *Snake Dance*.

A seven-year-old impishly offered me:

> There's a place in France, where the naked ladies dance.
> There's a hole in the wall, where the boys can see it all…

A mature senior citizen nostalgically recalled:

> There's a place on Mars where the ladies smoke cigars,
> Every puff they take is enough to kill a snake . . .

A forty-year-old woman gleefully burst forth with the following lyrics, accompanied by undulating movements and girlish giggles:

> All the girls in France do the hula hula dance,
> And the way they shake is enough to kill a snake.
> When the snake is dead they put roaches in his bed.
> When the roaches dine, it is 1959.

Snake Dance's biggest interval is a 4th. Circle the 4ths (*a* down to *e* in measures 3, 7 and 15), then read through the melody a few times. Knowing where the 4ths occur, can you play *Snake Dance* without the music? If not, locate and mark all the 3rds as well, then try again.

Mysterioso

This five-finger position song has *d* as its tonal center. Accompany it with the all-white triad on *d*—either on the downbeat of every measure, every other measure or whenever it sounds good to you.

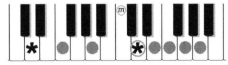

Chording Finesse In 4/4

While you can waltz or minuet in 3/4, you can fox trot, tango, square dance or line dance in 4/4. In fact, 4/4 is so *common* that we call it *common* time and sometimes mark the time signature as "**C**." Accent the first beat, and put a lesser secondary accent on the third beat. Try out some of these *Snake Dance* styles, then play it the way you like it.

Do you recognize this left hand rhythm? It sounds like "*Hello My Baby*" and lots of other snappy songs. I liked the accompaniment pattern, so I changed the melody to fit with it (*). No melody is sacrosanct to the Lone Arranger!

See p. T-6 & 7

Hear the Intervals of the Major Scale

How you hear each interval depends on you. Some people hear a certain quality. Others associate a familiar song or solfege syllables. A few say they taste or smell intervals! How do you hear each interval? Jot down your favorite memory pegs.

THE SOUND OF THE COMMON INTERVALS

Interval	Keyboard	Song	Quality
Perfect Unison *c – c* *do – do*		*Yan - kee* (Doodle)	Two voices in unison
Major 2nd *c – d* *do – re*		*Are you* (sleeping?) *Doe a* (deer)	Clashy, spicy, like *Chopsticks* Tastes bitter
Major 3rd *c – e* *do – mi*		*Mic - hael* (row the boat))	Pretty, harmonious Tastes sweet
Perfect 4th *c – f* *do – fa* or usually *g – c* *so – do*		*. . . cry. Oh* (Susanna) *A - maz -* (ing grace) *Here comes* (the bride)	Regal, chime-like, Olympian Tastes like low-fat cream
Perfect 5th *c – g* *do – so*		*Twinkle twinkle* (little star)	Hollow, ancient, fanfare Tastes like water
Major 6th *c – a* *do – la*		*Mama's little* (baby loves, Short'nin')	Pretty, harmonious, sweet Smell of freshly mowed grass
Major 7th *c – b* *do – ti*		*Ce - or - (a)*	Clashy, spicy Tastes bitter
Perfect Octave *c – b* *do – do*		*Some - where* (over the rainbow)	Doubles the note No taste

Add Intervals under the Melody

Imagine a soprano and an alto singing together. While the soprano sings the melody, the alto might sing the same melody an octave lower or harmonize by singing a 6th or 3rd below the melody. Similarly at the piano, you can sometimes beef up your right hand by adding octaves, 6ths or 3rds below the melody.

- If your hand is big enough, you can strengthen any melody by playing it in octaves.
- Playing 3rds or 6ths under the melody will often sound good.

Melody in octaves with left-hand fifths

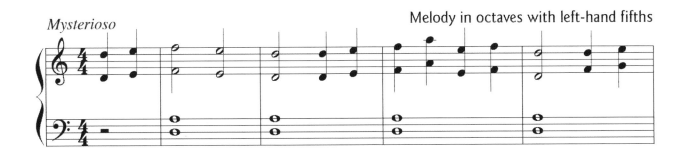

Melody in 6ths with left-hand octaves

Melody in 3rds with R 5 8 power chords

Melody in 6ths with left-hand broken octaves

DRILL 5: INTERVALS OF THE C MAJOR SCALE

To improve your reading and ear-playing, learn the sound, look and feel of each interval.

• Play and say each melodic interval.

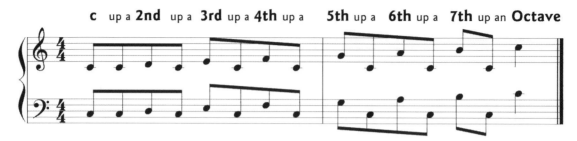

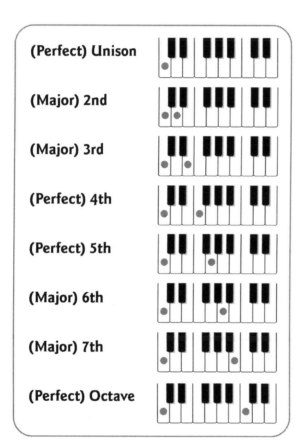

Rotate your wrists as if turning a doorknob to play melodic intervals.

Dangle loose, arched wrists to play harmonic 6ths, 7ths and 8ths. Use your elbow as a fulcrum, rather than your wimpy wrist.

• Play and say each harmonic interval.

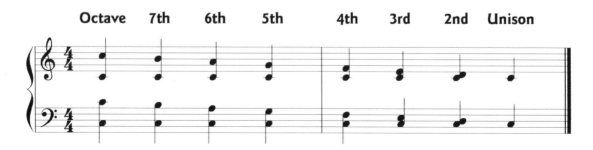

Thrills with Intervals

Choose the thrills that suit your interests and skill level.

Develop Your Technique

1. **Sing solfege syllables.** While letter names *(c c d c e . . .)* change for each scale, solfege syllables *(do do re do mi . . .)* stay the same. To install these great aural memory pegs, play and sing:

do do **re** do **mi** do **fa** do **so** do **la** do **ti** do **do**

2. **Play the melodic intervals of other major scales.** Use your ear, the memory of how you once diligently practiced it, or the major scale's formula: whole-whole-half-whole-whole-whole-half.

3. **Doubles**, page 5-3. Improvise with right hand intervals and a left hand boogie bass.

4. *Happy Birthday to You* by Patty Hill and Mildred Hill, page 5-12. Remember the order of the four big leaps (4th – 5th – 8th – 6th), and trust your ear for the rest.

5. **Add Sweeteners.** Add 3rds or 6ths to *Short'nin' Bread* (3-10) and *Amazing Grace* (5-14). For left hand fun, add a boogie bass to *Bread* or a R 5 8 bass to *Grace*.

6. *Snake Dance* **Your Own Way,** page 5-13. Start with any of the suggestions on pages 5-6 to 9. Add your own reptilian ideas, then snake, rattle and slither.

7. **The *Amazing Grace* of Added 3rds & 6ths**, page 5-14. Add intervals under the melody over a R 5 8 bass.

8. *Minuetto* by Ignaz Joseph Pleyel (1757-1831), page 5-15. A student of Haydyn, this French-born Austrian composer owned a factory that sold over 100,000 pianos.

9. **Boogie with a Friend** using the boogie bass (R 5 - R 6) shown in # 3 above.

   <u>Person on the left:</u> To set the tempo, play the boogie bass in both hands. Experiment with different rhythms and styles, then end on *c - g* 5ths in each hand..

   <u>Person on the right:</u> Improvise on the white keys. Follow your ear, play what you hear, and remember that "salvation's just a step away."

Happy Birthday to You

Words and Music by Patty Hill (1868–1946) and Mildred Hill (1859–1916)

Some day as the candles are being lit on a friend's birthday cake, you may be asked to play *Happy Birthday*. The song first appeared in 1893, when kindergarten principal Dr. Patty Hill collaborated with her sister, pianist and composer Mildred Hill. If you remember the order of the four big leaps and trust your ear for the rest, it will be a piece of cake.

To play *Happy Birthday* on the white keys:

1. Start on *g (so)*.

2. Remember the order of the song's four big leaps: 4th – 5th – 8th – 6th.

3. Use your ear to fill in the repeated notes, 2nds and 3rds.

4. Mark fingerings and other helpful reminders on keyboard diagrams.

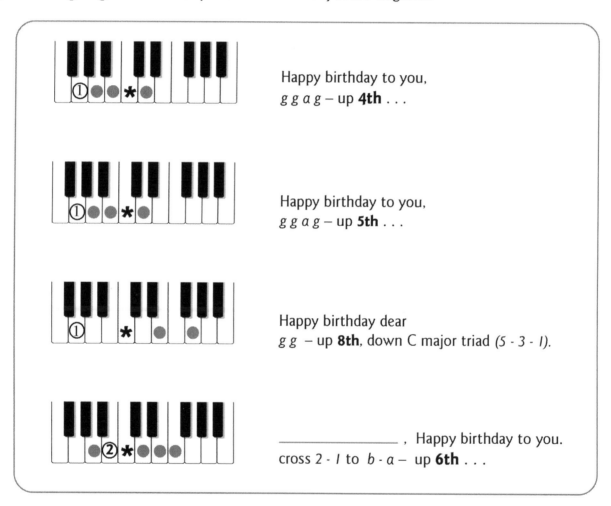

Happy birthday to you,
g g a g – up **4th** . . .

Happy birthday to you,
g g a g – up **5th** . . .

Happy birthday dear
g g – up **8th**, down C major triad *(5 - 3 - 1)*.

_____ , Happy birthday to you.
cross 2 - 1 to *b - a* – up **6th** . . .

Happy copyright freedom for *Happy Birthday!*

On September 22, 2015, a U.S. District Judge in Los Angeles ruled that Warner/Chappell did not own a copyright to the lyrics for Happy Birthday. While people could always legally sing the song at private parties, Warner had been collecting about two million dollars a year for its commercial use in films or performances. Now, finally, the song can be sung by anyone, anywhere at no cost.

Snake Dance Your Own Way!

Now create and learn your own arrangement. Combine some of the style suggestions in this chapter with your own slithery snake music.

Mysterioso

If you like arranging, get organized!

Buy a music notebook. To keep a chronological record of what you've done, use a spiral-bound music book. To organize songs, new style ideas and your own compositions in separate, expandable sections, use a loose-leaf book with blank staff paper.

The Amazing Grace of Added 3rds and 6ths

Minuetto

by Ignaz Joseph Pleyel (1757–1831)

♯ = Raise the note a half-step. See p. 2-7

CHAPTER 5 REVIEW

1. The distance between any two notes is called an _____ .

2. Identify the following intervals on the treble clef.

    a._____   b._____   c._____   d._____   e._____   f._____   g._____   h._____

3. Identify the following intervals on the bass clef.
   (Even if you don't read bass clef, you can still see the intervals.)

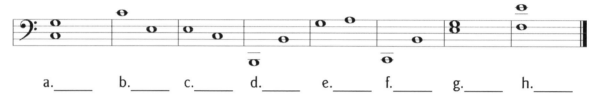

    a._____   b._____   c._____   d._____   e._____   f._____   g._____   h._____

4. Name these tunes: _____

5. Which of the following statements about intervals are true?

    a. The 3rds, fifths and sevenths have one line note and one space note.

    b. The 3rds, fifths and sevenths have two line notes or two space notes.

    c. An *interim value* added.

    d. The 2nds, 4ths, 6ths and 8ths have one line note and one space note.

    e. The 2nds, 4ths, 6ths and 8ths have two line notes or two space notes

> When you feel comfortable with this chapter,
> go on to **Chapter 6,** where you'll meet and
> start drilling the all-white triads.

PART II:
MEET THE CAST OF CHORDS

MEET THE CAST OF CHORDS

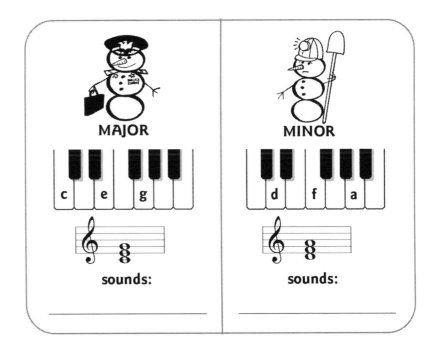

Play all-white triads on the notes of the C major scale, listening to their changing qualities. Some, like the triad on *c*, are major; others, like the triad on *d*, are minor. People often describe major as sounding happy and minor as sounding sad. How do you hear the mood, color or feeling of these chords?

To identify the quality of a chord that you are hearing:

1. Listen for the distinctive mood, color or feeling of the chord.

2. Decide whether the chord you are hearing sounds like the beginning of *Michael Row the Boat Ashore* or *St. James Infirmary*.

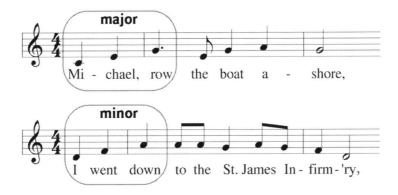

Play and listen to each all-white triad, then label it major or minor.
(The triad on *b* belongs to a strange, clashy category called diminished.)

To check your labels, turn the page.

Understand Major Triads

While every triad is made up of a pair of 3rds, all 3rds are not created equal. Although the two 3rds of a major triad look the same on the staff (both line-to-line or both space-to-space), they sound different. If you look at a major triad on the keyboard, you'll see that the bottom 3rd is actually bigger than the top 3rd. When you count the white *and* black keys jumped over, you find that the bottom 3rd contains four half-steps, but the top 3rd contains only three half-steps. In other words, a *major* triad has the bigger, *major* 3rd (four half-steps) on the bottom and the smaller, minor 3rd (three half-steps) on the top.

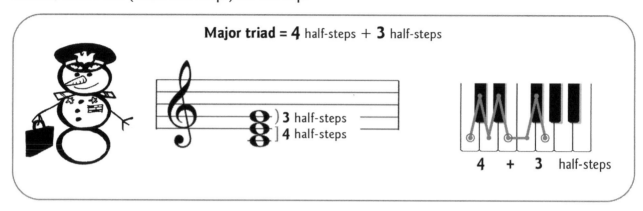

The major triad is the most common type of chord, its symbol is just its letter name, capitalized.

C major triad = C

C, F & G are the only all-white major triads. As an aid to remembering them, think of them as the **C**ool **F**rosty **G**ingerale majors.

THE ALL-WHITE MAJOR TRIADS

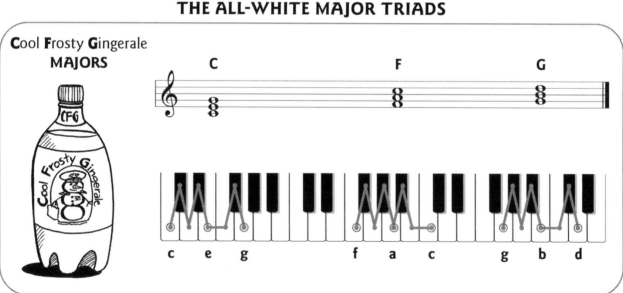

Cool Frosty Gingerale Jingle

For your own Cool Frosty Gingerale jingle, experiment with chord progressions that use C, F & G. You can block, break or arpeggiate the chords in whatever rhythm sounds good to you.

Understand Minor Triads

The reverse of a major triad, the minor triad has the smaller, minor 3rd (three half-steps) on the bottom and the bigger, major 3rd (four half-steps) on the top.

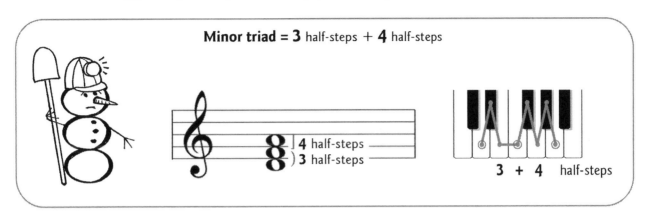

Minor triad = **3** half-steps + **4** half-steps

4 half-steps
3 half-steps

3 + 4 half-steps

The usual symbol for a minor triad is its letter name followed by a lowercase *m* (Dm). However, you might also see the letter name followed by *min* or − (Dmin or D−), or just the lowercase letter name itself (*d*).

D minor triad = Dm = (Dmin = D− = *d*)

Am, Dm & Em are the only all-white minor triads. My lemon-flavored aid for remembering them is lemon**ADE**.

THE ALL-WHITE MINOR TRIADS

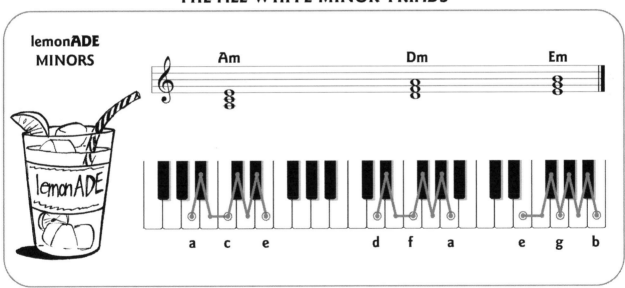

lemon**ADE**
MINORS

Am   Dm   Em

a c e   d f a   e g b

If Life Hands You a Lemon, Make LemonADE

Put the lemonADE minors in your hands and make a bittersweet song out of them.

Listen as you've never listened before. Play the major chord, feel it tickle the body internally, then play the minor chord and every desperate, terror-stricken, anger-ridden moment in your life will become that experience.

Lorin Hollander

Understand Diminished Triads

The jarring, melodramatic all-white triad on *b* is diminished—a pair of three half-step, minor 3rds.

Diminished triad = 3 half-steps + **3** half-steps

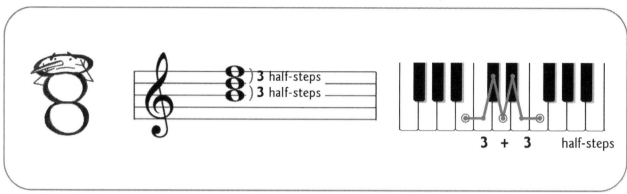

The symbol for a diminished triad is its letter name followed by *dim* or °.

B diminished triad = B dim = B°

The outside of a major or minor triad is a seven half-step *perfect* 5th (4 + 3 or 3 + 4). In contrast, diminished triads have a six half-step, *diminished* 5th (3 + 3), the ugly *diabolus in musica* that was banned in the Middle Ages! While majors and minors are the everyday staples of a healthy musical diet, diminished chords are merely condiments. When a musical recipe calls for a diminished chord, think of it as an optional dash of cayenne. If you're a novice, leave it out; if you're a connoisseur of fine chords, put it in to add spice.

The Fourth (and Final) Type of Triad

Triads are stacks of thirds, and thirds come in two sizes: 4 half-steps or 3 half-steps. You've already learned about major (4 + 3), minor (3 + 4) and diminished (3 + 3). Can you find the formula for the fourth (and final) type of triad?

See p. T-26

Learn the Key of C's Seven All-White Triads

When playing in the *key of C major,* expect that *c* will be the tonal center, with a note palette of (mostly) notes from the C major scale and a chord palette of (mostly) all-white chords.

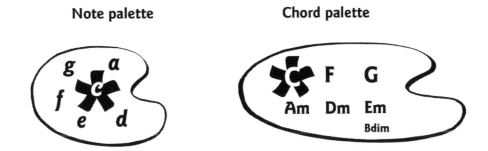

To have a satisfying ongoing relationship with each new chord, learn its sound, look, feel and spelling. Since you'll be spending your precious time, be efficient. Instead of learning each chord as a separate case, learn them in groups. By filing similar chords in the same mental file folder, they'll take up less room in your memory and be easier to access. By making a small investment of time now, you'll avoid the nuisance of stumbling and fumbling over chords, and you'll gain incredible musical dividends!

Learn the all-white triads by group.
Each one looks all white and feels like a pitchfork.

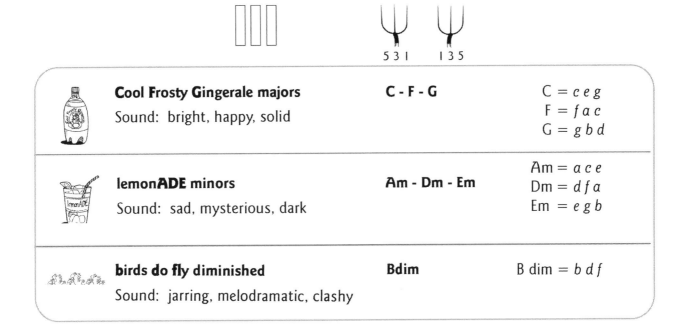

Do it your way.

How you learn these chords will depend on your learning style. Examine the learning strategies, drills and thrills in this chapter, then do whatever works best for you.

COOL FROSTY GINGERALE MAJORS

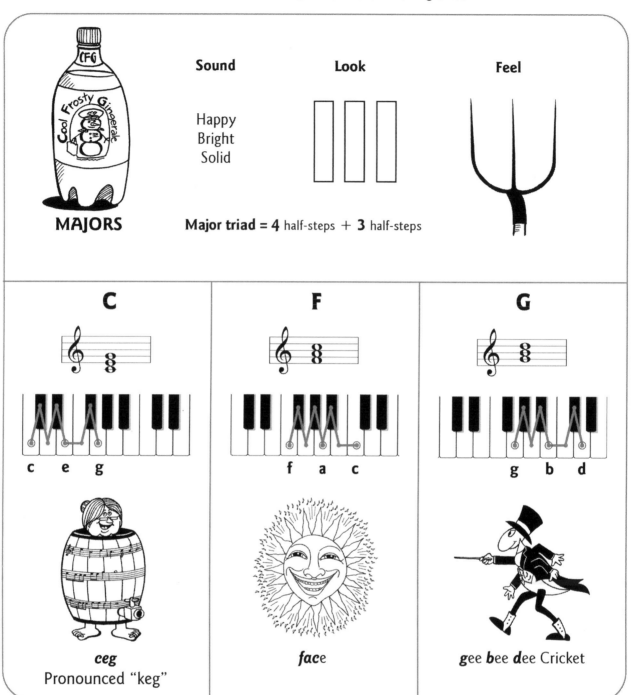

MAJORS

Sound

Happy
Bright
Solid

Look

Feel

Major triad = **4** half-steps + **3** half-steps

C

c e g

ceg
Pronounced "keg"

F

f a c

*fac*e

G

g b d

gee bee dee Cricket

bIRDS dO fLY

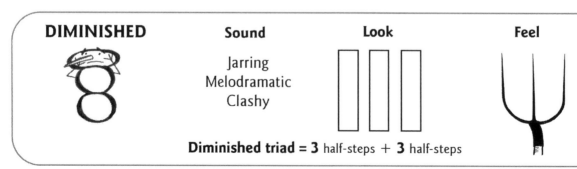

DIMINISHED

Sound

Jarring
Melodramatic
Clashy

Look

Feel

Diminished triad = **3** half-steps + **3** half-steps

LEMON**ADE** MINORS

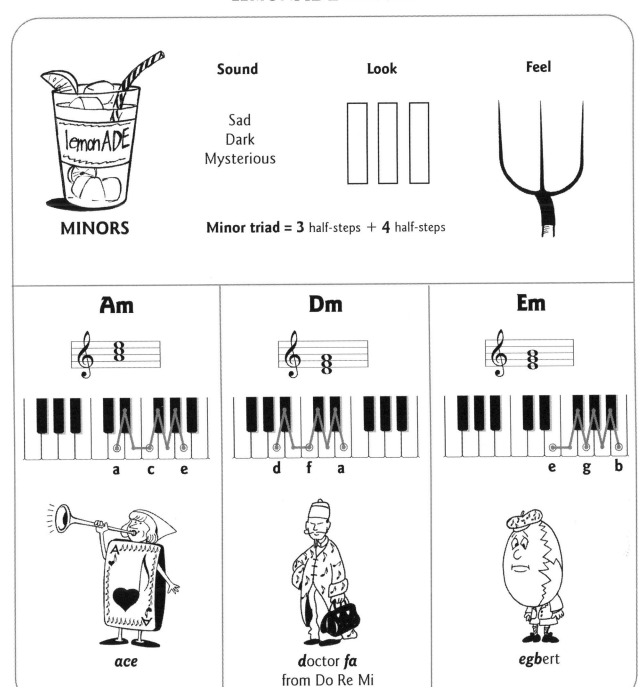

	Sound	Look	Feel
MINORS	Sad Dark Mysterious		

Minor triad = **3** half-steps + **4** half-steps

Am
a   c   e

ace

Dm
d   f   a

*d*octor *fa*
from Do Re Mi

Em
e   g   b

*egb*ert

DIMINISHED

B dim
b   d   f

*b*irds *d*o *f*ly

The Key of C Major's Primary Chords

As you would guess, the *major* chords are of *major* importance in a *major* key. Like painting with just primary colors, you can play most simple songs with just C's three primary chords (C, F & G). For others, you might add C's secondary chords (Am, Dm & Em), its tertiary chord (B dim) and/or some chords from outside this basic palette.

C = *c e g*

(pronounced "keg") feels like home, the place that music in the key of C usually starts, often returns and almost always ends.

Built on C's **first** scale tone, the tonal center, C is called the **tonic** chord.

G = *g b d*

(alias "**geebeed**ee cricket") has a tense, forceful sound that demands resolution home to C. The most common way to end a phrase, song or symphony in the key of C, G→C (a falling fifth) sounds like dramatically saying, "Go home!"

Built on C's **fifth** scale tone, G is called the **dominant**, because it forcefully pushes you home to C. Expect to also find bigger, tenser versions, especially G7 (*g b d f*).

F = *f a c*

(alias "**fac**e") has a mellow, churchy sound that either resolves home to C or goes someplace else. A gentle way to end a phrase in the key of C, F→C (a rising fifth) sounds like a heavenly choir sublimely singing "Amen."

Built on C's **fourth** scale tone, F is called the **sub-dominant** because, in contrast to the 5th-*above*-the tonic dominant, it is a 5th *below* the tonic.

When the Saints Go Marching in Root Position

African-American gospel hymn

In New Orleans, bands play this song for funerals—slowly (as a dirge) on the way to the cemetery and fast (as a jazzy parade) on the way back! Use these *root position voicings* (root on the bottom), the suggested rhythm or whatever sounds good to you.

For chord jumping strategies, see page 6-14 & 6-15.

When the Saints Go Marching in Closest Position

While jumping from C to F or G gets the job done, it's hard to jump smoothly, especially at fast tempos or without looking at your hands. Fortunately, with practice, *closest position voicings* will sound smooth and feel as easy as shifting gears on a bike or car. Use the suggested rhythm or whatever sounds good to you.

To learn how to grab closest position voicings, see pages 6-20 & 6-21.

When the Saints Go Marching in a Lead Sheet

Instead of reading a grand staff arrangement, you can look at a *lead sheet* — the melody with chord symbols and lyrics. Then, like a folk, rock or jazz player, you can interpret the chord symbols using whatever voicings, styles and melodic fills sound good to you.

Slowly or lively

                           C

Oh, when the Saints,_____ go march - ing in,_____

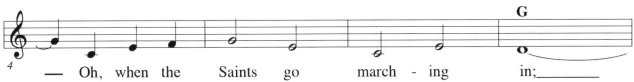

    G

— Oh, when the Saints go march - ing in;_____

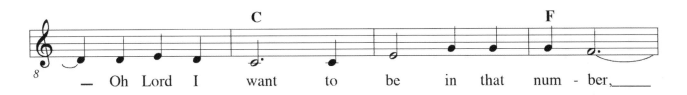

    C   F

— Oh Lord I want to be in that num - ber,_____

    C   G   C

_____ When the Saints go march - ing in._____

Style Suggestions

DRILL 6: ALL-WHITE TRIADS

A. ALL-WHITE TRIADS

Drill your left hand *(5 3 I)*,
your right hand *(I 2 5)*
and/or both hands together.

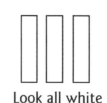

Look all white

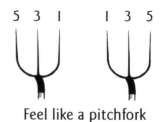

Feel like a pitchfork

- **Drill by group**

Cool Frosty Gingerale majors
Say, play and spell C, F and G.

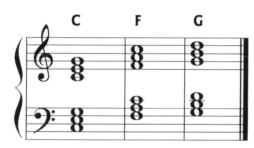

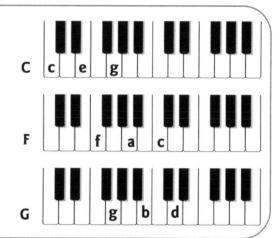

lemonADE minors
Say, play and spell Am, Dm and Em.

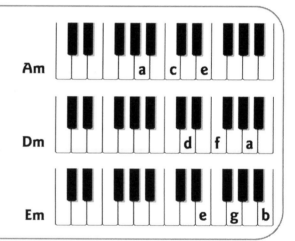

birds do fly diminished
Say, play and spell Bdim.

- ## Drill stepwise

  Play all-white triads on every note of the C major scale, identifying the quality of each triad.

  | C | Dm | Em | F | G | Am | B dim |

- ## Drill randomly

  Choose a white root at random, then play an all-white triad on it and identify its quality. "The chord on ___ is _____ (major, minor or diminished)."

Play: *Drunken Sailor (6-27)*

Learning Strategies

1. **Use memory aids** like the Cast of Chords, or create your own memory aids— perhaps **c**ows **e**at **g**rass for C or **d.f.a.** (**d**octor **of** **f**ine **a**rts) for Dm. If you already use "**e**very **g**ood **b**oy **d**oes **f**ine" to remember the lines of the treble staff, you might use "**e**very **g**ood **b**oy" for Em, "**g**ood **b**oy **d**oes" for G and "**b**oy **d**oes **f**ine" for B dim. One student made up a song that began, "A **ceg** was sent to **d**octor **fa** and **eg**bert . . ."

2. **Quiz yourself with flash cards** while watching T.V., standing in check-out lines or whenever you like. Buy flash cards at a music store or make your own.

3. **Play, spell and sing chords** on tabletops or in the air.

4. **Write chord spellings** on paper or in the air. Some people make magnificent, multi-colored charts that they refer to later. Others sloppily write the spellings over and over again, never bothering to reread what they've written.

5. **Post chord spellings** where you'll see them often, perhaps on your bathroom mirror or the dashboard of your car.

6. **Visualize yourself playing chords** on the keyboard and imagine how their distinctive qualities sound.

7. **Get together with a music buddy** to quiz one another on playing, spelling and singing chords. Then start jamming!

Learn the seven spellings, then recycle them!

Since there are seven letters in the musical alphabet, there are only seven possible triad spellings. Consequently, once you've learned a spelling, you can recycle it in many ways. For instance, you'll use the letters *c, e* and *g* to spell C *(c e g)*, Cm *(c e♭ g)*, C♯ *(c♯ e♯ g♯)*, C♯m *(c♯ e g♯)* and other C-family chords.

See p. T-27

B. LEFT HAND C→F→C AND C→G→C JUMPING

Like batters and golfers grooving their swing, practice C→F→C and C→G→C jumping until they feel automatic. Go up for several octaves, then come back down, switching between C, F and G in whatever ways you like. (In low registers, omit the murk-making third.) Rather than relying on rote repetition, use some of the strategies on the facing page. When you feel confident, practice jumping with your eyes closed.

- **Drill:**   C   →   F   →   C
  Sounds like: *Home.*   *A*   -   *men.*

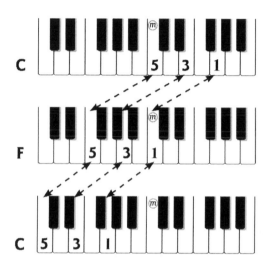

- **Drill:**   C   →   G   →   C
  Sounds like: *Home.*   *Go*   *home.*

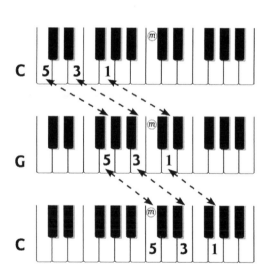

> **Play:** C→F: *Oh! How Lovely* (6-29), C→G: *Can Can* (6-28),
> C→F→C→G: *When The Saints Go Marching* (6-10), *Amazing Grace* (6-30), *Silent Night* (6-31)

Good news for reluctant jumpers.

If jumping still feels too dangerous, do not fear. Learn easier-to-play,
smoother-sounding voicings on pages 6-20 (left hand) and 6-21 (right hand).

How to Unbump Any Jump

LOOKING AT YOUR HANDS

Sneak a peak: While playing C, look down at your hands, jump to G or F, then look back up at the music. To avoid unseemly pauses, practice looking down, playing the chord and re-finding your place.

Memorize the whole song or section.

NOT LOOKING AT YOUR HANDS

C down or up a 5th: Play left hand C. To go down to F, move your hand to replace your pinkie with your thumb. To go up to G, replace your thumb with your pinkie.

C up or down a 4th: Play left hand C. To go up to F, move your hand to replace your pointer with your pinkie. To go down to G, replace your ring finger with your thumb.

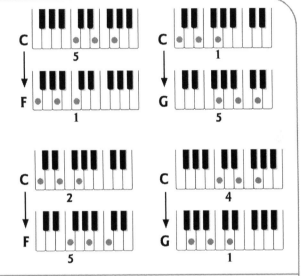

C → F: Play left hand C. Move your left hand so it brushes across the black keys. When you feel three black keys under fingers *4, 3* and *2*, bring *3* up a half-step to play F with *5, 3* and *1*.

C → G: Play left hand C, noticing that fingers *3* and *2* (on *e* and *f*) are not separated by a black key. Brushing across the black keys, move your hand until *3* and *2* lodge themselves on feel-alike white keys *b* and *c*. Play G.

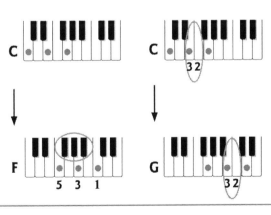

Position your arm: When playing each chord, feel the angle your arm makes with your body. Practice moving between these two positions.

C. FIVE-FINGER PATTERNS FOR C, F & G and Am, Dm & Em

Teach your fingers to grab major five-finger patterns—fingering's basic default settings. When you grab a major triad, you're plucking the first, third and fifth notes from a major scale. To play a major five-finger pattern, simply reinsert the missing second and fourth notes.

- **Build a major (or minor) five-finger pattern from a major (or minor) triad.**

  1. Grab a major (or minor) triad.

  2. Insert the missing scale tones a whole-step up from the bottom and down from the top.

  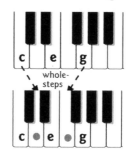

- **Play up and down five-finger patterns for C, F & G and Am, Dm & Em.**

C and G are all white;
F has one black key ($b\flat$).

Am and Dm are all white;
Em has one black key ($f\sharp$).

 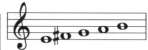

If a pattern has any black keys, move gradually into the black keys.

Prepare yourself to play the black key(s), instead of awkwardly lunging back and forth from white keys to black keys. Exactly where you place your fingers will depend on their size and shape—long, short, skinny or sausage-like. Place your fingers as close into the black keys as you can to design a choreography that works well for you.

Play: Five-Finger Pattern Ear Tunes (6-24#5),
Clouds And Sunshine by Beyer (6-40), *Halling* by Grieg (6-37)

D. INVERSION VOICINGS FOR ALL-WHITE TRIADS

Imagine all of the *c*'s, *e*'s and *g*'s lit up on your piano. How many ways can you play a C major triad that include all three chord tones consecutively? There are three compact options: the basic stack of 3rds voicing plus two *inversions*—rearranged versions that each contain one 3rd and one 4th. In *root position* (*c e g*), the root of the stack of 3rds is on the bottom; while in either inversion (*e g **c*** or *g **c** e*), the root is at the top of the "big gap" 4th.

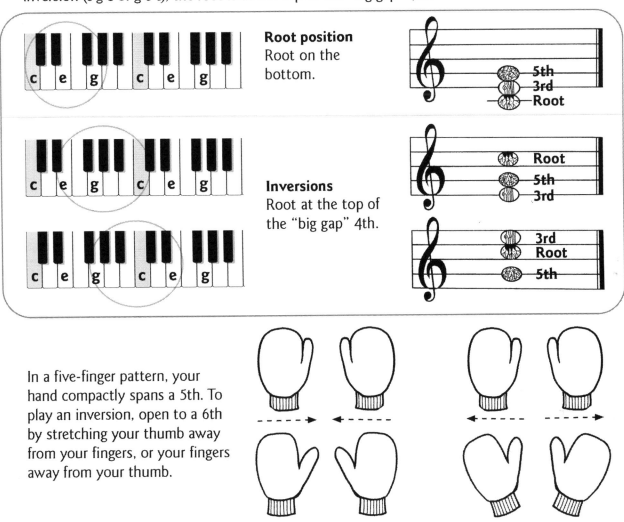

Root position
Root on the bottom.

Inversions
Root at the top of the "big gap" 4th.

In a five-finger pattern, your hand compactly spans a 5th. To play an inversion, open to a 6th by stretching your thumb away from your fingers, or your fingers away from your thumb.

Having stretched out to a 6th, take off your imaginary mitten. Play the outside notes with fingers *1* and *5*, and put the "big gap" 4th under the root with finger 2 or 3.

For each hand, play one inversion with *1 3 5* and the other with *1 2 5*.
For each inversion, play one hand with *1 3 5* and the other with *1 2 5*.

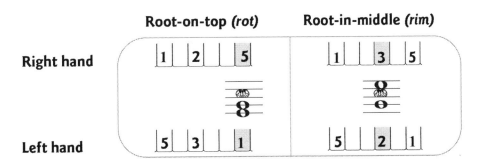

D1. ALL-WHITE ROOT-ON-TOP TRIADS (rot)

Put your top finger on the root. Drill your left hand *(5 3 1)*,
right hand *(1 2 5)* or hands together. (C *rot* = C/e = e g c.)

Look all white   Feel like a mitten

- ## Drill by group

Cool Frosty Gingerale root-on-top majors
Say, play and spell C, F and G *rot*.

C/e   F/a   G/b

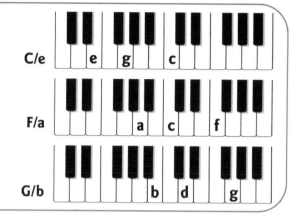

C/e | e | g | c

F/a | a | c | f

G/b | b | d | g

lemonADE root-on-top minors
Say, play and spell Am, Dm and Em *rot*.

Am/c   Dm/f   Em/g

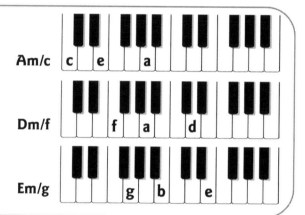

Am/c | c | e | a

Dm/f | f | a | d

Em/g | g | b | e

**birds do fly
root-on-top diminished**
Say, play and spell Bdim *rot*.

Bdim/d

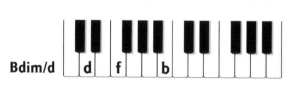

Bdim/d | d | f | b

- ## Drill stepwise

Play root-on-top triads on every note of the C major scale, identifying the quality of each.

C/e   Dm/f   Em/g   F/a   G/b   Am/c   B dim/d

- ## Drill randomly

Choose any white root, then play and identify an all-white root-on-top triad on it.

Play: Inversion Shape Ear Tunes (6-24), *Lean On Me* Revisited (6-24), *Oh! How Lovely* (6-29)

D2. ALL-WHITE ROOT-IN-MIDDLE TRIADS (*rim*)

Point your left *pointer* at the root, or make a *rim* around the *right middle finger*. Drill your left hand (*5 2 1*), right hand (*1 3 5*) or hands together. (C *rim* = C/g = g c e.)

Look all white   Feel like a mitten

- ### Drill by group

Cool Frosty Gingerale root-in-middle majors.

Say, play and spell C, F and G *rim*.

C/g   F/c   G/d

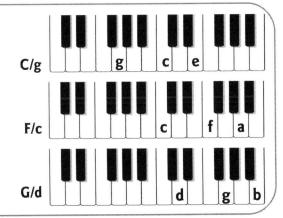

C/g   g c e

F/c   c f a

G/d   d g b

lemonADE root-in-middle minors

Say, play and spell Am, Dm and Em *rim*.

Am/e   Dm/a   Em/b

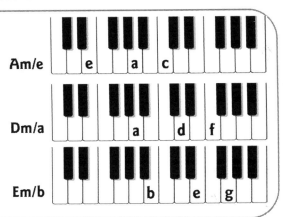

Am/e   e a c

Dm/a   a d f

Em/b   b e g

birds do fly root-in-middle diminished

Say, play and spell Bdim *rim*.

Bdim/f

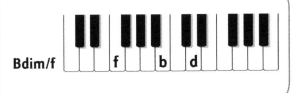

Bdim/f   f b d

- ### Drill stepwise

  Play root-on-top triads on every note of the C major scale, identifying the quality of each.

  C/g   Dm/a   Em/b   F/c   G/d   Am/e   B dim/f

- ### Drill randomly

  Choose any white root, then play and identify an all-white root-in-middle triad on it.

Play: Inversion Shape Ear Tunes (6-24), *Oh! How Lovely* (6-29)

E. CLOSEST POSITION VOICINGS FOR C→F→C and C→G→C

Imagine four men singing barbership. While Mel sings the melody, Low, Middle and High sing chords below him. Instead of all three jumping to every new chord, one of them usually holds or repeats his note, while the others add the missing chord tones over, around or under him.

Left hand

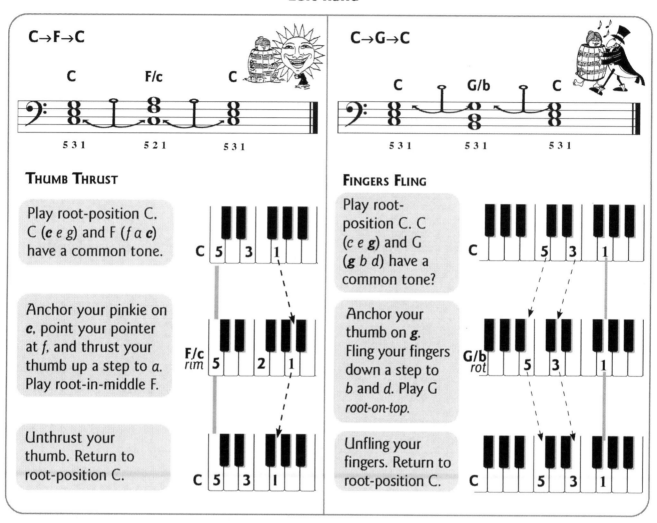

C→F→C

C   F/c   C

5 3 1   5 2 1   5 3 1

THUMB THRUST

Play root-position C. C (*c e g*) and F (*f a c*) have a common tone.

Anchor your pinkie on *c*, point your pointer at *f*, and thrust your thumb up a step to *a*. Play root-in-middle F.

Unthrust your thumb. Return to root-position C.

C 5 3 1
F/c *rim* 5 2 1
C 5 3 1

C→G→C

C   G/b   C

5 3 1   5 3 1   5 3 1

FINGERS FLING

Play root-position C. C (*c e g*) and G (*g b d*) have a common tone?

Anchor your thumb on *g*. Fling your fingers down a step to *b* and *d*. Play G *root-on-top*.

Unfling your fingers. Return to root-position C.

C 5 3 1
G/b *rot* 5 3 1
C 5 3 1

Play: C→F: *Oh! How Lovely* (6-29), C→G: *Can Can* (6-28),
C→F→C→G: *When The Saints Go Marching* (6-10), *Amazing Grace* (6-30), *Silent Night* (6-31)

FINDING CLOSEST POSITION VOICINGS FOR ANY TWO TRIADS

Play the first triad in a position that sounds good—around middle *c*, or in the octave below it.	
Find the new root. **Shape** a triad over, around or under it.	**Spell** the next triad. Do these chords have any tone(s) in common? • If so, anchor on the common tone and add the missing tones over, around or under it. • If not, lift the shape next door or change shapes and move in the opposite direction.

Play: *Canon* by Pachelbel (6-33), *All The Pretty Little Horses* (6-39)

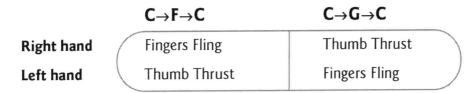

	C→F→C	C→G→C
Right hand	Fingers Fling	Thumb Thrust
Left hand	Thumb Thrust	Fingers Fling

Right hand

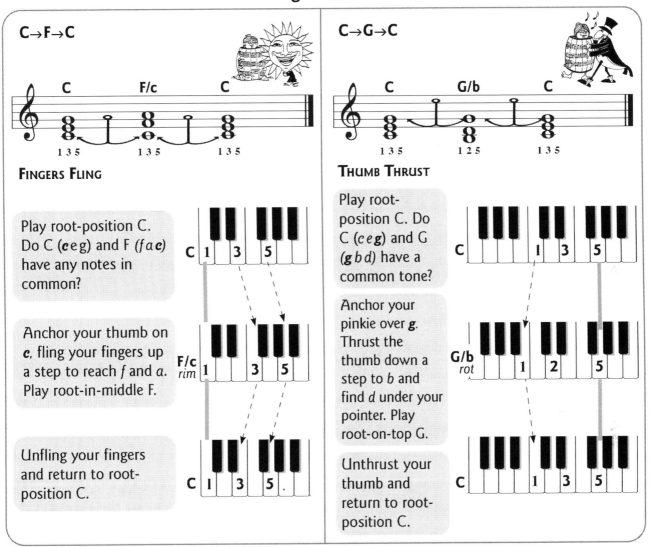

C→F→C

C   F/c   C

1 3 5   1 3 5   1 3 5

FINGERS FLING

Play root-position C. Do C (*c e* g) and F (*f a c*) have any notes in common?

Anchor your thumb on *c*, fling your fingers up a step to reach *f* and *a*. Play root-in-middle F.

Unfling your fingers and return to root-position C.

C→G→C

C   G/b   C

1 3 5   1 2 5   1 3 5

THUMB THRUST

Play root-position C. Do C (*c e* g) and G (*g b d*) have a common tone?

Anchor your pinkie over *g*. Thrust the thumb down a step to *b* and find *d* under your pointer. Play root-on-top G.

Unthrust your thumb and return to root-position C.

Play: C→F: *Oh! How Lovely* (6-29), C→G: *Can Can* (6-28), C→F→C→G: *When The Saints Sing Along* (6-35)

Can you find the closest position voicings for C→F→C and C→G→C starting with both C *rot* and C *rim*? Do these moves feel familiar? (See page T-34.)

Spelling Versus Shaping

Spelling chords keeps you in your head and slows you down.

Shaping chords lets you play intuitively and fluently.

Go back to pages 6-18 to 19. Learn the *rot* and *rim* shapes right now!

F. CONSECUTIVE POSITIONS OF ALL-WHITE TRIADS

Move back and forth from root position, through the two inversions, to root position in the next octave. With hands alone and/or together, first arpeggiate the chords (so you can think about the notes and fingerings), then block the chords.

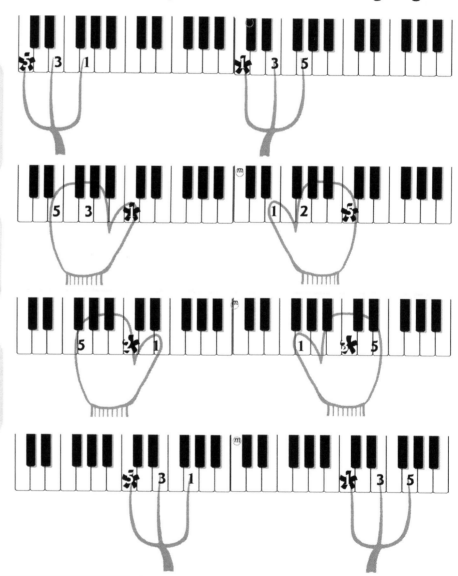

Root position	Root-on-top	Root-in-middle	Root position
1 3 5	1 2 5	1 3 5	1 3 5
5 3 1	5 3 1	5 2 1	5 3 1

For consecutive positions, switch between "pitchfork" and "mitten" fingerings.

Root position to inversion
Play a root position triad. Lift your "pitchfork," open its outside 5th to a 6th and fill in the "mitten" with 2 or 3.

Inversion to inversion.
Lift the "mitten" and keep the outside 6th, but switch the inside from 3 to 2 or 2 to 3.

Inversion to root position
Close your "mitten" down to a 5th and grab a root position triad with 5 3 1 or 1 3 5

Play: Shifting Shapes (6-24), *Let It Be* (6-24), *Gavotte* (6-36), *Shalom Chaverim* (6-38).

G. ADDING PEDAL POWER

The *damper pedal* lifts the *dampers* off the strings, so that played notes keep sounding and overtones of unplayed notes ring out sympathetically.

"The pedal is the soul of the piano . . ."
Arthur Rubinstein

"And with the pedal, I love to meddle . . ."
Irving Berlin

- Put your right heel on the floor to serve as a fucrum.
- Depress the right pedal with the ball of your foot.
- Avoid unwanted banging sounds by keeping your foot in contact with the pedal as you depress ("down") or release ("up") the pedal.
- Learn different ways to pedal, then decide how and where to pedal each song.

1. Rhythmic (Simultaneous) Pedal

To emphasize the rhythmic, dancelike nature of a song, simultaneously play the first chord and depress the pedal. Before the next chord, lift your fingers off the notes and release ("up") the pedal in preparation for playing and pedalling the next chord. Always lift and lower your fingers and foot at the same time.

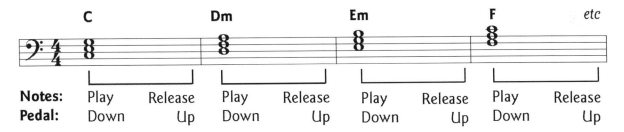

	C		Dm		Em		F		etc
Notes:	Play	Release	Play	Release	Play	Release	Play	Release	
Pedal:	Down	Up	Down	Up	Down	Up	Down	Up	

Play: *Can Can* (6-28), *Amazing Grace* (6-30) or whatever you like.

2. Legato (Overlapping) Pedal

To create a smooth, singing melody over a changing harmony, play and pedal the first chord. Keeping your foot on the pedal, lift your fingers off the notes to play the next chord. To make the sound continuous, be sure that either your fingers are holding down keys or your foot is holding down the pedal. When you hear the clash of overlapping chords, release ("up") and immediately depress ("down") the pedal. When you hear the clash, clear the clash!

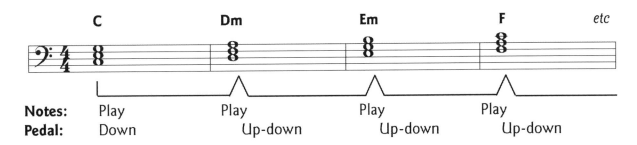

	C	Dm	Em	F	etc
Notes:	Play	Play	Play	Play	
Pedal:	Down	Up-down	Up-down	Up-down	

Play: *Amazing Grace* (6-30), *Silent Night* (6-31), *All The Pretty Horses* (6-39) or whatever you like.

Thrills with All-White Triads in Diatonic Music

DIATONIC PIECES IN THE KEY OF C MAJOR

Play on the white keys with *c* the tonal center (*) and C, F and G, the primary chords

3. **Cool Frosty Gingerale Jingle**, page 6-2. Make up jingles with just C, F and G.

4. **Shape Shifting**. Starting and ending on C, experiment with moving between chords in these three ways. (Don't slow yourself down by naming the intervening chords.)

LIFT	ANCHORED SHIFT	SHIFT LIFT
Keeping the same shape, lift your hand up or down the keyboard, like C→G→C jumping.	Keeping one finger anchored on its note, change one or both of the other notes, like closest position voicings.	While lifting your hand, shift to another shape, like consecutive positions.

5. **C, F and G Ear Tunes.** Expect the melody to either step next door or jump to a chord tone. To tune your internal dial to the key of C: play closest position C→G→C, sing the first note, then find it on the keyboard. *(5f = five-finger pattern)*

C & G	Clementine	La Cucaracha	Skip to My Lou	Yellow Rose of Texas
C, F & G	Aunt Rhody (5f)	Blueberry Hill	Lion Sleeps Tonight (5f)	Love Is a Rose
	Ode to Joy (5f)	Oh! Susanna	Spanish Harlem	This Land Is Your Land

6. **Joy to the World with Chords** (C, Dm, F and G). Add these chords or whatever sounds good to you. For hints on sounding out the meody, see page 2-11#13.

7. **Inversion Shape Ear Tunes.** Start on the bottom note and use only chord tones.

ROOT-IN-MIDDLE C/g	Reveille ("You got to get up . . .") and most of Taps ("Day is done . . .")
ROOT-ON-TOP C/e	Most of In the Mood ("Who's the livin' dolly . . . ")

8. **Lean on Me Revisited**, page 3-9. Ear out the melody. Add root-on-top shapes under the melody with left hand octaves (or low roots).

9. **Let It Be** by Lennon & McCartney. Finger using consecutive positions of C as a scaffolding. Start in C*rot* position with 2 on *g*.

10. **When the Saints Go Marching In** (C, F and G). Since Louis Armstrong recorded this gospel hymn in 1938, it's become a jazz standard. Use root positions triads (6-9), closest position triads (6-10), jump bass (6-11), walking bass (6-34), boogie bass (6-35) or something else.

11. **Can Can**, pages 6-28 (C and G). Jacques Offenbach wrote the *Infernal Galop* for his 1858 opera *Orpheus in the Underworld*. The French later renamed this gay, high-kicking dance the *can can*, which literally means "tittle-tattle" or "scandal."

12. **Oh! How Lovely Is the Evening**, page 6-29 (C and F). Experiment with both left hand and right hand styles on this lovely song.

13. *Amazing Grace* **of C, F and G**, page 6-30. For this pentatonic hymn, use root position triads (4-9), 3rds and 6ths under the melody (5-14), broken closest position voicings (6-30), arpeggios (6-30), jump bass (6-30) and/or add pedal (6-23).

14. *Silent Night*, pages 6-31 (C, F and G). On December 24, 1818, the assistant pastor of a small Austrian church showed the organist a poem he'd written. Joseph Mohr asked Franz Grüber to add a melody and guitar accompaniment. On Christmas Eve, the two men sang *Silent Night*, with Mohr on guitar and the choir harmonizing.

15. *Canon* by Johann Pachelbel, page 6-32 (C, Em, F, G, and Am). In the 1680's the German composer wrote this piece for three violins and a cello playing a repeating bass line. It remained unpublished until the early 20th century.

16. **Diatonic Lead Sheets in C.** Buy, borrow or download songs with no sharps or flats. If you find an extended chord (like G7), look it up on pages T-30 to 32.

Baby You're a Rich Man	*Golden Slumbers*	*Mack the Knife*
Born Free	*In the Still of the Night*	*Music Box Dancer*
Both Sides Now	*King of the Road*	*My Girl*
Casey Jones	*Lean on Me*	*The Rose*
Can't Buy Me Love	*Let It Be*	*Stand By Me*
Circle Game	*Love Is a Rose*	*Turn! Turn! Turn!*
Come Away With Me	*Love Is All Around*	*Whiter Shade of Pale*

17. **When the Saints Walk the Bass**, page 6-34. Dress up the walking bass (R 7 6 5) with connecting flourishes.

18. *Amazing Grace* **of Stepwise Triads**, page 4-14. Label the chords. Do the labels (and the act of labelling) help you remember the harmony?

19. *Gavotte* by Benjamin Carr (1768-1831), page 6-36. This *gavotte* (a lively French peasant dance from the seventeenth century) uses consecutive positions of C.

20. *Halling (Norwegian Dance)* by Edward Grieg (1843-1907), page 6-37. Imagine Grieg's friends and neighbors dancing happily overlooking the fjord.

21. **Diatonic Sheet Music in C.** Buy, borrow or download songs with no sharps or flats.

BYRD: *The Morris*	PURCELL: *Trumpet Tune*
DUNCOMBE: *Fanfare Minuet*	RAMEAU: *Minuet en Rondeau*
KABALEVSKY: *Little Song & Little Polka* from Opus 39	STRAVINSKY: *Five Finger Toccata*
KOHLER: *Soldier's Song*	For popular songs, see #16.

22. *Oh! How Lovely is the Evening*, page 6-29. Play this song as a two- or three-part round using whatever voicings you like.

23. **When the Saints Sing Along**, page 6-35. Accompany a friend playing or singing the melody with a boogie bass and closest position right-hand chords.

DIATONIC PIECES IN OTHER ALL-WHITE MODES

On the white keys, choose any of the 7 white keys as the tonal center. Sixth century Greeks named the 7 modes after states. Medieval monks sang them in Gregorian chants. By the 18th century, Bach & Co. were using only 2: C *Ionian* (now the key of C major) and A *Aeolian* (now the key of A minor). In the 20th century, jazz/pop players rediscovered all 7.

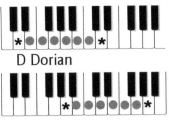
D Dorian

A Aeolian

24. **Changing Home.** Play melodies that begin, end and often return to any tonal center. Accompany by just repeating the tonal center or playing one of these progressions:

C Ionian (Major)	C→F→C or C→G→C	*Amazing Grace*
D Dorian	Dm→C→Dm or Dm→G→Dm	*Drunken Sailor, So What*
E Phrygian	Em→F→Em or Em→Dm→Em	
F Lydian	F→G→F or F→Em→F	
G Mixolydian	G→F→G or G→Dm→G	*On Broadway*
A Aeolian (Minor)	Am→Dm→Am or Am→Em→Am	*All the Pretty Little Horses*
B Locrian	Used in exotic jazz improvs	

25. *Drunken Sailor*, page 6-27 (Dm & C). The melody of this early 19th century sea chantey in D *Dorian* uses mostly chord tones of white-key neighbors Dm and C.

26. *Shalom Chaverim*, page 6-38 (Dm). *Shalom* is a beautiful Hebrew word that means *peace*. When used as a greeting or farewell, it's like saying "Peace be with you."

27. **Dorian Jazz Tunes.** Buy, borrow or download D Dorian songs.

Impressions	*Little Sunflower*	*So What*

28. *All the Pretty Horses*, page 6-39 (Am, Dm & Em). To accompany this lullaby in A *Aeolian*, practice Am→Dm and Am→Em by adapting the strategies on page 6-20.

29. **Clouds and Sunshine** by Ferdinand Beyer, page 6-40. This piece moves back and forth between "cloudy" A Aeolian and "sunny" C Ionian.

30. **Aeolian (Minor) Music.** Buy, borrow or download all-white A Aeolian songs.

BURGMULLER: *Arabesque* (first section)	WITHERS: *Ain't No Sunshine*
ROTA, arranged by MANCINI: *Love Theme from Romeo and Juliet* (first 16 and last 22 measures)	

31. *Shalom Chaverim* **Duet**, page 6-38 (Dm). Play this peaceful round with friends.

32. **Dorian Duet.** Make up your own duet to *Drunken Sailor*'s Dm→C→Dm progression.
- <u>Person on the left</u>: Set the tempo with a two-handed progression and end on Dm.
- <u>Person on the right</u>: Feel the groove, then begin to play on the white keys.

Drunken Sailor

Traditional 19th century American sea chantey

Brightly

What shall we do with the drunk-en sail-or, What shall we do with the drunk-en sail-or

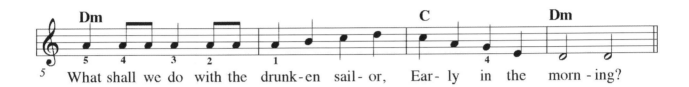

What shall we do with the drunk-en sail-or, Ear-ly in the morn-ing?

CHORUS

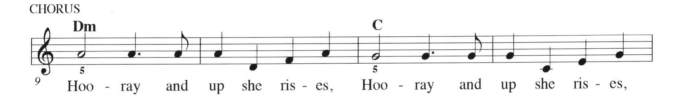

Hoo - ray and up she ris - es, Hoo - ray and up she ris - es,

Hoo - ray and up she ris - es, Ear - ly in the morn - ing.

2. Put him in the longboat 'til he's sober …

3. Shave his belly with a rusty razor …

4. Put him in a leaky boat and make him bale her …

5. Temperance lectures will never help him …

Style Suggestions

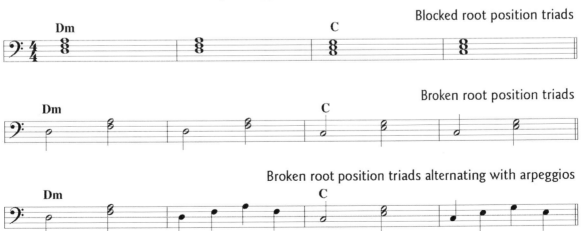

Blocked root position triads

Broken root position triads

Broken root position triads alternating with arpeggios

Can Can

Jacques Offenbach (1819–1880)

Energetically

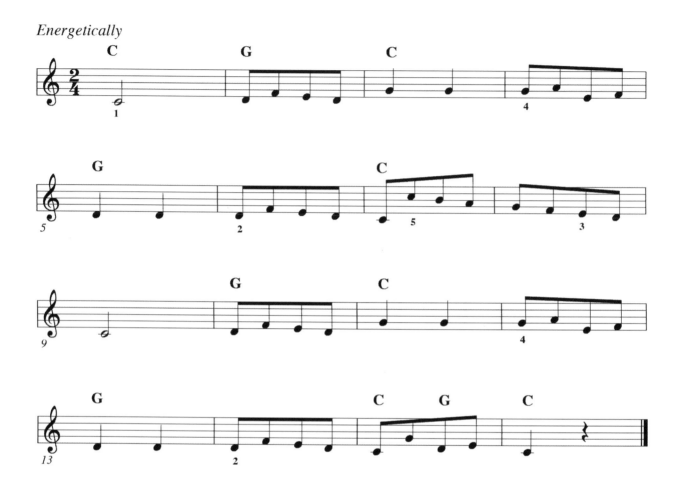

Style Suggestions

Closest position broken chords   Contrary motion C scale for ms. 7–8

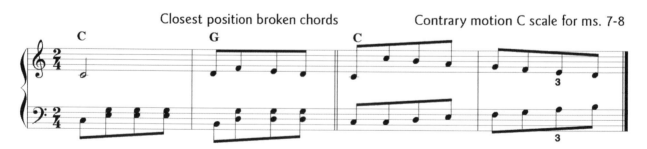

My Can Can Cover

As a sixth-grader, I wrote a report on France and put a high-kicking can can dancer on the cover. When you lifted her gauzy skirt, you saw the title—"France."

Oh! How Lovely Is the Evening

Traditional German folk song and round

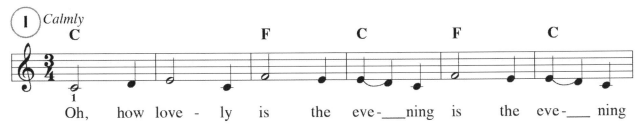

1 *Calmly*

Oh, how love - ly is the eve-___ning is the eve-___ ning

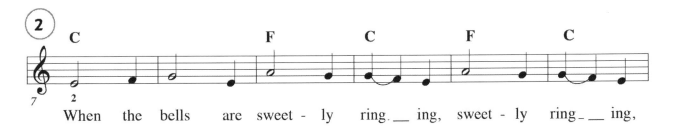

2

When the bells are sweet - ly ring.___ ing, sweet - ly ring ___ ing,

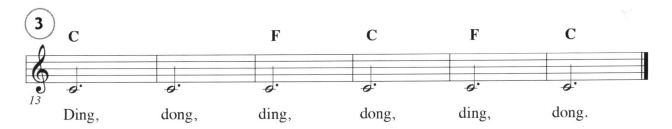

3

Ding, dong, ding, dong, ding, dong.

Style Suggestions

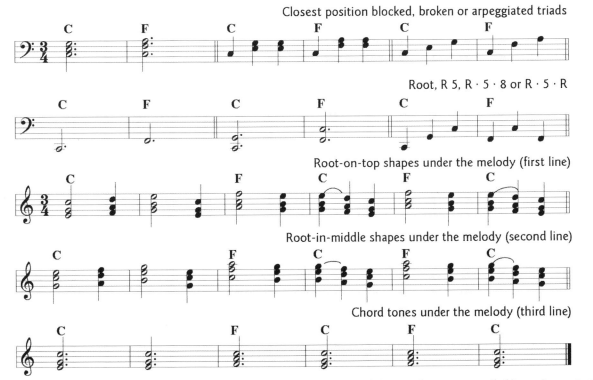

Closest position blocked, broken or arpeggiated triads

Root, R 5, R · 5 · 8 or R · 5 · R

Root-on-top shapes under the melody (first line)

Root-in-middle shapes under the melody (second line)

Chord tones under the melody (third line)

The Amazing Grace of C, F and G

Learn this song as is, then add pedal (page 6-23) and your choice of style(s).

- At fast tempos: rhythmic pedal on the downbeat of each measure and on the last G.

- At slow tempo: legato pedal at the beginning of each new chord or wherever you like.

Silent Night

Music by Franz Grüber (1787–1863) & Lyrics by Joseph Mohr (1792–1848)

To remember the harmony, notice that the second half of the song mirrors the first half, except for the last line's G.

C	C	C	C
G	G	C	C
F	F	C	C
F	F	C	C
G	G	C	C
C	G	C	C

Slowly

Si_____ -lent night, ho_____ -ly night!

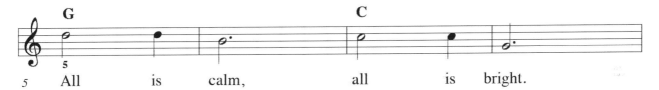

5   All   is   calm,   all   is   bright.

9   Round   yon   Vir_____ -gin   Moth - er   and   Child.

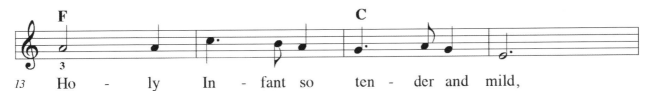

13   Ho - ly   In - fant   so   ten - der   and   mild,

17   Sleep   in   heav - en - ly   peace,_____

21   Sleep_____   in   heav - en - ly   peace.

Style Suggestions

R 3 5 arpeggios   R 5 8 arpeggios

Canon

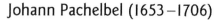

Pachelbel originally wrote this diatonic piece in the key of D for three violins and cello. While the violinists played a carefully notated *canon* (an imitative form similar to a round), the cello played a *basso continuo* (a repeating four-measure bass line). In the key of C, the bass line would be:

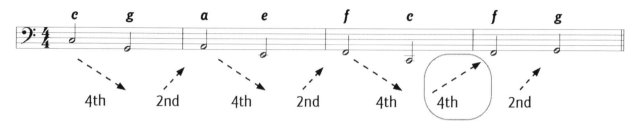

To turn the quartet into a piano solo:

- Memorize the progression—alternating falling 4ths and rising 2nds (except for one rising 4th).
- Build all-white triads on each bass note.
- Finger the melody.
- Play the chords however you like, for instance:

Canon Around

To play this piece as a modified round, each person repeats just those lines that feel easy enough, then ends on the coda.

Compare Canons

Find a grand-staff arrangement of the *Canon* in another key.

- Label the chords and learn any new ones.
- Do the chords follow the down a 4th, up a 2nd … pattern?
- Is the piece easier to read once you know the chords?
- Are there interesting style ideas to adapt to your own lead sheet version?

See p. T-7

When the Saints Walk the Bass

Like most walking bass arrangements, the bass line either:

- **Steps** from one chord tone to another (C: *c b a g*) or to the next chord's root (ms. 12-13).
- **Jumps** from one chord tone to another (C: *g* to *c*) or to the next chord's root (ms. 16-17).

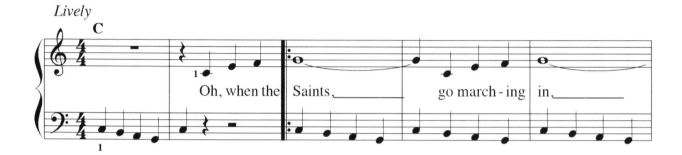

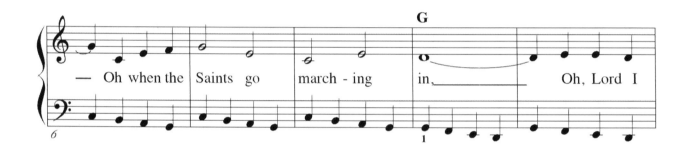

When the Saints Sing Along

To accompany a friend (or yourself) singing, play a boogie bass in your left hand and closest position chords in your right hand.

Gavotte

by Benjamin Carr (1768–1831)

Lively dance

Halling (Norwegian Dance)

by Edward Grieg (1843–1907)

- **Bass:** The left hand rhythmically repeats *g* to *c* (G's root to C's root, and also C's fifth to C's root.)

- **Melody:** The right hand dances between broken triads (ms. 3-6) and between five-finger positions and triads (ms. 7-11). If it helps you, label the treble clef chords as:

| Dm Bdim | C Am | Bdim F | G C/e |

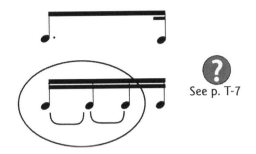

See p. T-7

Shalom Chaverim ("Farewell Good Friends")

Use the consecutive positions of Dm as a scaffolding for fingering this melody.

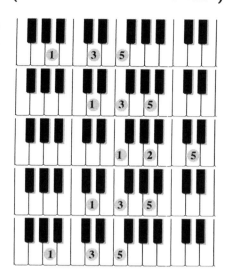

Traditional Israeli round

Lively

Sha- lom, cha -ve - rim! Sha -lom, cha -ve - rim! Sha - lom, sha - lom. Le -
Fare -well, good_ friends! Fare- well, good_ friends! Fare - well, fare - well. Till

hit ra__ - ot, le   hit - ra__ - ot, Sha - lom,   Sha__ - lom.
meet a__ - gain, till   meet a__ - gain, Fare - well,   Fare__ - well.

Style Suggestions

R 8 · 5

R · 3 5 · R

Play this song as a two-part round. Player one starts at the beginning ① and player two starts when player one reaches the fourth beat of measure two ②.

All the Pretty Little Horses

Traditional African-American lullaby

Tenderly

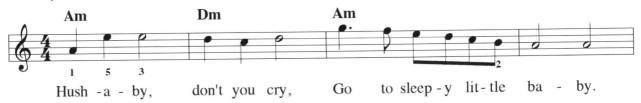

Hush-a-by, don't you cry, Go to sleep-y lit-tle ba - by.

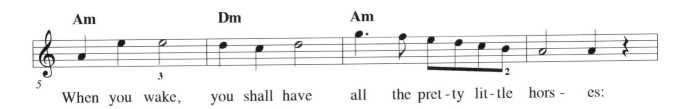

When you wake, you shall have all the pret-ty lit-tle hors - es:

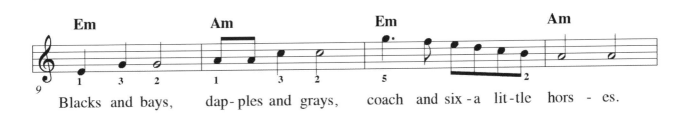

Blacks and bays, dap-ples and grays, coach and six-a lit-tle hors - es.

Hush-a-by, don't you cry, Go to sleep-y, lit-tle ba - by.

Style Suggestions

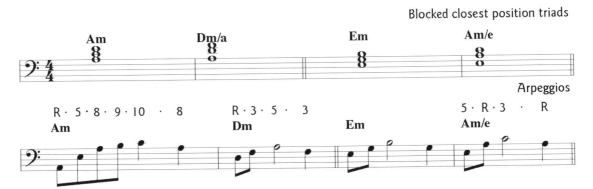

Blocked closest position triads

Arpeggios

Clouds and Sunshine

Ferdinand Beyer (1803–1863)

Play the "cloudy" eight-measure first phrase in the Am five-finger pattern. Then, move the phrase up to the C five-finger pattern, where it sounds "sunny." Finally, *D.C. al fine:* go back to the beginning and play until the *fine* sign. Look for imitation (like ms. 1 and 2), contrary motion (like ms. 3), parallel motion (like ms. 4) and both hands in the treble clef (ms. 10-16).

CHAPTER 6 REVIEW

1. Name and spell the three all-white major triads:

_____ = ___ ___ ___   _____ = ___ ___ ___   _____ = ___ ___ ___

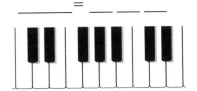   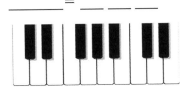   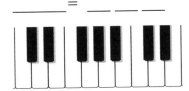

2. Name and spell the three all-white minor triads:

_____ = ___ ___ ___   _____ = ___ ___ ___   _____ = ___ ___ ___

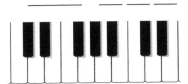      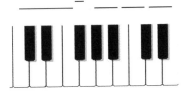

3. Name and spell the all-white diminished triad:

_____ = ___ ___ ___

4. Major triads are: (Circle all that apply.)
   a. A pair of thirds with four half-steps on the bottom and three half-steps on top.
   b. A pair of thirds with three half-steps on the bottom and four half-steps on top.
   c. All white chords built on *c*, *e* and *g*.
   d. All white chords built on *c*, *f* and *g*.
   e. Eligible for major discounts at fine music stores everywhere.

5. Minor chords are: (Circle all that apply.)
   a. A pair of thirds with four half-steps on the bottom and three half-steps on top.
   b. A pair of thirds with three half-steps on the bottom and four half-steps on top.
   c. All white chords built on *a*, *d* and *e*.
   d. All white chords built on *a*, *c* and *e*.
   e. Often heard at funerals and mid-eastern celebrations.

6. Which of these is a major five-finger pattern?

 a.    b.    c.    d.

7. Identify the following chords.

a_____ b_____ c_____ d_____ e_____ f_____ g_____ h_____

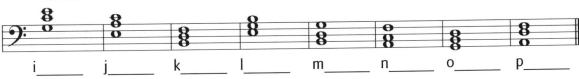

i_____ j_____ k_____ l_____ m_____ n_____ o_____ p_____

8. An inversion is:

    a. A rearranged version of a triad that contains one 2nd and one 4th.

    b. A rearranged version of a triad that contains one 3rd and one 4th.

    c. A chord whose root is at the bottom.

    d. A chord whose root is not at the bottom.

    e. An *in fashion version* of a chord.

9. Finger the three basic triad shapes.   (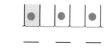 = the root)

    Right hand   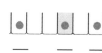

    Left hand   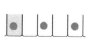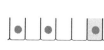

10. Show each C chord and the closest position of F.

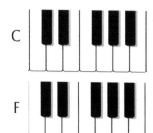

11. Show each C chord and the closest position of G.

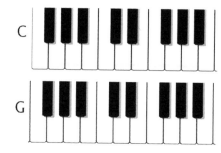

When you're comfortable with this chapter:

    If you skipped **Chapter 4**, learn about fingering, chording and voicing now. If you skipped **Chapter 5**, learn about intervals, sight-reading and ear-playing now.

            or

    Go to **Chapter 7**, where you'll learn how to convert majors to minors and minors to majors, so you know half of the major and minor triads!

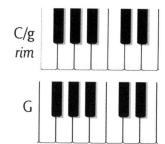

To apply what you've learned in the key of C to other keys, go to the **Coda**, "The Same, But Different, In Any Key."

CHAPTER 7
RECYCLE CHORD SPELLINGS

To double the number of chords you know, learn the major–minor conversion rules. Like baseball, going from majors to minors is a step down and going from minors to majors is a step up. Listen to the huge qualitative difference that a half-step makes.

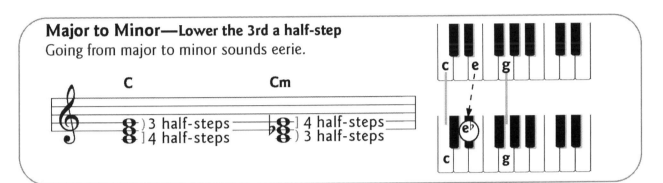

Major to Minor—Lower the 3rd a half-step
Going from major to minor sounds eerie.

Theme from 2001, A Space Odyssey (Thus Spoke Zarathustra by Richard Strauss)

Play Cm, Fm & Gm, then drill the Cool Frosty Gingerale minors on pages 7-8 and 7-9.

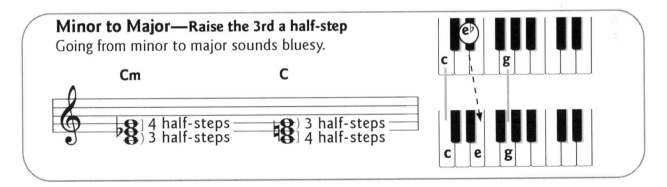

Minor to Major—Raise the 3rd a half-step
Going from minor to major sounds bluesy.

St. Louis Blues by W. C. Handy

Play A, D & E, then drill the lemonADE majors on pages 7-8 and 7-9.

Modern Major/Minor Tonality

During the 17th century, the western world's musical paradigm shifted from the seven diatonic modes to our modern, often non-diatonic, major and minor tonality. Musicians began adopting *equal temperament*—a tuning system that splits the octave into twelve *equal* half-steps. Only the octaves are truly in tune, and pairs of acoustically different *enharmonic* notes (like *f♯* = *g♭*) masquerade as the same pitch. By sacrificing exact in-tuneness, we gained the ability to play approximately in tune in any major or minor key, on any keyboard, using any chords.

In 1722, Johann Sebastian Bach showed modern tonality's harmonic depth and power with *The Well-Tempered Clavier*, the first set of pieces in each of the twelve major and twelve minor keys. At the beginning of each staff, a *key signature* announces the sharps or flats (if any) of either a major key or its *relative minor*.

Like baseball, going from a major to its relative minor is going down.

Key of C major and its relative minor: A minor.

To DETERMINE A SONG'S KEY:

- **Look at the last note.** About 99% of the time, the last note will feel like home and be the song's tonal center. (When it doesn't, just sing the note that does feel like home.) Play the song. If it sounds bright and happy, it's major. If it sounds dark and moody, it's minor. If it sounds oddly exotic, it's probably in one of the ancient modes.

- **Look at the key signature.** Once you're a "key club" member, this secret code will reveal the name of a major key and its relative minor. If the song's last note matches either, that's the name of the key. Moreover, you'll know what chords to expect and how they'll sound—in the key of C, expect C, F & G; in any key, expect chords built on the first, fourth and fifth scale tones.

Identify the key of these tunes (and perhaps name them).

For all of the key signatures, see page T-23.

THE KEY OF C MAJOR (formerly Ionian) is based on the C major scale. Expect some (or, in subsequent centuries, many) accidentals, either posted (like *Minuetto*, page 5-15) or hidden within a chord symbol (like *We Shall Overcome*'s Fm = *f a♭ c*, page 7-4).

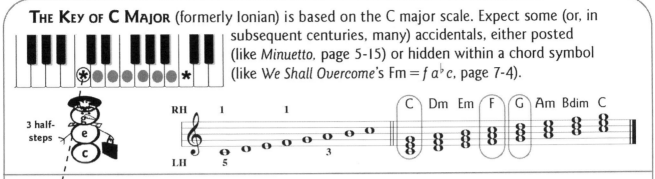

THE KEY OF A MINOR is based on one or more of several A minor scales, usually the five-finger pattern *(a b c d e)* plus *f, f♯, g* and/or *g♯.* Expect lots of accidentals, either posted or hidden within a chord symbol (like *Joshua*'s E = *e g♯ b*, page 7-5).

- **A natural minor** (formerly Aeolian) uses just white keys. *(All the Pretty Little Horses, 6-39)*

 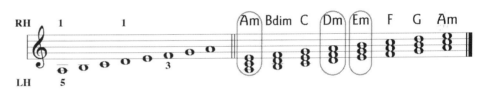

- **A Dorian** sharps every *f,* but is a diatonic mode in the Key of G. *(Scarborough Fair, 7-25)*

 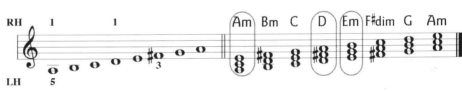

- **A harmonic minor** sharps every *g,* which changes the dominant from minor to major (Em→E) and makes the *harmony* of *harmonic* minor more satisfying. *(Joshua, 7-5, Wild Rider, 7-30)*

 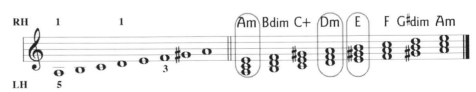

- **A melodic minor** ascends in melodic minor and descends with natural minor according to classical theorists, while jazz players go up and down with it. (Parts of *Greensleeves, 7-26*)

 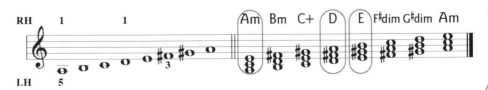

We Shall Overcome in the key of C major
African-American spiritual and international protest song

Use (and adapt as needed): thumb thrusts, finger flings, shift-lifts and a 3→♭3 (F→Fm).

Joshua Fit the Battle of Jericho in the key of A harmonic minor

African-American spiritual

Thumb thrust   Fingers fling

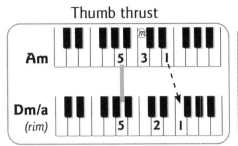
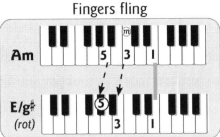

A harmonic minor's closest position primary chords feel like C's, give or take a half-step here or there.

Moderately fast

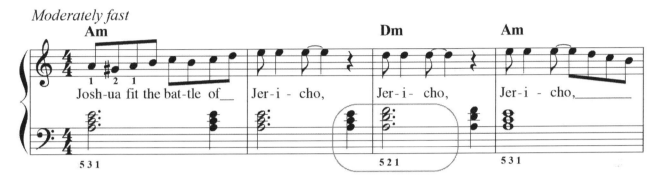

Josh-ua fit the bat-tle of__ Jer-i-cho, Jer-i-cho, Jer-i-cho,_____

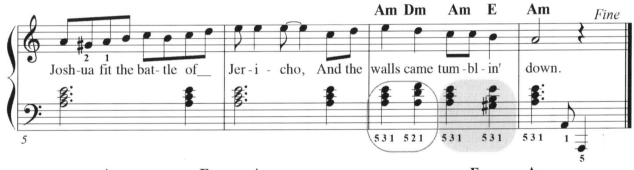

Josh-ua fit the bat-tle of__ Jer-i-cho, And the walls came tum-bl-in' down.

You may talk a-bout your man of Gid-e-on. You may talk a-bout your man of Saul, But there's

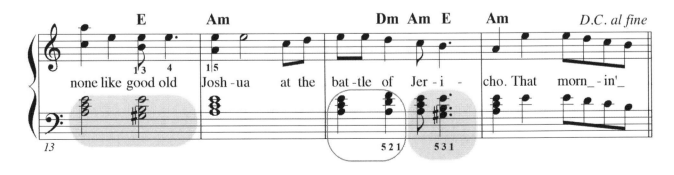

none like good old Josh-ua at the bat-tle of Jer-i-cho. That morn_-in'_

The Original Twelve Bar Blues

"The Blues, the most convenient harmonic progression ever discovered."

Benny Green

In the early 1900s, African-Americans in the southern United States combined traditional African music with American spirituals and folk music to create the *blues*. Often played in a *bar*-room, the twelve *bar* blues has twelve *bars* (measures), each containing four beats and a bluesy melody.

- **Harmony.** Learn the form—three four-measure phrases, each ending with two bars of C. The first half of each line starts in alphabetical order (C-F-G).

Original twelve-bar blues

C	C	C	C
F	F	C	C
G	G	C	C

- **Melody.** The flatted third *blue note* makes the blues chordally androgynous—both major (*c e g*) and minor (*c e♭ g*) at the same time! Play ♭**3–3** (alias ♯**2–3**) in any of these ways:

  1. **Grace note:** Slightly before the beat, snap ♭3 quickly, then play 3 on the beat.
  2. **Slide:** Slide a finger from ♭3–3 (which only works from a black key to a white key).

  3. **Crush:** Play both notes together.
  4. **Pull off:** Play both notes together, then pull off the lower note.

- **Rhythm.** Swing the melody, playing pairs of eighth notes unevenly.

STRAIGHT EIGHTHS	SWUNG EIGHTHS
Subdividing the beat evenly, play two equal eighth notes.	Play the first eighth note longer than the second, as uneven triplets in any proportion that feels right to you.

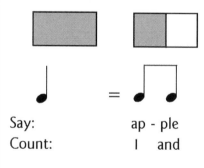 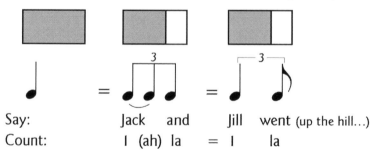

Walk to songs with even straight eighths for classical, Latin, ragtime, rock, folk and most other genres.

Skip or boogie to uneven swung eighths for blues, jazz, swing or any piece that says "swing the eighths," "moderate swing," or something similar.

St. Louis Blues

W. C. Handy (1873–1958)

In 1909, Handy wrote a campaign song for a Memphis mayoral candidate.
Mr. Crump, the first blues ever written down, won Mr. Crump the election and
made Handy famous. In 1914, Handy wrote *St. Louis Blues*, his most enduring song.

Tempo di Blues

Boogie bass (R 5 · R 6 · R 5 · R 6)

Got the St. Lou-is Blues just as blue as I can be, That

man got a heart like a rock cast__ in__ the sea, Or__

else he__ would-n't have gone__ so__ far__ from_ me.

To simplify the left hand, play just the root and fifth (C = c g) in whole, half or quarter notes. For help putting your hands together, see page T-11.

Fast lane. Play in the original key of G. Put 6ths under the melody and play the boogie bass in octaves (R 5 8 · R 6 8 · R 5 8 · R 6 8).

To improvise and play the blues with people, see pages 7-32 to 35.

DRILL 7: SANDWICH MAJORS AND MINORS

Each white-black-white chord looks like a sandwich and feels like a mountain. Once you learn the all-whites and sandwiches, you'll know half of the major and minor triads!

Look like a sandwich

5 3 1   1 3 5

Feel like a mountain

A. SANDWICH TRIADS

- **By group.** Say, play and spell the sandwich majors (A, D & E) and minors (Cm, Fm & Gm). You might spell A as "a c♯ e" or "a c e, sharp in the middle" or "a c e, black in the middle."

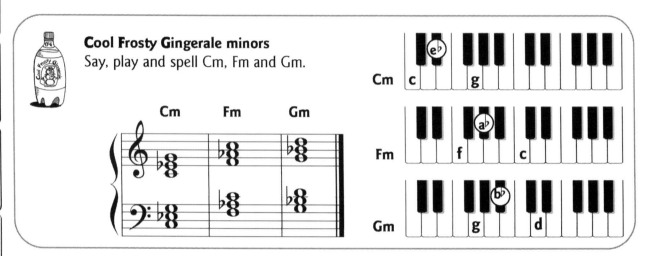

Cool Frosty Gingerale minors
Say, play and spell Cm, Fm and Gm.

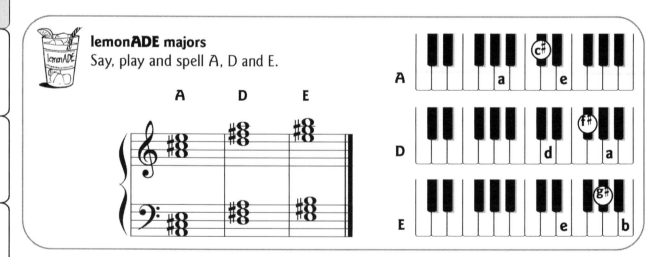

lemonADE majors
Say, play and spell A, D and E.

- **Stepwise white-root majors.** Say and play up and back down from C to A.

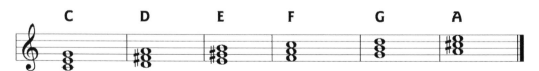

C   D   E   F   G   A

- **Stepwise white-root minors.** Say and play up and back down from Cm to Am.

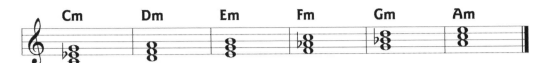

- **Randomly.** Say and play:

Cm	G	Dm	Em
Fm	A	C	Gm
D	F	Am	E

The all-white majors have sandwich minors.

COOL FROSTY GINGERALE TRIADS

The all-white minors have sandwich majors.

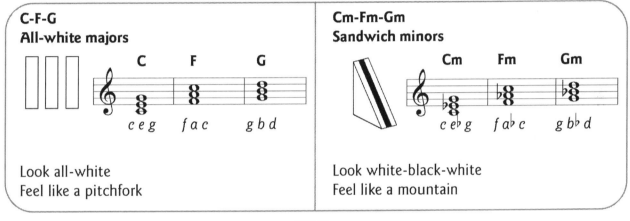

A-D-E
Sandwich majors

Look white-black-white
Feel like a mountain

LEMONADE TRIADS

Am-Dm-Em
All-white minors

Look all-white
Feel like a pitchfork

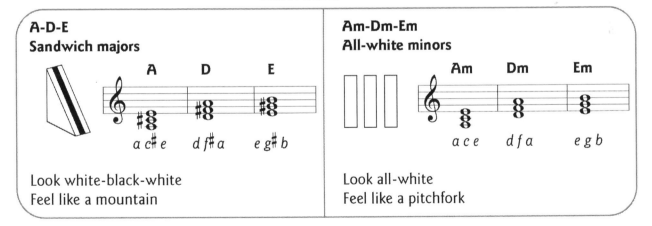

Play: *We Shall Overcome* (7-4), *Happy Birthday* (7-18#3),
Morning Has Broken (7-24), *Für Elise* (7-28) and *Wild Rider* (7-30)

B. LEFT HAND SANDWICH JUMPING

To jump confidently between sandwich chords, adapt the jumping suggestions on pages 6-14.

C. MAJOR AND MINOR FIVE-FINGER PATTERNS FOR C, F & G and A, D & E

Teach youself to grab these patterns—fingering's basic default settings.

- ### Build a five-finger pattern from a major (or minor triad).

  1. Grab a major (or minor) triad.

  2. Insert the missing scale tones— a whole-step up from the bottom and down from the top.

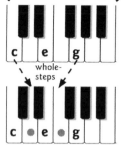
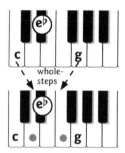

- ### Play up and down the major five-finger patterns: C, F & G, then A, D & E.

C and G are all white;
F has one black key (b♭).

A and D have one black key in the middle;
E has two black keys (f♯ and g♯).

- ### Play up and down minor five-finger patterns: Cm, Fm & Gm and Am, Dm & Em.

Cm and Gm have one black key in the middle;
Fm has two black keys (a♭ and b♭).

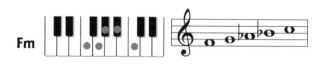

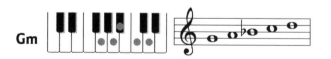

Am and Dm are all white;
Em has one black key (f♯).

If a pattern has any black keys, move gradually into the blacks. Don't awkwardly lunge at the last minute. Plan a choreography that works for your fingers—long, short or sausage-like.

- **Play and say major five-finger patterns up and down by fifths.**
  Replace your thumb with your pinkie (or vice versa).

- **Play and say minor five-finger patterns up and down by fifths.**
  Replace your thumb with your pinkie (or vice versa).

Play-prepare. Like biking up a hill, don't stop (and have to restart again). Instead, use the energy of lifting off *5* (or *1*) to propel you all the way to *1* (or *5*).

Play: *When the Saints Go Marchin'* in other major five-finger patterns (6-11) *and Snake Dance* in other minor five-finger patterns (5-5).

D1. SANDWICH ROOT-ON-TOP TRIADS (rot)

Put your top finger on the root. Drill your left hand (5 3 *1*), right hand (*1* 2 5) or both hands together. (C/e = *e g c*).

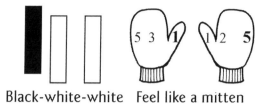

Black-white-white   Feel like a mitten

- **Drill by group**

lemonADE root-on-top majors
Say, play and spell A, D and E *rot.*

A/c#   D/f#   E/g#

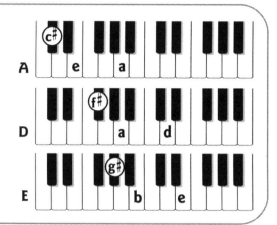

Cool Frosty Gingerale root-on-top minors
Say, play and spell Cm, Fm and Gm *rot.*

C/e♭   F/a♭   G/b♭

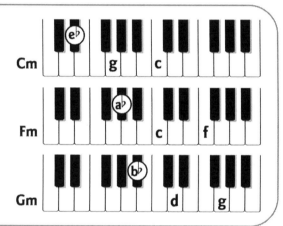

- **Drill stepwise**

Play root-on-top majors from C to A and play root-on-top minors from Cm to Am.

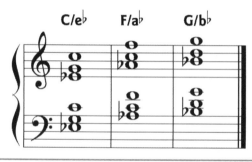

C/e   D/f#   E/g#   F/a   G/b   A/c#

Cm/e♭   Dm/f   Em/g   Fm/a♭   Gm/b♭   Am/c

- **Drill randomly**

Choose any white root, then play a root-on-top major or minor triad on it.

Play: *We Shall Overcome* (7-4) and *Joshua Fit the Battle of Jericho* (7-5)

D2. SANDWICH ROOT-IN-MIDDLE TRIADS *(rim)*

Point your *left pointer* at the root to make a *rim* around the **r**ight **m**iddle finger. Drill your left hand *(5 2 1)*, right hand *(1 3 5)* or both hands together. *(C/g = g c e)*.

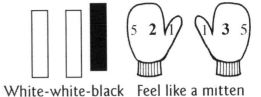

White-white-black   Feel like a mitten

- **Drill by group**

lemonADE root-in-middle majors
Say, play and spell A, D and E *rim*.

A/e   D/a   E/b

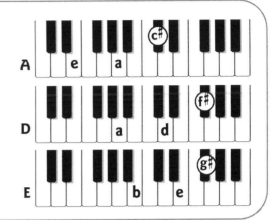

Cool Frosty Gingerale root-in-middle minors
Say, play and spell Cm, Fm and Gm *rim*.

Cm/g   Fm/c   Gm/d

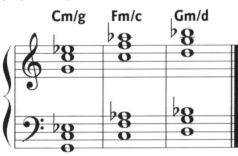

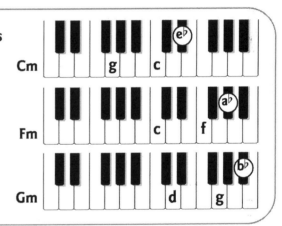

- **Drill stepwise**

Play root-in-middle majors from C to A and play root-in-middle minors from Cm to Am.

C/g   D/a   E/b   F/c   G/d   A/e

Cm/g   Dm/a   Em/b   Fm/c   Gm/d   Am/e

- **Drill randomly**

Choose any white root, then play a root-in-middle major or minor triad on it.

Play: *We Shall Overcome* (7-4) and *Danny Boy* (7-41)

E. DOMINANT SEVENTH CROSSOVERS

In the early 1600s, Claudio Monteverdi (1567–1643) broke the ban on carefully controlled dissonance by extending the dominant (G = *g b d*) to include its 7th (G7 = *g b d f*). Within the *dominant seventh* lurks the previously forbidden *diabolus in musica (b f)*! The oldest and most common type of seventh chord, G dominant seventh is simply called G7 ("G seventh"). While G→C says, "Go home," G7→C yells, "Go right home."

GO RIGHT HOME!

G7
geebeedeef

- **Build a dominant seventh from a triad.**

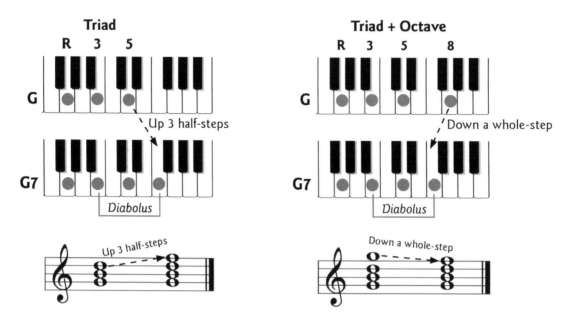

- **Arpeggiate G dominant seventh with each hand.**

  Fan out your fingers, using whichever fan fingering suits your hand.

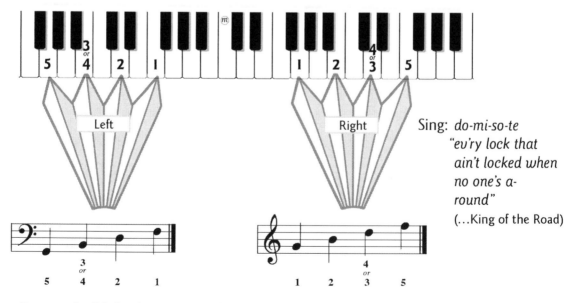

Sing: *do-mi-so-te*
"*ev'ry lock that ain't locked when no one's a-round*"
(…King of the Road)

Can you build dominant sevenths on other white roots? (See page T-30.)

- **Cross root position G7 hand over hand up the keyboard.**

   Start on G7, cross left over right up the keyboard and end by crossing your left pointer to *g*.

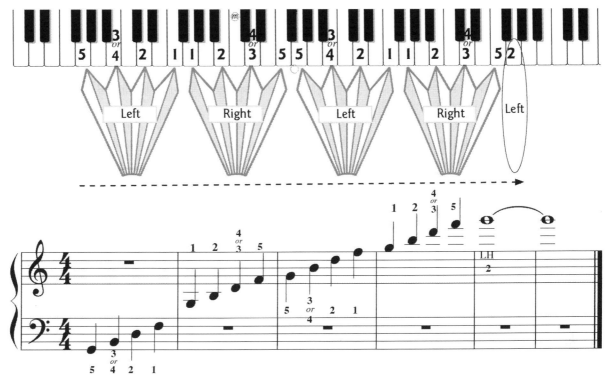

- **Cross each inversion of G7 hand over hand up the keyboard.**

   Grab a triad in any position. Insert the 7th a whole-step below the root.

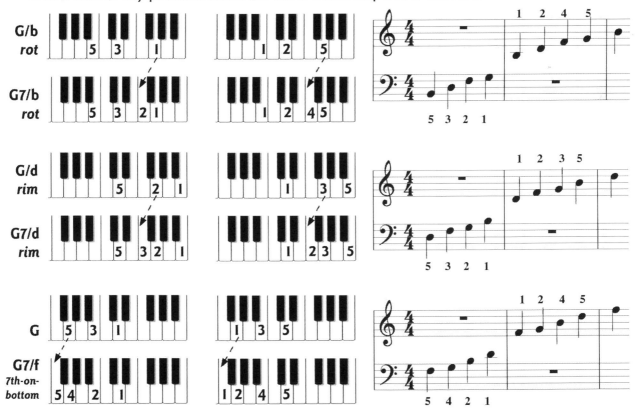

Play: G7: *Kum Ba Yah* (7-38), *Country Waltz* by Haydn (7-39) and *Danny Boy* (7-41)

F. CLOSEST POSITION OF C, F & G7

Mixing three- and four-note chords creates an uneven musical texture, like a trio enlisting a fourth singer in mid-song. Sometimes, you'll want dramatic textural changes, but usually, you'll keep the same number of voices in each phrase. To go from a triad to a seventh, omit the sevenths 5th (already included as its second overtone: g b ꬷ f), or try other voicings options.

1. Magic formula: Left hand three-note C→F→G7→C works like magic, but is hard to understand.

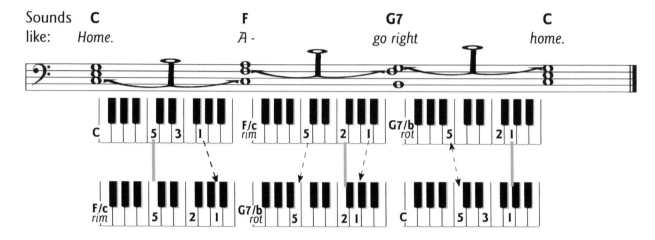

> **Anchor on the common tone and add the missing tone(s) over, around or under it.**
>
> Play C. Anchor pinkie on c. Put the pointer on f. Thrust thumb up a step to a. Play F/c.
>
> Anchor pointer on f. Swing the outside 6th down a step. Play G7/b.
>
> Anchor thumb on g. Shrink to five-finger pattern. Play C. For C→G7: keep thumb on g, put pointer on f, and lower pinkie to b. Play G7.

2. Big-handed only: Left-handed four-note C→F→G7→C

3. Choral voicings: Some of the many options for two-handed open voicings of C, F and G7

C	F	G7	C

> **Play:** C, F and G7: *Kum Ba Yah* (7-38); G7 and other sevenths (7-23)

G. CLOSEST POSITION DIATONIC SEVENTHS FALLING BY FIFTHS

If one falling 5th is exciting, how about a chain reaction of seventh chords?
Look & listen for chords falling down the circle of 5ths: "**B E A D G C F.**"

Inchworm. Fan out your fingers to play a root position
all-white seventh. Lower the top two fingers, then the
bottom two, then the top two . . . So suave, so easy!

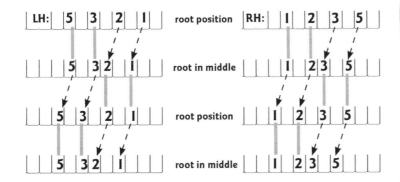

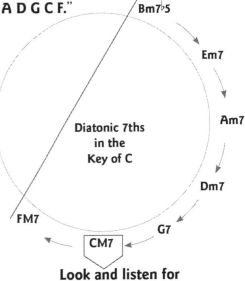

Diatonic 7ths
in the
Key of C

Look and listen for
"**B E A D G** (rhymes with *siege*) **C F.**"

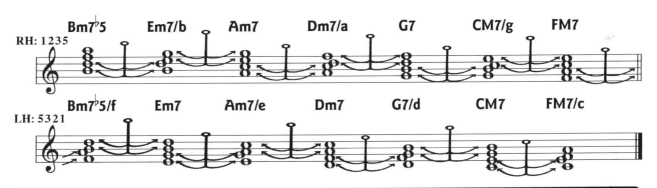

> **Play:** Root position diatonic sevenths (7-23 #32). Circle songs: *Heart & Soul, Danny Boy,*
> and *Prelude in C* by J. S. Bach (7-23). To play in G and learn more about chord travel, see 8-2 to 6.

FINDING CLOSEST POSITION VOICINGS FOR ANY TWO CHORDS

Play the first chord in a position that sounds good—around or in the octave below middle *c*.

Find the new root. **Shape** a chord over, around or under it. (**Insert** the 7th.)	**Spell** the next chord. Do these chords have any tone(s) in common? • If so, anchor on the common tone and add the missing tones over, around or under it. • If not, lift the shape next door or change shapes and move in the opposite direction.

1. Does the voicing sound good with the melody?
2. Can you learn it (and feel confident) within a reasonable amount of time?
3. Does the melody stay out of the harmony's turf?
4. Do the melody and harmony stay within an octave of each other? Add chord tones under the melody; or avoid moving too far apart by going the other way when a new phrase begins, a chord repeats or you find no common tones.
5. Does the bass line move stepwise and/or in contrary motion to the melody?

Thrills with Sandwich Triads

NON-DIATONIC PIECES IN THE KEY OF C MAJOR

Play mostly on the white keys, with *c* the tonal center (✱) and C, F and G the primary chords. Expect some sharps or flats.

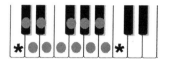

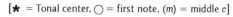

[✱ = Tonal center, ○ = first note, (m) = middle c]

1. **Sandwich Triads over All-White Triads.** Play the root or whole triad in your left hand. With your right hand, try different sandwich triads over the bass, for instance: LH=*c* or *c e g*, RH=D or Gm; or LH=*g* or *g b d*, RH=Fm or D.

2. **Add Melodic Embroidery.** Experiment with the ♭3 to 3 lick (page 7-6). Apply that to embroider any of the twelve bar blues songs (pages 7-32 to 35) and/or dress up the *Saints* (pages 7-36, 37).

3. ***Happy Birthday to You*** by Patty Hill and Mildred Hill, page 5-12. Ear out the melody starting on *g*, then accompany it with C, F, (Fm) and G, or whatever sounds good to you.

	C	G	G	C
Happy *g*	Birthday to	you, Happy	Birthday to	you, Happy

C	F	(Fm)	C	G	C
Birthday dear	_____ ,	Happy	Birthday	to	you.

4. ***We Shall Overcome***, page 7-4 (C, Dm, (D), Em, F, (Fm), G & Am). In the 1960s, union organizers and civil rights marchers sang this gospel hymn as their anthem. Since then, protestors in North Korea, South Africa, China's Tiananmen Square and elsewhere have sung it.

5. ***Morning Has Broken***, page 7-24 (C, Dm, (D), Em, F, G & Am). English author Eleanor Farjeon's 1931 lyrics turned a 16th century Scottish Gaelic ballad into a Christian hymn. Englishman Cat Stevens' arrangement topped the U.S. easy listening chart in 1972.

C		G		F	C
Morning has	bro -	ken	like the first	morn -	ing.

C	Em	Am	C	Dm	G
Blackbird has	spo -	ken	like the first	bird.	

C	F		C	Am	D
Praise for the	sing -	ing!	Praise for the	morn -	ing!

G	C	F	G	C	
Praise for them	spring -	ing	fresh from the	Word.	

⟶ = falling 5ths   ⌐‾‾ =stepping

6. **Non-diatonic Lead Sheets in C.** Buy, borrow or download songs that include some accidentals in the melody or harmony. When you find an unfamiliar chord, look it up on a chord chart (T-30 to 32), apply the formula (T-26, 27, 32), drill it along with its group-mates (T-27 to 30), simplify it (T-32) or omit it. (circle = circle of 5ths progression)

After You've Gone (circle)	*I Believe* (circle)	*Piano Man* (D7)
All of Me (D7, E7, Fm, Gm, A7)	*In the Still of the Night* (C7, G+)	*P. S. I Love You*
Blue Moon (circle)	*Imagine* (E7)	*Take the "A" Train*
The Best of My Love (Fm7)	*I'm Gonna Sit Right Down and*	*Sentimental Journey*
Candy Man	*Write Myself a Letter Imagine* (E7)	*Something*
Carry That Weight (E7, A)	*I Will Always Love You*	*Somewhere Out There*
Celebration (D, E)	*Louie Louie* (just C7 and G7)	*Suzanne* (all white chords)
Chattanooga Choo Choo	*On the Sunny Side of the Street* (circle)	*Tennessee Waltz* (C7, E7)
Climb Ev'ry Mountain	*Maybe This Time* (from *Caberet*)	*Tiny Dancer*
Fire and Rain (C9, Gm7, B♭)	*Moon River*	*Vision of Love*
The First Time Ever I Saw	*Morning Has Broken/Stevens* (circle)	*When I'm 64*
Your Face (Dm7, G7, B♭)	*Nobody Knows You When You're*	*When Sunny Gets Blue*
Fly Me to the Moon (circle)	*Down and Out* (D7, E7, G7, A7, B7)	*White Christmas*
Homeward Bound	*Paper Roses* (C7, A+)	*You'll Never Walk Alone*

7. **Non-diatonic Sheet Music in C.** Buy, borrow or download music that is mostly all-white, but includes a few accidentals. Look for and label familiar chords.

BACH: *Applicatio*, BWV 994 and *Prelude in C*, BWV939
CLARKE: *Trumpet Tune*
DEBUSSY: *Le Petit Négre*; *Doctor Gradus ad Parnassum* from *Children's Corner*
GRIEG: *Sailors' Song* from *Lyric Pieces*, Op. 68, No. 1
HANDEL: *Fughetta in C major*
JOPLIN: *The Cascades* and *The Entertainer*
MENDELSSOHN: *Faith* from *Songs Without Words*, Op. 67
MOZART: *Menuet in C*, K. 315; *Sonata in C*, K. 545; *Variations on "Ah, vous dirai-je, maman"*
SATIE: *Second Gymnopedie*
SCARLATTI: *Minuetto*, K. 73b (second movement)
TCHAIKOVSKY: *Sweet Dream* from *Album for the Young*, Op. 39, No. 21
Any of the popular songs in #6

8. **When The Saints Keep on Jamming**, page 7-36. The person on piano left plays a walking bass with right-hand closest position chords, while the person on piano right plays and embroiders the melody on page 7-37.

9. *Imagine* **Your Friends Singing Along.** Learn John Lennon's *Imagine* arranged for voice and piano.

10. **Non-diatonic Duets in C.** Buy, borrow or download sheet music in the key of C that includes some accidentals. Look for and label familiar chords.

DIABELLI: *Sonatina in C*, Op. 24, No. 1	SCHUBERT: *Allegro Moderato in C Major*
GRETCHANINOV: *In the Meadows*, Op. 99, No. 1	SCHUMANN: *Birthday March*, Op. 85, No. 1
MOZART: *Sonata*, K. 19 D	VON WEBER: *Sonatina in C*, Op. 3, No. 1

PIECES IN THE KEY OF A MINOR

A minor is mutable, to many inscrutable. It uses *a* as the tonal center (✱) of a palette that includes the A minor five-finger pattern *(a b c d e)* plus *f, f♯, g* and *g♯*. Learn the A harmonic minor scale and perhaps other minor scales.

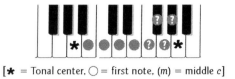

[✱ = Tonal center, ◯ = first note, *(m)* = middle *c*]

11. **Scarborough Fair**, page 7-25. *(a b c d e f♯ g* • Am, Ⓓ, G and C • Dorian.)* In medieval England, the town of Scarborough hosted a trade fair each summer. The narrator, who'd been jilted, sang about his herbal remedy—parsley to remove bitterness; sage for strength; rosemary for faithfulness, love and remembrance; and thyme for courage. Simon and Garfunkel's 1966 recording made the song a pop hit.

12. **Greensleeves**, page 7-26. *(a b c d e f f♯ g g♯* • Am, Dm, Ⓔ, F, G and C • Natural, Harmonic & Melodic.)* In the 1580s, several English printers published this anonymous ballad. William Dix turned it into *What Child Is This?* in 1865.

13. **Joshua Fit the Battle of Jericho**, page 7-5. *(a b c d e f g♯* • Am, Dm and Ⓔ • Harmonic.)* This nineteenth century African-American spiritual retells the biblical story of Joshua's men circling the walls of Jericho blowing ram's horn trumpets. When Joshua commanded the men to shout, the walls came tumbling down.

14. **Hava Nagila**, page 7-27. *(a b c d e f g♯* • Am, Dm and Ⓔ • Harmonic.)* When people hear this song at a Jewish gathering, many join hands for an energetic Israeli circle dance—the hora. At weddings, several strong men lift the bride and groom up on chairs, as their dancing friends and relatives encircle them with love and laughter.

15. **Für Elise** by Ludwig von Beethoven, page 7-28. *(a b c d d♯ e f g♯* • Am, Ⓔ, C and G • Harmonic and Major.)* In 1810, Beethoven fell in love with Terese Malfatti and wrote a piano solo for her. When "Elise" didn't return his love, Ludwig didn't publish the piece. Published posthumously, *Für Elise* starts in the key of Am, moves to its relative major (key of C), then returns to Am.

16. **Wild Rider** by Robert Schumann, page 7-30. *(a b c d e f g♯* • Am, Dm and Ⓔ • Harmonic.)* Start moderately loud *(mf = mezzo forte)*, observe the strong accents *(sfz = sforzando)*, and play fast enough to feel like you're galloping on your bench.

17. **Alla Turca** by Wofgang Amadeus Mozart, page. 7-31. *(a b c d♯ e f♯ g♯* • Am, Bdim, Ⓑ, C, Em, Ⓔ, Ⓕ7 and G • Harmonic with chromatic curlicues.)* Mozart imitates the sound of Turkish military bands popular in late 18th-century Austria, which had been in and out of war with the Turks for two centuries.

18. **Lead Sheets in A minor.** Buy, borrow or download songs that include the white keys plus *f♯*, *g♯* and/or other accidentals. For unfamiliar chords, use chord charts (T-30 to 32); learn formulas (T-26, 27 & 32); and/or drill more chords (7-14 to 17; T-27 to 30). If a song seems too hard for now, save it for learning later.

Angie	*Gentle Rain* (circle)	*Stairway to Heaven*
Avinu Malkenu	*Goldfinger*	*Summertime*
Bei Mir Bist Du Schon	*I Will Survive* (circle)	*Sunny*
Black Orpheus (circle)	*Jesus Is Just Alright*	*Those Were the Days* (circle)
Dust in the Wind	*Killing Me Softly With His Song*	*25 or 6 to 4* (B♭7, C9)
Fever	*Moondance* (Bm7, E11, E7+)	*You've Got a Friend*

19. **Sheet Music in A minor.** Buy, borrow or download music that includes *f♯*, *g♯* or other accidentals. Look for and label familiar chords.

BARTOK: *Sorrow* from *For Children*, Volume 1 ("Based on Hungarian Folk Tunes"), No. 7
BEETHOVEN: *Russian Folk Song* ("Little Minka"); *Bagatelle in A minor*, Opus 119, No. 9
BRAHMS: *Hungarian Dance No. 5* (circle!); *Intermezzo*, Opus 76, No. 7
BURGMULLER: *Arabesque*
CHOPIN: *Mazurka in A minor*, Op. 68, No. 2; *Waltz in A Minor* (circle!)
GRIEG: *Anitra's Dance* from *Peer Gynt Suite*, No.1; *Solveig's Song* from *Peer Gynt Suite*, No. 2
MOZART: *Alla Turca* from *Sonata in A*, K. 331
SATIE: *Third Gymnopedie*
SCHUMANN: *The Poor Orphan, Echoes from the Theatre & Sheherazade*, Op. 68: No. 6, 25 & 32
Any of the popular songs in #18

20. **A Minor Steps Down** (Am→G→F→Ⓔ)
Person on left: Begin by playing this exciting A minor *vamp* as an introduction.

Person on right: Listen, feel the groove, then start to play using an A minor palette that includes both *g* and *g♯*. If clash happens, salvation's a step away—just repeat and resolve.

21. ***Moondance* with a Friend.** Accompany a friend singing or playing Irishman Van Morrison's 1970 song, an A Aeolian melody with jazzy non-diatonic chords.

22. **Sheet Music for Four Hands in Am.** Buy, borrow or download music that is mostly all-white, but includes a few accidentals. Look for and label familiar chords.

GRIEG (arranged for duet by Adolf Ruthardt): *Anitra's Dance* from *Peer Gynt Suite No. 1*
SCHUBERT: *Andante in A Minor* (Sonatine) D. 968
    (arranged for duet by Johannes Brahms): *Eleven Landler*, #3 and #5

TWELVE BAR BLUES SONGS IN THE KEY OF C MAJOR

In the early 1900s, African-Americans began playing the blues—a melody with *blue notes* (in C: $e^{\flat}$, $g^{\flat}$ and $b^{\flat}$) and/or chords that follow the *twelve bar blues* form.

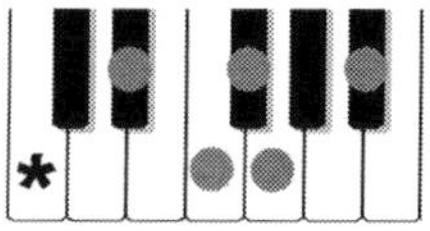

[✱ = Tonal center, ○ = first note, (*m*) = middle *c*]

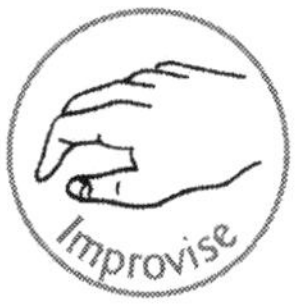

23. **Basic Twelve Bar Blues,** pages 7-32, 33. Memorize this form, learn blues scales and licks, play the examples and enjoy.

♭3 to 3 triad lick — 5-tone blues scale

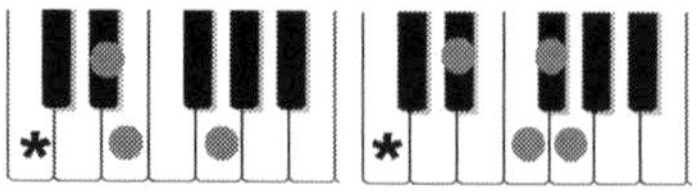

C	**C**	**C**	**C**
F	**F**	**C**	**C**
G	**F**	**C**	**G** to repeat (:‖) **C** to end (‖)

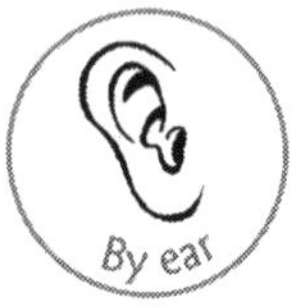

24. ***Kansas City***. Jerry Leiber & Mike Stoller, nineteen-year olds from L.A., wrote *K.C.* in 1952. The Beatles, Peggy Lee, Fats Domino and others recorded it. Start on *c*, swing the eighths and follow the basic blues form. Use either a boogie bass or this Kansas City bass:

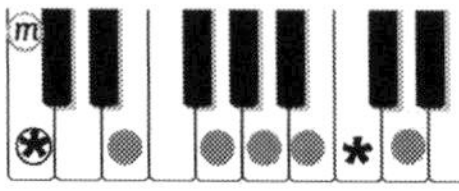

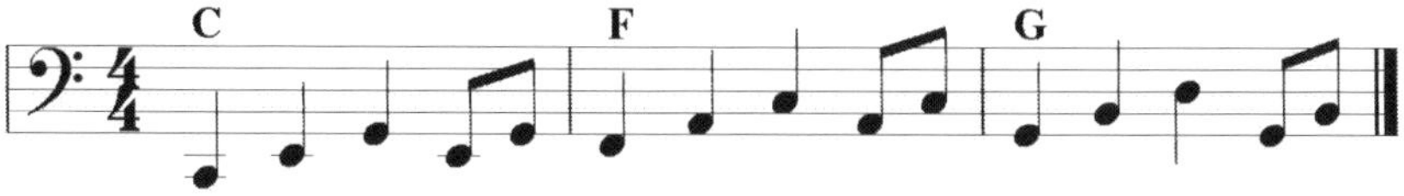

25. ***Rolling in the Deep***. Londoners Paul Epworth & Adele Adkins recorded this smash hit in 2010. Play the first section out of the C five-tone blues scale, starting with *4* on *f*♯ and using straight eighths. Next, refinger to start with *3* on *f*♯, slide and then stretch up to the bawdy flatted seventh ($b^{\flat}$). To end the phrase, insert *d* between $e^{\flat}$ and *c*.

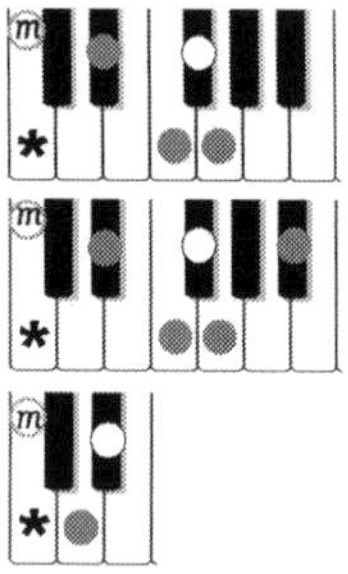

Cm	**Gm**	**B♭**	**Gm B♭**

To learn the whole song, find a YouTube tutorial, download the sheet music or a lead sheet, and/or use page T-11's learning strategies.

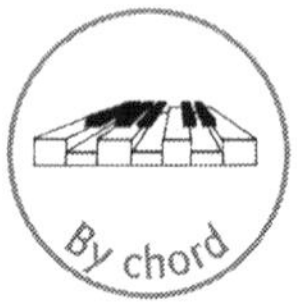

26. ***St. Louis Blues*** by W. C. Handy, page 7-7, uses the original twelve bar blues form.
27. ***Pay Your Dues Blues, Bittersweet Blues*** and ***Blues Scale Blues***, page 7-32 to 35.
28. **Lead Sheets for Blues in C.** Buy, borrow or download blues.

Back in the U.S.S.R.	*Don't Be Cruel*	*Night Train*	*Watermelon Man* (16 bars)
Can't Buy Me Love	*Kansas City*	*Shake, Rattle and Roll*	*Wipe Out*

29. **Sheet Music for Blues in C.** Buy, borrow or download music that is mostly all-white, but includes a few rousing accidentals. Look for and label familiar chords.

AMMONS: *Shout for Joy*	LEIBER/STOLLER: *Kansas City*	JOHNSON: *Roll 'Em Pete*
EPWORTH/ADKINS: *Rolling in the Deep*	LEWIS: *Bear Cat Crawl*	Any song in #27

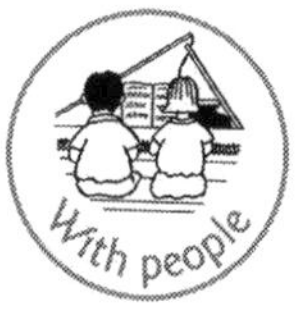

30. **Jamming on the Twelve Bar Blues**, page 7-34. Practice the two-handed comping patterns. Then, ask a friend to play any of the blues songs on pages 7-32 to 35 or improvise a solo. If your friend plays piano or guitar, switch roles so you can discover the fun of soloing over an accompanist.

SEVENTH HEAVEN IN C

To enjoy luscious, sophisticated sevenths, simply add another third to a triad.

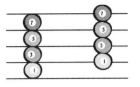

32. **Progress with Sevenths**. On page 3-3, fan out your fingers to play with diatonic sevenths. (See all five types on page T-30.)

CM7	Dm7	Em7	FM7	G7	Am7	Bm7♭5
Major 7th	Minor 7th	Minor 7th	Major 7th	Dominant 7th	Minor 7th	Half-diminished 7th

33. *Heart & Soul* **Ear Tunes**. Seventh chords often fall by fifths (➞) around the circle of fifths. Play ♥ & Soul, *Blue Moon* and/or *26 Miles* with this familiar progression.   C   Am7 ➞ Dm7 ➞ G7 ➞

34. *Kum Bah Yah*, page 7-38. Use magic formula voicings.
C ➞ F   G7 ➞ C ➞ F

35. *Wanderin'*, page 7-40. During the depression, a million men rode the rails. Follow the tracks of their falling 5ths.   Em7 ➞ Am7 ➞ Dm7 ➞ G7 ➞ C

36. *Danny Boy*, page 7-41. Expect dominant sevenths to fall by 5ths, part of a "**BEADGCF**" chain reaction.   A7 ➞ D7 ➞ G7 ➞ C ➞ F

37. *Country Waltz* by Joseph Haydn, page 7-39. Dance diatonically with C and G7 arpeggios, then end the next section with falling 5ths.   Dm ➞ G7 ➞ C
f

38. *Prelude in C from The Well-Tempered Clavier* by J.S. Bach, page 7-42. (C, C7, D, D7, F, FM7, G, G7, G7*sus*, Am, Am7 and five mysterious *diminished sevenths*). Block and label the chords, find falling 5ths (➞), and make your own cheat sheet.

C   Dm ➞ G7 ➞ C   Am ➞ D ➞ G ➞ C
      c   *b*   *c*   *c*   *b*   *b*

39. *Heart & Soul* by Hoagie Carmichael.

To accompany a friend, play LH roots, RH closest position chords and/or whatever you like.
(See drill on page 7-17.)

C   Am7 ➞ Dm7 ➞ G7 ➞

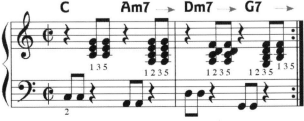

Morning Has Broken

16th century Scottish-Gaelic ballad
Lyrics by Eleanor Farjeon
(1881–1965)

Moderately

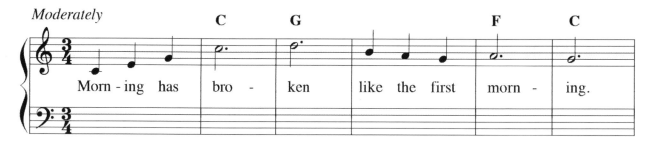

Morn - ing has bro - ken like the first morn - ing.

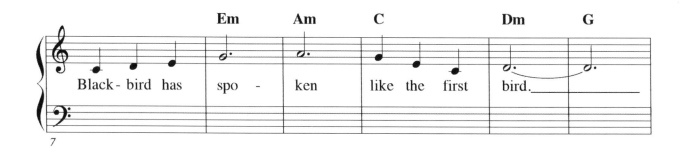

Black - bird has spo - ken like the first bird._____

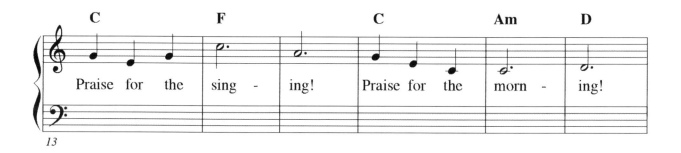

Praise for the sing - ing! Praise for the morn - ing!

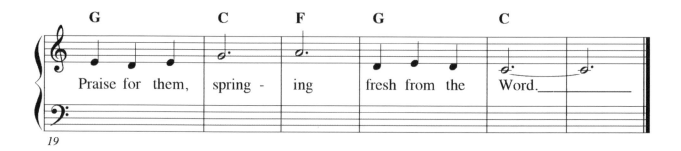

Praise for them, spring - ing fresh from the Word._____

Scarborough Fair

Medieval English ballad

Moderately

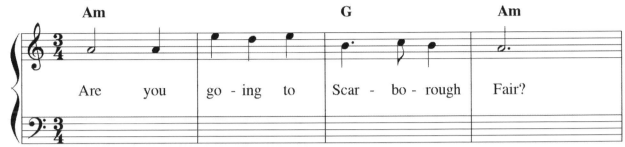

Are you | go - ing to | Scar - bo - rough | Fair?

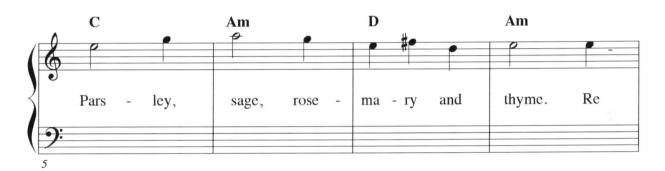

Pars - ley, | sage, rose - | ma - ry and | thyme. Re

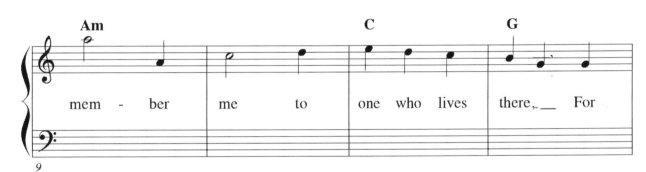

mem - ber | me to | one who lives | there,___ For

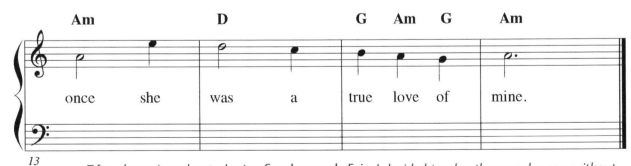

once she | was a | true love of | mine.

After dreaming about playing Scarborough Fair, I decided to play the song by ear, without looking at the music or jotting down any notation. Changing my learning channel from analytic to aural felt so exhilarating, that I tinkered merrily for months. Years later, when I notated my arrangement, I realized that I'd used 4/4 as the meter, R 4 5 sus voicings for each Am (A sus = a d e) and mostly five-measure phrases! Have fun playing Scarborough Fair the way you hear it.

Greensleeves

16th century English folk song
Melody used for *What Child Is This?*
Lyrics by William Dix (1837–1898)

Moderately

Am   **G**   **F**

A - las my love__, you do me wrong__, To cast me

E   **Am**

off____ dis - court - eous - ly, And I have loved___ you

G   **F**   **E**   **Am Dm Am**

oh so long__, De light___ -ing in__ your com - pa - ny.

CHORUS:

C   **G**   **F**

Green - sleeves___ was all my joy_____, Green_____

E   **C**

sleeves___ was my de - light, Green - sleeves was my

G   **F**   **E**   **Am Dm Am**

heart of gold___ and who but my la___ -dy Green - sleeves.

Hava Nagila ("Let Us Rejoice")

Israeli circle dance from a Ukrainian/Romanian folk melody
Lyrics by Abraham Zevi Idelsohn (1882–1938)

Let's rejoice, let's rejoice, let's rejoice and be happy.
Let's sing, let's sing, let's sing and be happy.
Awake, awake brothers, awake brothers with a happy heart.
Awake brothers, awake brothers with a happy heart.

See p. T-46

Für Elise (excerpt)

Ludwig von Beethoven (1770–1827)

Harmony: Two pairs of triads—Am & E and C & G. Label the chords. Finger to perfection.

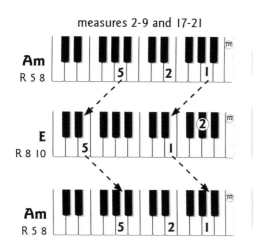

measures 2-9 and 17-21

Pivot!

Play R 5 8 and look down to find the next root.

Play R 8, pivot on your thumb to reach the 10th, but keep your thumb poised over its note.

As you pivot back to *e*, grab a fifth down from it (*a*), then play R 5 8 (*a e a*).

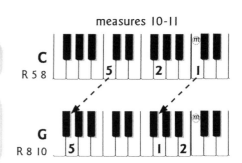

measures 10-11

To simplify these chords, see page T-35.

Form: Four 8-measure **A** phrases and two 3-measure **B** phrases

AA' Weave right hand around Am [*e d♯ e d♯ e b d c a*], then arpeggiate Am→E→Am from left hand to right. At ms. 7, play left hand E, then right hand [*e c b*]. Take the 1st ending and play **A'**, then the 2nd ending to go on to the **B** section.

BA' At ms. 10, play the **B** melody [*e g f e d*] and move it down a step with each chord: C→G→Am→E. For E, scale the keyboard hand to hand with 9 octave *e*'s and 3 [*d♯e*]'s. Then, launch *d♯* [*e d♯ e d♯ e b d c a*] and [it's a joy to play this lovely tune] to the first ending.

BA Repeat **BA**, then take the 2nd ending to leave Elise.

Meter: Originally in 3/8, this excerpt appears in the more common 3/4.

If you love Für Elise, learn the entire piece, like my mom did in her 90s.

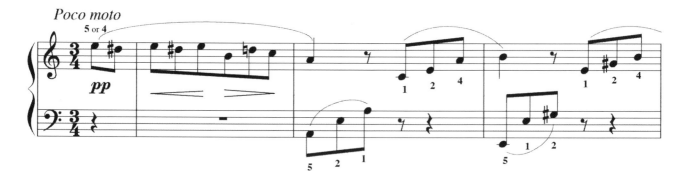

Wild Rider, Opus 68, No. 8 (excerpt)

Robert Schumann (1810–1856)

Harmony: Both Am→Dm/a and E→Am/e feel like thumb thrusts.

Meter: To get galloping, look at or listen to the original in 6/8 meter, then accent the first beat of every other measure.

Piano Freedom for Frustrated Pianists

Alla Turca from *Sonata* K. 331 (excerpt) — by Wolfgang Amadeus Mozart

B major triad (ms. 7)

To learn the **b**irds **d**o **f**ly majors and minors, see pages T-28 to 29.

tr = **trill** (ms. 23)
Rapidly alternate the note (b). with its upper neighbor (c).

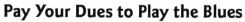

Pay Your Dues to Play the Blues

The blues is a dialect with a language of licks
(♭3 to 3, used in *St. Louis Blues* in 1914), blues scales
(R · ♭3 · 4 · ♭5 · 5), bass patterns (R5 · R6 · R5 · R6),
and form variants (change to F in ms. 2). Collect licks,
scales, bass patterns and form variants, then start improvising.

*"I love the blues,
they hurt so nice."*

Ben Sidram

Basic twelve-bar blues

C	C	C	C
F	F	C	C
G	F	C	**G** to repeat (𝄇) **C** to end (𝄇)

♭3 to 3 triad lick

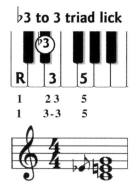

Pay Your Dues Blues

Improvising with ♭3 to 3 = ♯2 to 3

When the rhythm gets complex, arrangers often reduce the visual clutter of lots of ♭'s and ♮'s in a measure (page 7-32) by showing ♭3 as ♯2. Here, the melodic palette has been extended to include the tense, forceful, bluesy ♭7.

♯2 to 3 seventh lick

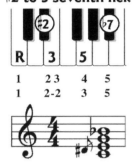

To improvise:

- Play the notes of this lick in any order, octave or rhythm.
- Stay on the C lick throughout, move for each chord, or play whatever sounds good to you.
- Replace crushes (in ms. 5, 6, 9, 10) with grace notes, slides or pull offs (page 7-6).

Bittersweet Blues

On the repeat, play the left hand an octave lower.

Jamming on the Twelve Bar Blues

The ac*comp*anist (on the left)
*comp*s for the soloist (on the right).

Comper, agree on the tempo, then play (and count) the first two or four measures as an introduction. Use one pattern throughout, mix and match, or create your own variation.

Soloist, enter on beat 4. Play as written on page 7-35, or do your own thing with the blues scale(s) or whatever sounds good to you.

- Listen! Respond to what your partner's doing, so it's a conversation, not a monologue.
- Keep track of where you are. Chant, (**C**-2-3-4, **2**-2-3-4 …), watch the form or memorize.
- If your partner gets lost, chant aloud until you're in sync. To end, feel the flow, nod, or say, "Last time."

Jazzy twelve-bar blues with 7ths

C⁷	C⁷	C⁷	C⁷
F⁷	F⁷	C⁷	C⁷
G⁷	F⁷	C⁷	G⁷ to repeat / C⁷ to end

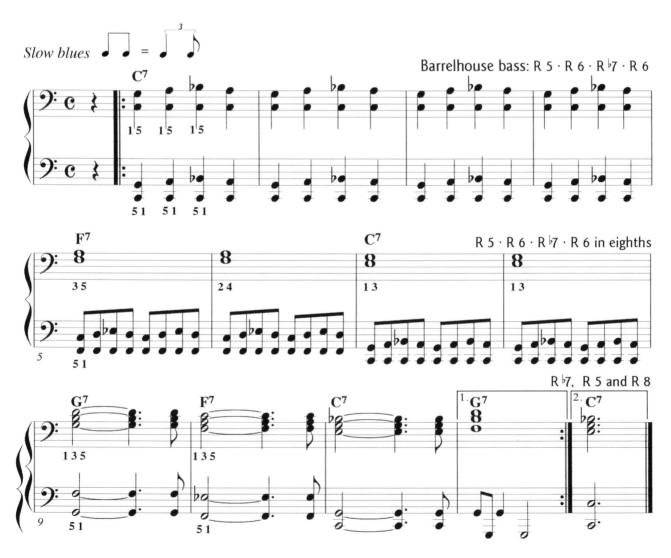

The Blues Scale

The feisty five-tone blues scale has two *blue notes*—♭3 (the minor 3rd) and ♭5 (the previously-forbidden *diabolus*). It fits conveniently under your five fingers and sounds great!

When you're comfortable with five tones, add another *blue note*—♭7 (the minor 7th), giving you a gritty six-tone blues scale with three *blue notes* and multiple fingering options.

To improvise:

• Play the scale tones in any order, octave or rhythm.

• Stay on C blues throughout, move for each chord or . . .

• Add grace notes, slides, crushes and pull offs (page 7-6).

• Ask a friend to accompany you, playing one or both hands.

Five-Tone Blues Scale

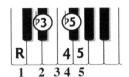

Six-Tone Blues Scale

Fast lane: Change the form to include an F in measure 2.

Blues Scale Blues—Soloist

As a duet, play both hands an octave higher.

Slow blues

Sixths or thirds: R 6 or R 3

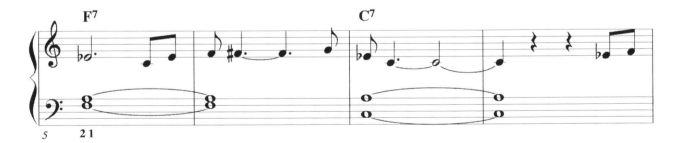

When the Saints Keep on Jamming

Invite a friend to sing or play (and embroider?) the melody
while you play the walking bass accompaniment (and embellish?).

Piano Freedom for Frustrated Pianists

When You Dress Up the Saints

Musicians have always liked to embroider melodies by filling in their empty spaces. What we now call grace notes (page 7-6) and neighbor notes, Baroque musicians called appogiaturas and mordents. To absorb the following basic improvisation ideas, focus on each one in isolation. Read the description and play the example, then apply just that idea to the *Saints*. Mix and match these ideas until you like what you're playing. Finally, ask a pianist (or guitarist) to accompany you by reading a duet arrangement (page 7-36 or 6-35) or faking one.

Grace notes. Just before the main note, play a quick note. Use two different fingers (2 3) or slide a finger (3-3).

Neighbor notes. Play the note and its upper or lower neighbor, then return to the note.

Passing tones. Fill in the note(s) between the given notes.

Rhythmic changes.

- Play notes earlier or later;
- Subdivide long notes;
- Play eighth notes unevenly as swung eighths:

Echoes. Move a note or phrase an octave or other interval.

Chord tones. Jump around between chord tones.

Combination of any of these improvisation ideas plus your own creative meanderings.

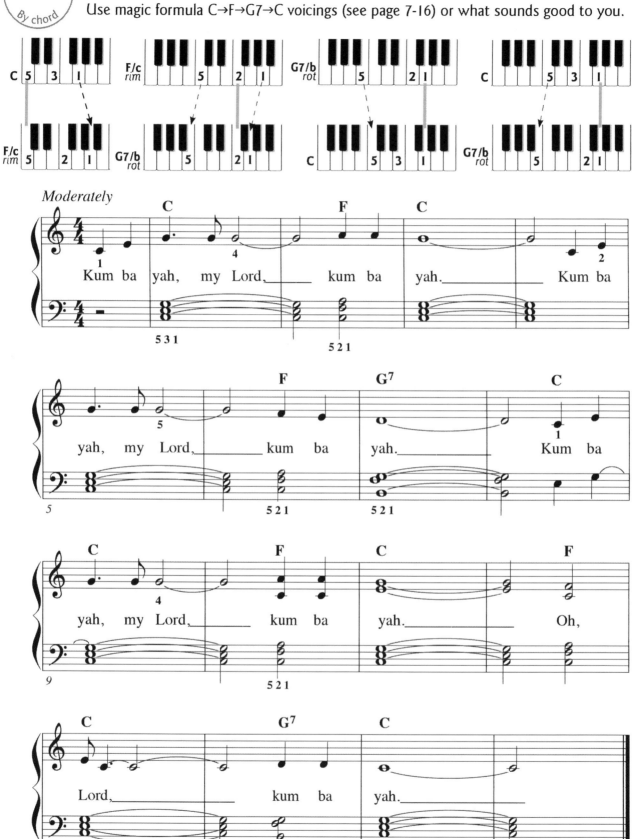

Kum Ba Yah ("Come By Here")

Traditional African-American spiritual

Use magic formula C→F→G7→C voicings (see page 7-16) or what sounds good to you.

Country Waltz

Joseph Haydn (1732–1809)

Imagine peasants dancing energetically *(animato)* with firm, heavy *(pesante)* steps at a German beer garden. **Oom** pah pah, **oom** pah pah, **oom** pah . . .

Wanderin'

For a greater gravitational push home, phrases often end with chain reactions of falling fifths. The greater the tension, the more satisfying the ultimate resolution!

B (E A D G C) F

This wanderer leaves C, goes to Em, then follows the gravitational force of falling fifths home to C. Look for:

- walking bass, ms. 1
- arpeggios, ms. 2-3
- jump bass, ms. 5-6
- diatonic inchworm voicings, ms. 6-7 (see page 7-17)
- 3rds and 6ths under the melody, ms.1-4

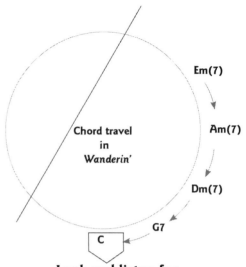

Chord travel in *Wanderin'*

Em(7)

Am(7)

Dm(7)

G7

C

Look and listen for
"**B E A D G** (rhymes with *siege*) **C F.**"

Moderate swing

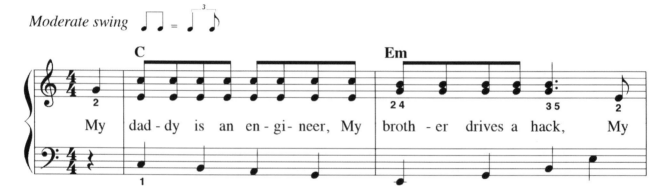

My dad-dy is an en-gi-neer, My broth-er drives a hack, My

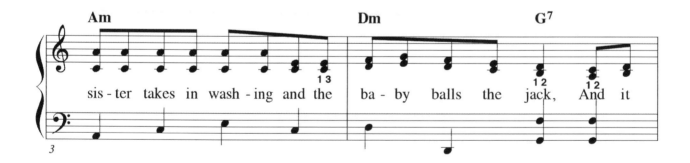

sis-ter takes in wash-ing and the ba-by balls the jack, And it

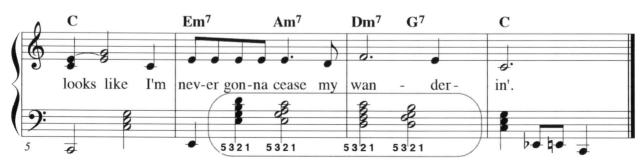

looks like I'm nev-er gon-na cease my wan - der - in'.

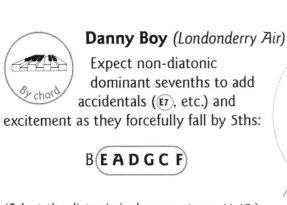

Danny Boy (Londonderry Air)

Expect non-diatonic dominant sevenths to add accidentals (E7, etc.) and excitement as they forcefully fall by 5ths:

B E A D G C F

(Adapt the diatonic inchworm at ms. 11-12.)

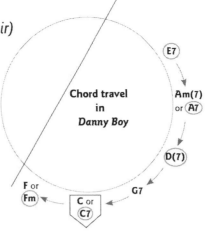

Chord travel in *Danny Boy*

19th century Irish folk tune
Lyrics by Frederic Weatherly
(1848–1929)

For more about chord travel, see pages 7-23. 8-5 and 8-6

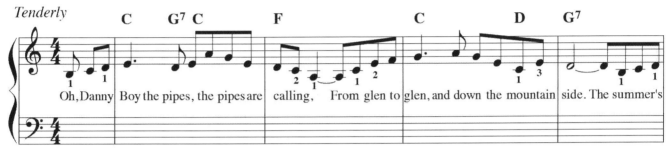

Tenderly

Oh, Danny Boy the pipes, the pipes are calling, From glen to glen, and down the mountain side. The summer's

gone, and all the roses falling, it's you, it's you must go, and I must bide. But come ye

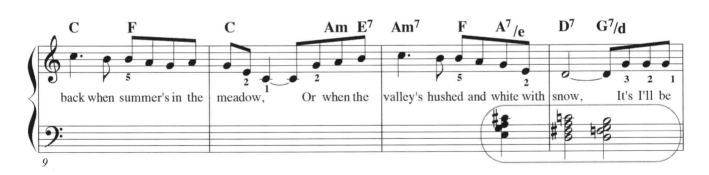

back when summer's in the meadow, Or when the valley's hushed and white with snow, It's I'll be

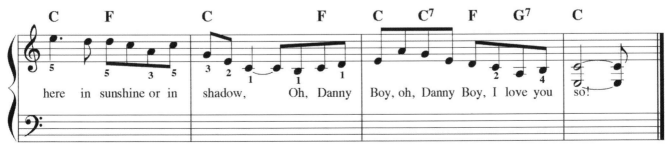

here in sunshine or in shadow, Oh, Danny Boy, oh, Danny Boy, I love you so!

Prelude in C from *The Well Tempered Clavichord*

Johann Sebastian Bach (1685–1750)

Andante con moto

CHAPTER 7 REVIEW

1. To convert a minor triad to a major triad _____.

2. Name and spell the 3 white-black-white "sandwich" majors & show them on the keyboard:

   __A__ = _a_ _c♯_ _e_   ____ = __ __ __   ____ = __ __ __

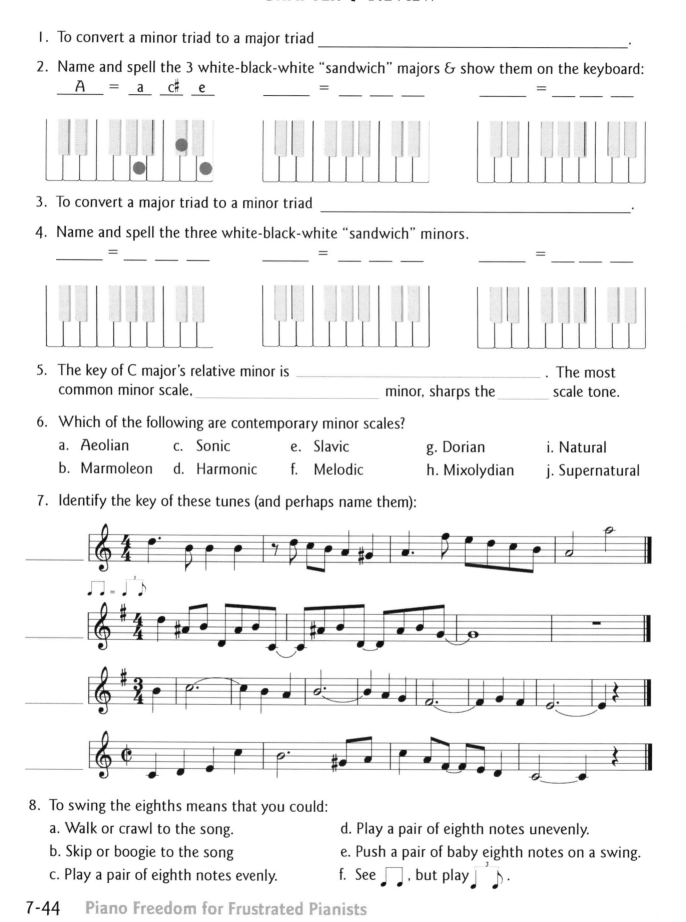

3. To convert a major triad to a minor triad _____.

4. Name and spell the three white-black-white "sandwich" minors.

   ____ = __ __ __   ____ = __ __ __   ____ = __ __ __

5. The key of C major's relative minor is _____. The most common minor scale, _____ minor, sharps the _____ scale tone.

6. Which of the following are contemporary minor scales?

   a. Aeolian   c. Sonic   e. Slavic   g. Dorian   i. Natural
   b. Marmoleon   d. Harmonic   f. Melodic   h. Mixolydian   j. Supernatural

7. Identify the key of these tunes (and perhaps name them):

8. To swing the eighths means that you could:

   a. Walk or crawl to the song.   d. Play a pair of eighth notes unevenly.
   b. Skip or boogie to the song   e. Push a pair of baby eighth notes on a swing.
   c. Play a pair of eighth notes evenly.   f. See ♪♪ , but play ♩ ♪ .

9. Show each Am chord and the closest position of Dm.

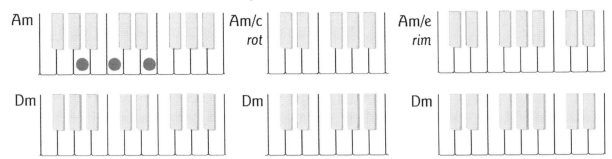

10. Show each Am chord and the closest position of E.

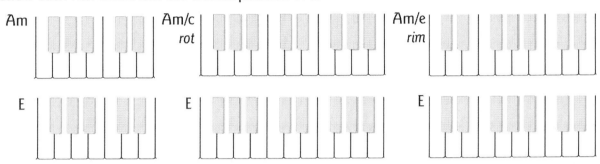

11. What is a dominant seventh?
   a. A four-note stack of 3rds built on the fifth scale tone.
   b. The seventh scale tone after taking assertiveness training.
   c. A dominant triad plus the note a whole-step down from the octave.
   d. The bigger, badder bully of the Sevenths family.

12. Show root-position G7.  or  or

13. What are falling fifths? (Pick *a* or *b*, and fill in *c*.)
   a. Musical bottles falling from the sky.
   b. Interlinked fifths whose roots are the fifths of the next chord.
   c. Progressions such as this all-white one in the Key of C:

   B___ → ___ → ___ → ___ → ___ → ___ → ___

When you feel comfortable with this chapter:

Go directly to the **Coda**, where you'll find out how it's the same, but different, in any key,

THE SAME, BUT DIFFERENT, IN ANY KEY

Like players on a baseball team, the names of the chords are different for each key, but the positions and rules of play remain the same. To generalize what you know about the key of C, call each chord by its *Roman numeral name,* based on its scale degree. Use UPPERCASE Roman numerals for MAJOR triads (**I**, **IV** and **V**) and lowercase for minor (**ii**, **iii** and **vi**) and diminished (**vii**) triads. Then, you can predict how the primary chords—**I**, **IV** and **V**—will function in the key.

C major:	C	Dm	Em	F	G	Am	B dim
Any key:	**I major**	**ii minor**	**iii minor**	**IV major**	**V major**	**vi minor**	**vii diminished**

I ("one") feels like home, where a piece of music usually starts, often returns and almost always ends.

Built on the key's **first** scale tone, the tonal center, **I** is called the **tonic** chord.

V ("five") has a tense, forceful sound that demands resolution home to **I**. The most common way to end a phrase, song or symphony, **V**→**I** (a falling fifth) sounds like dramatically saying "Go home!"

Built on the key's **fifth** scale tone, **V** is called the **dominant**, because it forcefully pushes you home to **I**. Expect to also find bigger, tenser versions, such as **V7** or **V9**.

IV ("four") has a mellow, churchy sound that either resolves home to I or goes someplace else. A gentle way to end a phrase, **IV**→**I** (a rising fifth) sounds like a heavenly choir sublimely singing "Amen."

Built on the **fourth** scale tone, **IV** is called the **sub-dominant**. Whereas the dominant (**V**) is a fifth *above* the tonic, the *sub*-dominant (**IV**) is a fifth *below* the tonic.

The rules of the game
As in baseball, when you understand the function of each of the players and the rules of the game, the game makes more sense. To underline this point, I once asked a class, "Have you ever seen a game where you didn't know the rules?" "Yes," said a student, "Life!"

Orienting Yourself in G Major (or Any Key)

When visiting foreign lands, seasoned travelers read guide books, look at maps, and listen to language lessons. When you visit a new key, orient yourself—play the key's scales, chords and progressions.

1. Play an eight-fingered G major scale.

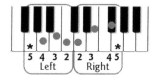

Put your pinkies on octave apart g's. Play the G major scale using your fingers, but no thumbs. Savor G's sound.

Adjust your fingers to easily reach the black key, then hold down all eight notes and take a mental snapshot. Closing your eyes, feel G's topography.

In the key of C, you'd see a sharp sign in front of each *f* on the staff.

In the key of G, you'd see one *f♯* posted up front in the *key signature*.

The *key signature* tells you what to sharp (or flat) and announces the key.

- **Key of G major**, if *g* is the tonal center,
    expect: G (I), C (IV) and D or D7 (V or V7); or

- **Key of E minor** (G's relative minor), if *e* is the tonal center,
    expect: Em (i), Am (iv) and E or E7 (V or V7).

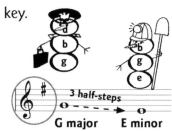

G major   E minor

2. Play one-handed G major scales.

Practice with each hand alone and with hands together.
Be sure to gradually glide into the black keys to easily reach each *f♯*.

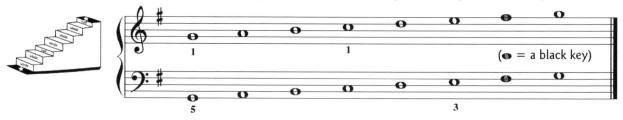

(● = a black key)

3. Play diatonic triads on each scale tone.

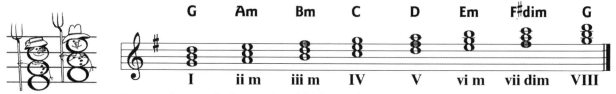

G	Am	Bm	C	D	Em	F♯dim	G
I	ii m	iii m	IV	V	vi m	vii dim	VIII

Do you know all these chords? If not, learn them now, or wait until you need one for a song. (For unfamiliar chords, see pages T-26 to 32.)

4. Play the primary chords in closest position. Gradually glide into the black keys to easily reach each *f* sharp. As a memory aid, you might mark the *f* sharps or pencil in some sharp signs.

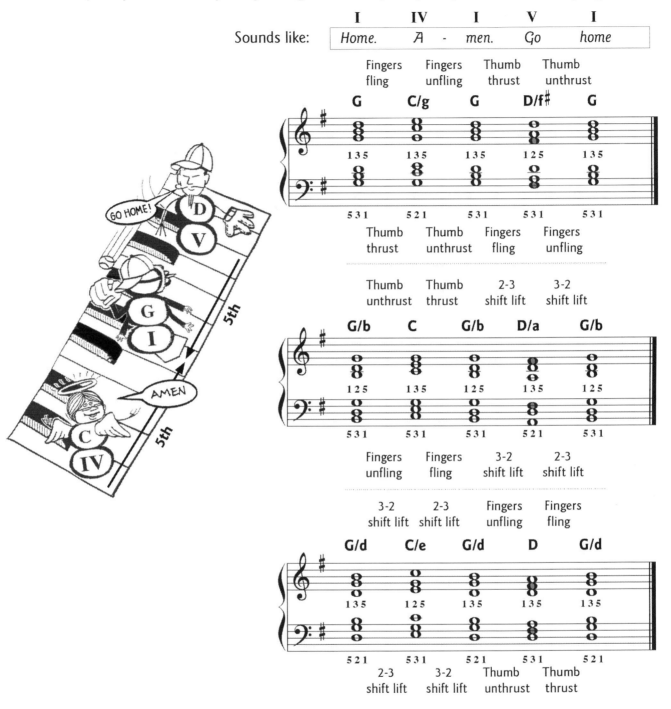

5. Play diatonic sevenths on each scale tone. Learn G's dominant seventh (D7) first. Then, tackle the other types of sevenths as you need them. (See page T-30).

6. **Inchworm diatonic sevenths around the circle of fifths.**

Leaving C, turn the *wheel of fifths* so that the new key (G) lands on the bottom. G becomes home base, ⬠ I , the center of gravity of this musical reality.
Alternate *root* and *rim* sevenths with *1 2 3 5* throughout.

F#m7♭5 Bm7/f# Em7 Am7/e   D7 GM7/d CM7

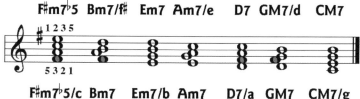

F#m7♭5/c Bm7 Em7/b Am7   D7/a GM7 CM7/g

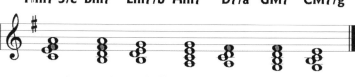

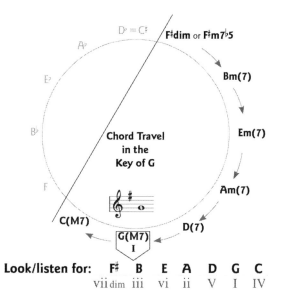

Chord Travel in the Key of G

Look/listen for: F#   B   E   A   D   G   C
                 vii dim iii vi ii   V   I   IV

Diatonic pieces in G

Five Hundred Miles	*I Walk the Line*	BACH: *Minuet (first part)* BWV Anh. 114
From a Distance	*Unchained Melody*	HAYDN: *Allegro* from *Sonata in G Major*
Heart of Gold	*Yellow Submarine*	L. MOZART: *Burlesque*

Non-diatonic pieces in G

Blackbird	*Longer*	BACH: *Minuet in G*, BWV 841
Blue Moon (circle)	*More* (circle)	BEETHOVEN: *Minuet in G*, WoO 10; *Écossaise*, WoO 23;
Chapel of Love	*Norwegian Wood*	Sonatina in G; Sonata in G, Op. 49, No. 2;
Desperado	*St. Louis Blues*	Rondo a Capriccio, Op. 129 (circle)
How High the Moon	*Stormy Weather*	HAYDN: *German Dance, Easy Divertimento*
Lady Madonna	*Try to Remember* (circle)	SCHUMANN: *Soldiers' March, Little Cradle Song*

7. **Play G major's relative minor scale(s) and primary chords.**

To play an E minor scale, follow the key signature, sharp the 6th (c#), and/or sharp the 7th (d#). Since the f# appears in the key signature, the signs of non-diatonic intruders pop out.

Play E minor's primary chords in closest position.

Em Am/e *or* A/e Em Bm/d *or* B/d# Em

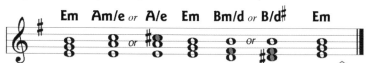

On the G wheel, move "home" to Minorville, where ⬠ i is surrounded by other minors. Inchworm around the circle with sevenths, but start and end at minor's home, expecting accidentals along the way.

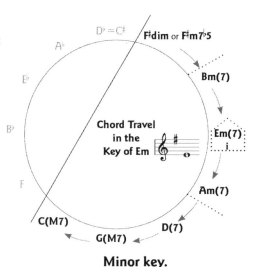

Chord Travel in the Key of Em

**Minor key.
Expect accidentals!**

Non-diatonic pieces in Em

Autumn Leaves (circle)	*Perhaps (Quizas)* (circle)	BACH: *Bourée* from *Suite in E Minor*, BWV 996
Eleanor Rigby	*The Pink Panther*	CHOPIN: *Prelude in E Minor*, Op. 28, No.4
Green-Eyed Lady	*Scarborough Fair/Canticle*	GRIEG: *Elfin Dance & Album Leaf*, Op. 12, No. 4 & 7
Nights in White Satin	*What Child Is This?*	SCHUMANN: *Child Falling Asleep, First Loss, Phantasy Dance & About Strange Lands and People* (circle)

The Wheel Way to Predict Chord Travel

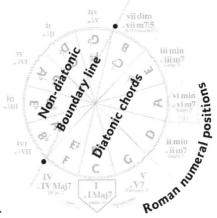

The Wheel of Fifths on page 8-6 shows the key of C's diatonic chords with their Roman numeral positions and common travel routes. A boundary line separates the **7** diatonic roots from the **5** spicy non-diatonic roots.

To make a spinnable wheel that will work in any key:

- Photocopy this page and the next onto cardstock. For longer use, laminate or cover with clear contact paper.

- Cut out the circle of letter names below. Place it at the center of the circle of Roman numeral positions. Fasten the wheel with a brad or a bent paper clip.

- To replace the wheel's now hidden stretch of boundary line, cut open a long, skinny rubber band. Insert each end at a black dot, and turn the wheel over. Tape the ends of the rubber "string" slightly taut, then take your wheel out for a spin with a song and twang along.

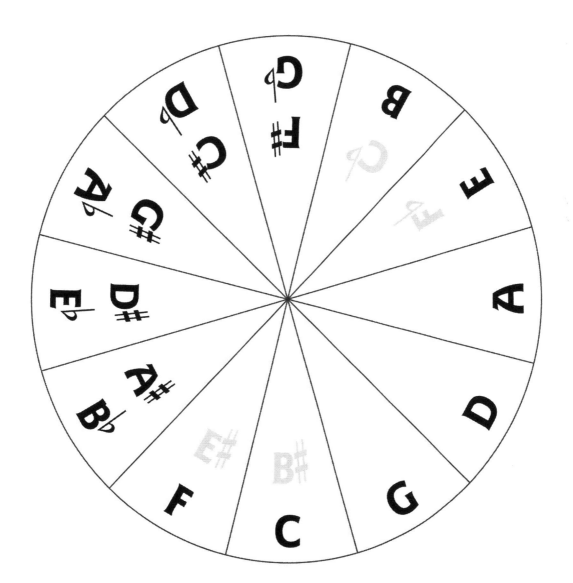

THE WHEEL OF FIFTHS

- For a major key, put the name of the key on the bottom of the circle as ⬠ I , the middle major.
- For a minor key, keep the relative major on the bottom, but call the middle minor chord ⬠ i , (not "vi," as it appears from the major's perspective). Renumber, if desired.
- Expect chord progressions to start at home and go someplace diatonic, then return home directly, by fifths or stepwise. If a chord goes someplace else, requires an accidental or crosses the boundary line to grab a non-diatonic root, feast your ears and take note.

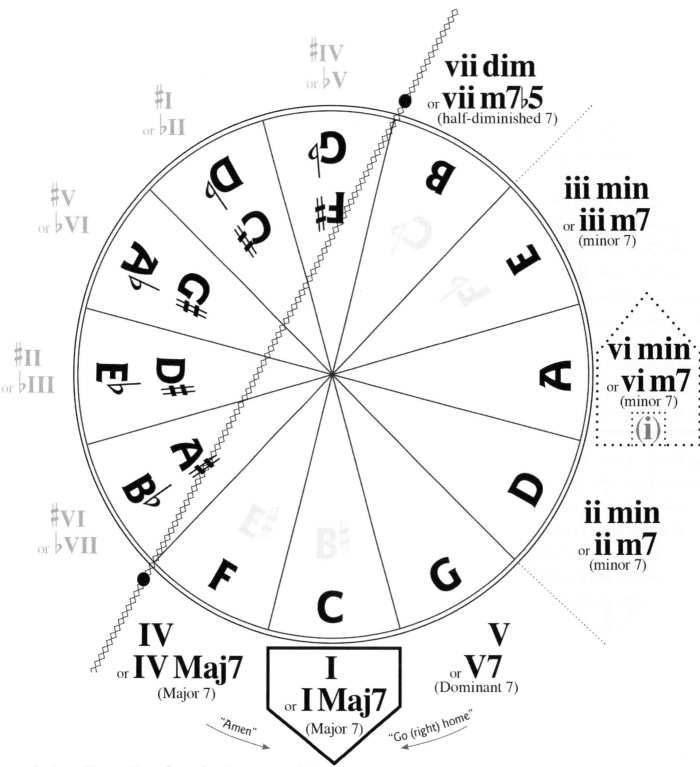

Live Out Your Piano Dreams!

Only you can live out your piano dreams. There's an old story about an aspiring pianist who travels to New York to launch his career. He hails a taxi and asks the driver, "Can you tell me the quickest way to get to Carnegie Hall?"

"Sure," says the driver. "Practice, practice, practice."

To live out your piano dreams, make a commitment to practice regularly. Do what excites and delights you, as well as whatever it takes to efficiently learn that music. I once read a letter in an Ann Landers column by a man who had taught his pet poodle to play *Tea For Two* on the piano. If he could teach his dog to play a song with one paw, you can certainly teach your ten fingers to play a song that you want to learn! Work on music you love. Put your heart and soul into the learning process. Eventually, as if by grace, with your mind singing, your fingers dancing and your ears listening, you'll experience the thrill of piano freedom.

WHERE TO GO FROM HERE

Practice scales, chords and progressions clockwise around the circle of falling fifths.

B→E→A→D→G→C→F→B♭→E♭→A♭→D♭→G♭=F♯→B→E→A→D→G . . .

Think: *BEADG* (rhymes with *siege*)→C→F.

For gospel and rhythm 'n' blues, practice rising "Amens" (counterclockwise): B♭→F→C→G . . .

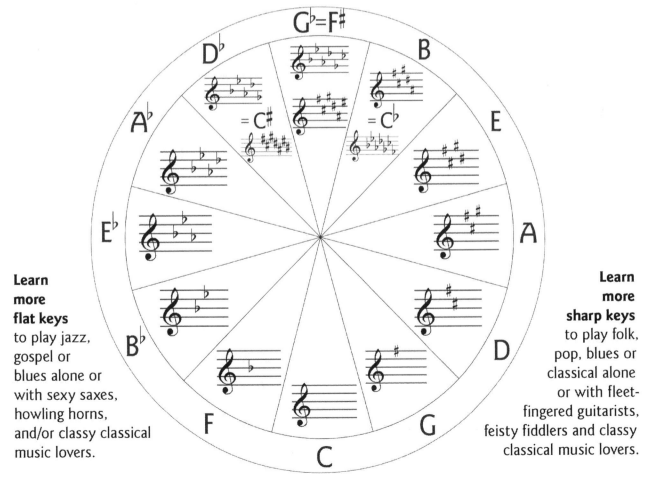

Learn more flat keys to play jazz, gospel or blues alone or with sexy saxes, howling horns, and/or classy classical music lovers.

Learn more sharp keys to play folk, pop, blues or classical alone or with fleet-fingered guitarists, feisty fiddlers and classy classical music lovers.

CODA REVIEW

TO ORIENT YOURSELF IN ANY MAJOR KEY:

1. Play an 8-fingered major _____ with LH _ _ _ _ and RH _ _ _ _, so you see the whole palette. Then, install default fingerings by practicing the major _____ in each hand. Gradually learn all _ _.

2. Play majors on the _____, _____ and _____ scale tones.
    Play minors on the _____, _____ and _____ scale tones.
    Play diminished on the _____ scale tone.

3. Play primary chords, I, __ and __ in closest position. Start with I in root position, then play the other chords in their most convenient _in_____, with the root either on _____ or in the _____.

4. Play _dia_____ sevenths on each scale tone. Expect a dominant seventh on the _____ scale tone, for example, in the key of C, G7 = _ _ _ _ and in the key of G, _7 = _ _ _ _ .

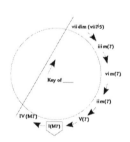

5. Inchworm closest position _dia_____ sevenths around the _____ of _____. Expect no _acci_____ as you simply alternate _____ position and root-in-_____ seventh shapes.

TO ORIENT YOURSELF IN ANY MAJOR KEY'S RELATIVE MINOR:

6. From a major key's tonal _____, go down _____ half-steps to find its relative _____. To play the harmonic minor's scale and primary chords, follow the _____ signature but sharp the _____ scale tone.

Go have lots of musical fun!

TOOLBOX

HOW TO MASTER A PIECE OF MUSIC

When you begin to learn a piece, be efficient—start by seeing the big picture. Like looking at the picture on a jigsaw puzzle's box, your overview will help you know how to put the pieces of the musical puzzle together. After looking at the big picture on the box, efficient puzzle solvers might divide the pieces into groups of edges, corners and insides. Similarly, after getting an overview of a piece, efficient pianists divide their learning process into manageable learning chunks. For instance, you might tap difficult rhythms before playing the notes and learn each hand alone before putting your hands together. The more memory pegs and strategies you have, the easier it will be to assemble the whole piece. Savor the satisfaction of solving one chunk at a time, knowing that slowly but surely, you'll conquer the entire piece!

Right now, how would you go about learning *St. James Infirmary* on the facing page? Internalize the procedure described in this section, then apply it to any piece you want to master.

St. James Infirmary

Anonymous eighteenth-century British ballad

Went up to see the doctor, "She's very low," he said;
Went back to see my baby, Good God! She's lyin' there dead.

I went down to old Joe's barroom, on the corner by the square,
They were servin' the drinks as usual, and the usual crowd was there.

On my left stood Joe McKenny, on my right stood my old friend Fred,
I gazed at the crowd around me, and these were the words that I said:

Let her go, let her go, God bless her, wherever she may be,
She may search this wide world over, an' never find a better man than me.

Yes, sixteen coal black horses, to pull that rubber tied hack,
Well it's seventeen miles to the graveyard, but my baby's never comin' back.

Now that's the end of my story, let's have another round of booze,
And if anyone should ask you, just tell them, I've got the St. James Infirmary blues.

See the Big Picture

To learn any piece, start by seeing the big picture.

Title and Composer

St. James Infirmary

The anonymous eighteenth-century English composer probably sang his sad song and sold broadside printings on the streets of London. In the 1900s, the song came to New Orleans, where it took on the city's jazzy, bluesy style.

Listen to recordings by Louis Armstrong, Billie Holliday, Janis Joplin, Van Morrison and others.

Key Signature and Key

Flat every *b*: you're in the key of F major or D minor.
Since *St. James'* tonal center (✱) is *d*, it's in the key of D minor.
Expect mostly: Dm, Edim (or Em7♭5), F, Gm (or G), Am (or A or A7), B♭ (or B♭7) and C.

For more about key signatures, see pages 7-2, 3 and T-23. To predict the chords in any key, see Chapter 8.

Meter

$\frac{4}{4}$

The time signature (4/4) tells you the meter, the song's recurring rhythmic pattern. Feel the quarter note ($\quarternote = 1/4$) as the beat. Expect 4 beats (4/4) per measure. Accent the first beat of every measure and give a lesser accent to the third beat.

For more about time signatures, see page 2-2 (4/4); page 4-5 (3/4); or page T-33 (6/8 and 12/8).

Tempo and Feel

Slowly

Play this song at a slow, mournful tempo. To give it a bluesy feeling, play swung eighths instead of straight eighths.

To learn about straight eighths versus swung eighths, see page 7-6.

Form

Four two-measure phrases.

Each phrase starts (○) on beat four at the tonal center *d* (✱). All play out of Dm 5-finger pattern, except the second phrase. It goes up Dm triad+octave and comes down from *d* to *b♭*, then *a*.

Meanwhile, the left hand walks the bass (*d c g a*), except for flourishes at phrase endings.

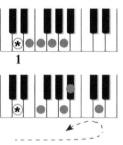

Walking bass harmony, page T-3

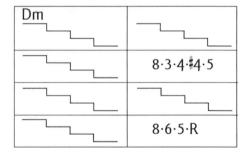

Dm		
	8·3·4·#4·5	
	8·6·5·R	

Chordal harmony (one of many)

Dm	A7	Dm	
Dm	Gm	Dm	A7
Dm	A7	Dm	
Dm	A7	Dm	

For blank keyboard diagrams, see pages T-16 and 17. For blank cheat sheets, see T-18.

Divide and Conquer

Once you've gotten an overview, begin to divide and conquer the piece.

Where will I start?

While most people always start at the beginning, efficient learners often start at the hardest part. That way, when you eventually perform the piece, your confidence grows, rather than your fear that the hard part's coming! Work on several measures, a phrase, or whatever chunk seems small enough to learn easily. (Start learning *St. James Infirmary* by tackling its second phrase, where most of the rhythmic and fingering challenges occur.)

As you work on the piece, rather than always repeating the sections you already know, practice starting at different spots. By efficiently focusing on what still needs work, you'll also be cultivating re-entry spots—places to pick up the music if you get lost in performance. (To learn *Für Elise* on page 7-28, start practicing at measures 1, 10 and 13.)

How will I tackle the challenges of this chunk?

Decide which of the following strategies to use:

- Learn each hand alone, page T-6.
- Put your hands together, page T-11.
- Diagnose and treat musical problems, page T-12.
- Memorize on multiple channels, page T-13.

How will I be sure I've mastered this chunk?

After several unsuccessful attempts at playing a chunk, you finally get it right. Do you blithely go on to the next chunk? Not if you want to cancel out all of your incorrect renditions and correctly reprogram your brain/fingers. To properly reprogram your internal computer, repeat the chunk until you can play it correctly three times in a row.

How will I add this chunk to what I've already learned?

Once you've learned a chunk, tack it onto the previously learned chunk(s). Then practice playing the joined-together chunks. Just as seams are usually the weakest parts of garments, transitions between chunks are usually the weakest parts of songs. To make each transition feel secure, go for three-in-a-row correct repetitions to reinforce each "seam." Continue this process one chunk at a time until you've learned the whole song.

Learn Each Hand Alone

If a piece is easy, play both hands together right away. If not, master one chunk at a time, first with each hand alone, then with hands together. That way, you reinforce what you've just learned and enjoy an aural pay-off. For each chunk, use any or all of the following strategies:

- ## Learn the rhythm.

    If a piece's rhythm is confusing, isolate the rhythmic challenge. (Why compound the rhythm problem by also trying to read the notes?) Pencil in the counting. Count and tap the rhythm until you know it.

    1. **Learn the time values for the piece's notes** (pitches) and rests (silences). In 2/4, 3/4 or 4/4:

Notes	o	𝅗𝅥.	𝅗𝅥	𝅘𝅥	𝅘𝅥𝅮	𝅘𝅥𝅯
	whole 4 beats	dotted half 3 beats	half 2 beats	quarter 1 beat	eighth 1/2 beat	sixteenth 1/4 beat
Rests	▬	▬·	▬	𝄽	𝄾	𝄿
	Dot (·): Add half again as much			**Beam:** 𝅘𝅥𝅮𝅘𝅥𝅮 = 1 beat = 𝅘𝅥𝅯𝅘𝅥𝅯𝅘𝅥𝅯𝅘𝅥𝅯		

    2. **Always say the numbered beats** (1 2 3 4). Only say subdivisions like *and* (**+**) when a note or rest begins on them. A single eighth note holds a *flag* (𝅘𝅥𝅮); pairs *beam* together (𝅘𝅥𝅮𝅘𝅥𝅮).*

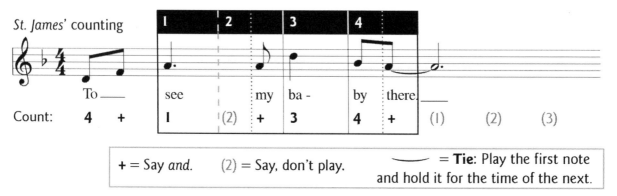

	+ = Say *and*.	(2) = Say, don't play.	⌣ = **Tie**: Play the first note and hold it for the time of the next.

3. **Think of each note as a television show** and each rest as silent time when the TV is off. A grandfather clock chimes and you call out the time. (In 4/4 time, this magical metric clock repeatedly strikes 1:00, 2:00, 3:00, 4:00.) Like shows on a TV schedule, each note starts when the last one ended.

4. **Transfer rhythmically confusing measures to a rhythm grid**, like those on T-7 and T-8. Using two columns for 2/4, three for 3/4, or four for 4/4, draw boxes to represent the duration of each note or rest. Then, write in the counting. Once you're comfortable counting, just imagine a grid superimposed over the notes of a song, and pencil in the counting.

5. **Remember new rhythms by associating them with familiar songs.** You might associate 𝅘𝅥𝅮𝅘𝅥 𝅘𝅥𝅮𝅘𝅥 𝅘𝅥 with *Hello my baby* or *Hang down your head Tom* (Dooley). Personalize the rhythm grid on the facing page in whatever way works for you.

6. **Practice counting the rhythms of new songs** or get help from a sympathetic teacher.

7. **Play songs you know and fake the rhythm.**

> * Were you taught that if a measure has any eighth notes, you should say all of the the subdivisions—
> 4 + | 1 (+) (2) + 3 (+) 4 + | (1) (+) (2) (+) (3) (+)? If this works for you, keep doing it. If it feels too mechanical, like plotting rhythms on graph paper, retrain yourself using the method described above.

RHYTHM GRID FOR 4/4

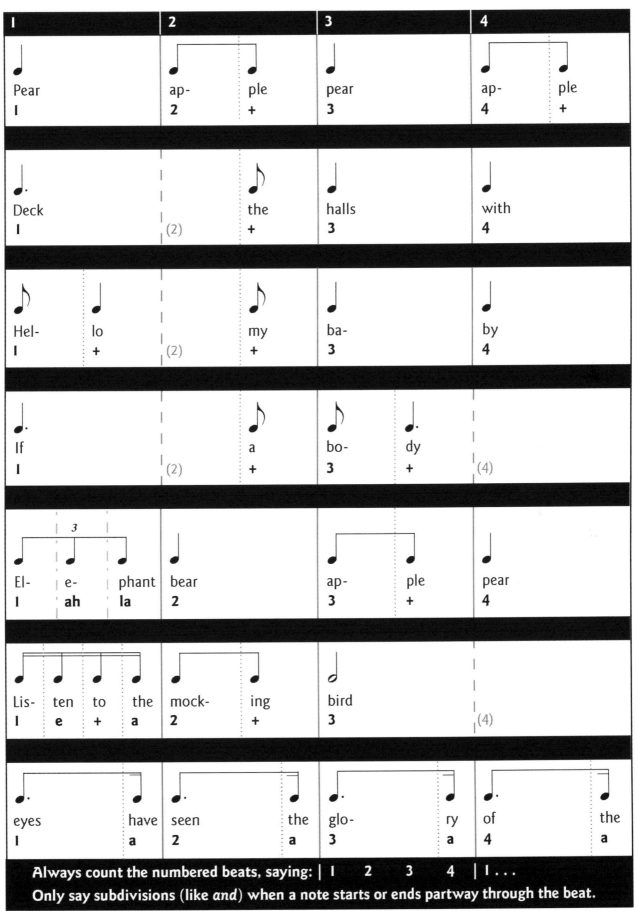

Write-on Rhythm Grid for 4/4

| I | (+) | 2 | (+) | 3 | (+) | 4 | (+) |

Always count the numbered beats, saying: | 1 2 3 4 | 1 . . .

Only say subdivisions, like *and* (+), when a note starts or ends partway through the beat.

• Learn the notes

Read the notes in each chunk, observing the key signature. (If you often forget to sharp or flat a particular note, draw a "reminder" flat or sharp in front of it.) Decide how to finger that chunk and pencil in your fingering. Use one of the following fingerings or whatever works for you.

St. James' fingering

	1	3	5	2	5	3	2	
or	1	2	3	3 or 2	5	3	- 3	(Slide *3* from *b♭* to *a*.)

If something feels awkward, choreograph more efficient, graceful movements. Perhaps you can leave out or rearrange problematic note(s). Once you've worked out your fingerings, consistently play the chunk the same way every time, until your fingers just dance and your ears delight.

• Find memory pegs

Analyze the music to find memory pegs for holding onto groups of notes. Use familiar musical shapes, patterns and concepts as ready-made memory pegs. Invent new memory pegs based on anything you can hear, see, feel or figure out.

How many memory pegs you use depends on the song and your learning style. If you are highly analytic, use lots of memory pegs. If your ear takes in each phrase as an indivisible chunk, only pull out your analytic microscope to focus on trouble spots.

St. James' memory pegs

I went down to the St. James In-firm-'ry,   To__ see my ba-by there.   She was

ly- in' on a long white__ ta- ble,   So__ sweet, so__ cool__ so fair.

Each of the four phrases starts (○) on beat four at the tonal center *d* (✱).

1. For the first phrase, start with *1* on *d* and stay in Dm five-finger pattern until the phrase ends on *d*.

Dm 5-finger

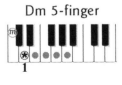

2. For the second phrase, start at *"To,"* and go up Dm triad+octave. At *"baby there,"* come down from *d* to *b♭*, then *a*.

Dm triad+octave

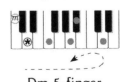

Dm 5-finger

3. For the third and fourth phrases, start at *"she,"* with *1* on *d*, then stay in Dm five-finger until the song ends on *d* (✱).

- ## Give life to the music

Pay attention to not only which notes you play, but also what those notes express and how you will play them. To clarify your musical intent, describe or draw the mood, feelings and images of the piece. (How did the man *feel* when he was at Saint James Infirmary, seeing his girlfriend lying dead on a long white table?) To capture the subtle shadings of the melody, sing it. To feel the rhythm in your body, dance to the song. To bring out expressive nuances, experiment with the dynamics, tempo, phrasing, articulation and pedaling.

The Troubles She's Seen

Although Karen had lost 95 percent of her hearing as a child, she considered herself quite musical. At forty-three, after a cochlear implant had allowed her to hear seventeen distinct frequencies, she began teaching herself piano. When she came to me for help, she played Nobody Knows the Trouble I've Seen. *All the notes were correct, but her playing sounded mechanical, devoid of feeling and nuance. I asked her to think about the troubles she'd seen in her life, and then play the song again. This time, the beauty and depth of her playing brought tears to my eyes.*

- ## Practice slowly and perfectly

"Remember when you are practicing you are teaching yourself."
Tobias Matthay

Practice at a tempo that's slow enough to play the notes correctly. If you learn the notes at a slow tempo, you can gradually get faster. If you start out too fast, you'll develop sloppy habits that you'll need to laboriously reprogram later.

Remember that "only perfect practice makes perfect." To program a chunk in your memory, play it correctly at least three times in a row before continuing. If you make a mistake, diagnose the cause of the error, treat the underlying problem, then play it correctly three times in a row.

Put Your Hands Together

1. Learn to coordinate the two-handed rhythm.

Make sure you know each hand's rhythm alone, then do any or all of the following:

- **Move to the beat.**
  Walk one hand's rhythm while singing, clapping or counting the other. (This only works if one hand plays a consistent pattern, like all quarter notes.)

- **Away from the keyboard, tap the two-handed rhythm on a table top or your thighs.**
  To establish the tempo, slowly count a measure or two ("*1 2 3 4 . . .*"), then start tapping on "*4 and.*" Experiment with the following steps, then cycle through the ones you like best.

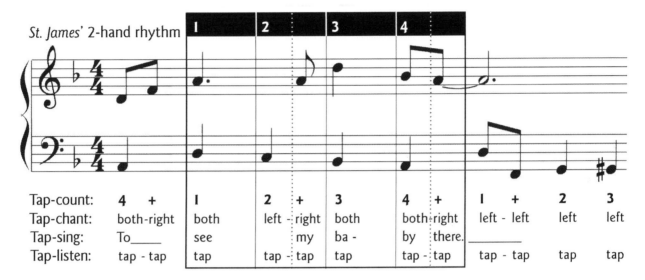

Tap-count:	4	+	1		2	+	3		4	+	1	+	2	3
Tap-chant:	both-right		both		left -	right	both		both	right	left -	left	left	left
Tap-sing:	To___		see			my	ba -		by	there.	___			
Tap-listen:	tap - tap		tap		tap -	tap	tap		tap -	tap	tap - tap		tap	tap

- **At the keyboard, count, chant and/or just play the rhythm.**
  Play one hand and tap the other hand.
  Play one hand and a simplified version of the other hand.
  Repeat the previous steps with opposite hands.
  Play both hands together with or without a metronome.

2. Coordinate fingerings and choreography.

Some things feel fine with hands alone, but awkward with hands together. When necessary, refinger, rechoreograph or redistribute the notes. For instance, play a treble clef note with your left hand or a bass clef note with your right.

3. Find memory pegs.

Do the hands imitate one another, move parallel, move contrary or spell chords?

4. Give life to the music.

Experiment with phrasing, articulation, dynamics, tempo and pedaling. Also, consider the balance between the hands so that you bring out the melody over the accompaniment.

5. Practice.

The way to learn quickly is to practice slowly. Perfect practice makes perfect.

"Mistakes are your best friends. They bring a message. They tell you what to do next and light the way. They come about because you have not understood something, or have learned something incompletely. They tell you that you are moving too fast, or looking in the wrong direction . . . The goal is not to make music free of mistakes. The goal is to be complete in learning and to grow well."

W. A. Mathieu

Diagnose and Treat Musical Problems

At persistent trouble spots, don't assume that more practice will solve the problem. (Isn't that a definition of insanity, doing the same thing over and over and expecting a different result?) As Albert Einstein said, "You can't solve a problem on the same level that it was created. You have to rise above it to the next level."

At trouble spots:

1. Diagnose the cause of the problem.

If you keep making the same mistake, look for the underlying problem that's causing that mistake. It's hard to solve a problem if you don't know what the problem is.

2. Prescribe and apply a treatment.

Once you've identified the problem, come up with possible solutions. As with medical problems, if your first treatment plan doesn't work, reconsider your original diagnosis and look for another treatment plan. If you have chronic problems with technique, fingering, reading or rhythms, seek the help of a specialist. In addition to diagnosing and treating your problems, a good teacher will help you learn to diagnose and treat them yourself.

3. Create a healthy new habit.

Rehearse the trouble spot until you can play it correctly three times in a row. Then, rehearse the trouble spot along with what immediately precedes and follows it. When you can play that correctly three times in a row, you've created a healthy new habit.

Memorize on Multiple Channels

To memorize a piece, do you just play it over and over until you know it? If so, you've probably already discovered that if the dog barks, the phone rings or your concentration wavers, the piece may fall apart. When I was thirteen, I was performing my favorite Chopin nocturne at a camp talent show. Suddenly, I had a memory lapse. Stranded in the middle of the piece, I didn't know how to jump back into it. Instead, I got up from the piano and fled the hall in tears.

Learning researchers tell us that the more ways you input information, the stronger the memory. (Neurons that fire together wire together.) Now, I combine aural, kinesthetic, visual and analytic memory, so that if one "channel" goes blank, I can jump back in on another channel. I once had to do just that while performing at a friend's nursing home. Since Paulette was French and loved classical music, I was playing *Claire de Lune* by Claude Debussy. Midway through, just when I was thinking how beautifully I was playing, I forgot what came next. Remaining calm, I improvised my way to the beginning of the next section and ended the piece as if nothing had happened. Afterwards, people who didn't know the piece told me how beautifully I'd played. Later, as I wheeled Paulette back to her room in her wheelchair, she knowingly whispered, "Highly original!"

Read about each of the four main memory channels and experiment with the strategies that appeal to you the most. Mark the ones you've tried, then gradually over time, try out more strategies. You may use all four channels equally or rely primarily on one or two channels. (If you perceive chords or intervals as having a particular taste, smell or color, feel free to use that channel too.) At first, memorizing will take a lot of effort. But like weight lifting, start out small and gradually flex your memory muscle with bigger challenges. Even if you later prefer the security blanket of performing from music, the process of memorizing will have helped you master the piece. And, speaking of blankets, when you can't sleep, try mentally playing songs. You may find that it works even better than counting sheep!

♪ *"Memorizing is a personal process, and each pianist has to find the way that suits him best. I simply play a piece over and over until I know it by heart ..."*   John Browning

♪ *"I am fortunate in that I was blessed with the ability to memorize quickly. It's not a photographic memory because I don't see the music; I hear it."*   Rudolf Firkusny

♪ *"I've devised what I call my "system," which I believe anyone can learn . . . I break down the form of the piece into its larger structural sections. In the smallest possible sense, I memorize intervallic relationships and harmonic blocks that are common through the entire movement of the complete piece."*   Misha Dichter

♪ *"When it comes to memorizing the music, I do perhaps ninety-five to ninety-eight percent of it away from the piano. I look at the score, study it, go through it in my mind, and piece it all together."*   Jorge Bolet

♪ *"I memorize in three ways: I have a visual memory, I have a harmonic memory, and I have a digital memory—that is, I know what chords are involved and I know the fingering."*   Janina Fialkowska

AURAL CHANNEL

Focus on how the music sounds.
Playing by heart, turn your left ear toward the keyboard and/or close your eyes.

1. **LISTEN!**

2. **Trust your ear when the melody steps or skips,** and create memory pegs for bigger intervals ("up a fifth" or "up to *g*").

3. **Develop your harmonic sense** to gradually recognize common chords (C= *c e g* = major triad) and chord progressions. (Key of C: C→F→C sounds like "*Home. Amen,*" while C→G→C sounds like "*Home. Go home.*")

4. **Sing along,** either out loud or in your imagination. Play the notes along with whatever nuances of expression, dynamics, phrasing and articulation you hear.

5. **Listen to the music that you want to learn.** Search the Internet, visit the library, borrow recordings from friends or ask someone to record it.

Develop your ear: sound out many melodies (page 1-7); learn to hear and play common intervals (5-8; T-24, 25); learn to recognize common chords (6-2 to 7; 7-8, 9, 14); inversions (6-17 to 19; 7-12, 13, 15); chord progressions (6-8, 14, 20, 21; 7-6, 16, 17; 8-1, 8-3 to 6); do ear-training drills alone or with a partner (T-24); play with people; and listen to lots of music. If you're predominantly aural, please nurture your talent by also tuning in to other channels.

KINESTHETIC CHANNEL

Focus on how the music feels in your fingers, wrists, arms and shoulders.
Playing by heart, close your eyes.

1. **Use consistent fingering and choreography.** When you start learning a piece, pencil in your fingering, choreograph the trouble spots and jot down helpful kinesthetic cues. Play the song so many times that your fingers just know what to do. (See pages 4-2 to 4.)

2. **Divide and conquer.** Memorize a measure or two until you can play it automatically with both hands together, enjoying both the aural payoff and the kinesthetic glue. Tackle the next chunk, then combine the two chunks. Proceed to other chunks until you've mastered the whole piece. (See pages T-5 to 12.)

3. **Make keyboard diagrams** (T-16, 17) to show how the music moves and feels. Pencil in notes and fingerings. Write words and symbols that show jumps, crosses and other complicated finger gymnastics. Mark the starting note (o), tonal center (*), middle *c* (m) and/or whatever helps you. (See pages 4-2, 3, 8; 5-12; 6-14, 15, 20, 21; 7-16 to 22, 28; T-16, 17.)

4. **Watch someone play the piece,** imagining *your* fingers, wrists, arms and torso playing. Ask a teacher or friend to play it, find an instructional video, or watch an on-line performance.

5. **Notate what you want to learn** on staff paper (T-19); or use notation software (such as Encore), which will allow you to hear what you've just transcribed.

6. **Play through the piece on a table-top or closed piano,** imagining the sound. Playing a piece without aural feedback exposes the insecure spots, so you know what still needs practice.

Develop your kinesthetic channel: drill intervals, scales, chords, arpeggios and progressions; practice technique exercises on and off the keyboard; tap or walk rhythms; and dance a lot.

VISUAL CHANNEL

Focus on how the music looks on the keyboard or staff.
Playing by heart, look at the keyboard or close your eyes and visualize the staff notation.

1. **On your music, pencil in fingerings, voicings and choreographies.** Use colored pencils to circle accidentals, label familiar chord shapes and create your own clever cues.

2. **Make keyboard diagrams.** On columns of keyboards (T-16, 17), pencil in the notes each hand will play. Label chords, scales, starting note (o), tonal center (*), middle c (m) and/or whatever helps you. (See pages 4-2, 3, 8; 5-12; 6-14, 15, 20, 21; 7-17; T-16, 17.)

3. **Create a cheat sheet** (T-18) to show the form of the piece and other helpful details. Describe how the music looks, for instance, A (a c♯ e) is a white-black-white "sandwich" chord. (See pages 6-31; 7-18 & 7-23#38; T-4, 18.)

4. **Watch someone play the piece** live or on YouTube, then finger, phrase, choreograph and interpret the piece the way you like it.

Develop your visual channel: use flash cards to learn notes, intervals and chords. Write and rewrite what you want to learn on staff paper or keyboard diagrams.

ANALYTIC CHANNEL

Focus on how the notes relate to each other and the structure of the whole piece.
Playing by heart, look at a cheat sheet, talk through the progression or do it *your* way.

1. **Analyze the music.** *What is the form?* (How many measures per phrase and phrases in the piece? Which sections or parts of sections repeat?) *What are the key, meter, tempo and feel?* (Do any of these change?) *Are there familiar melodic ideas?* (Is the melody diatonic? If it's non-diatonic, where do accidentals occur? Do you play five-finger patterns, major scales, minor scales, blues scales or sequences?) *What is the harmonic structure?* (How do the chords move? Are there unusual chords or voicings? Do any chords require accidentals?) *How do the melody and harmony relate to each other?* (Is there parallel or contrary motion? Does the melody outline a chord?) *Are there other helpful details?*

2. **Mark the music.** Pencil in fingerings, label chords and voicings, and create as many memory pegs as you like. Copy challenging measures or chord voicings on staff paper. (See page T-19.)

3. **Make a cheat sheet** (T-18). Chart the phrase structure of the song, showing the chords plus helpful melodic, harmonic and voicing details. Color code similar sections, circle unexpected chords and make up your own symbols. Deciding what to write down helps you focus on what's important. Writing down the information, reading and rereading (or rewriting) it drives the memory pegs in deeper. (Adapt page T-18's generic form—number the measures, add or subtract measures per phrase and/or tape on more sections.)

4. **Rehearse the piece in your imagination.** Tell yourself what chords to play and let your ears, fingers and memory pegs supply the melody and chord voicings.

Develop your analytic channel: learn scales (1-1 to 4; 2-1, 2, 6, 8, 9; 6-16; 7-3, 10, 11; 8-2; T-22, 23), chords (3-1, 2, 5 to 7; 4-5, 6; 6-1 to 8, 12, 13, 17 to 19; 7-1, 8, 9, 12 to 15, 23; 8-2 to 6; T-26 to 32) and progressions (3-3, 4; 6-20, 21, 26#24; 7-4 to 6, 16, 17, 22, 23; 8-1 to 6). When learning a piece, identify the key (2-5; 7-2, 44; 8-1 to 8), and play the expected scale(s), chords and progressions. Gradually expand your musical vocabulary with words describing form, meter, tempo, intervals, voicings, rhythm and other details.

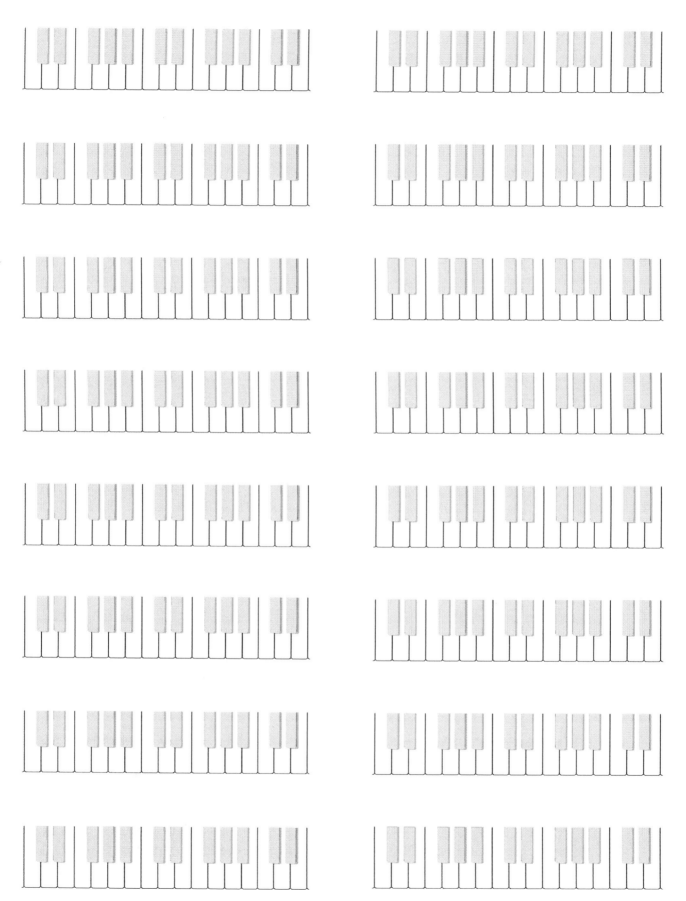

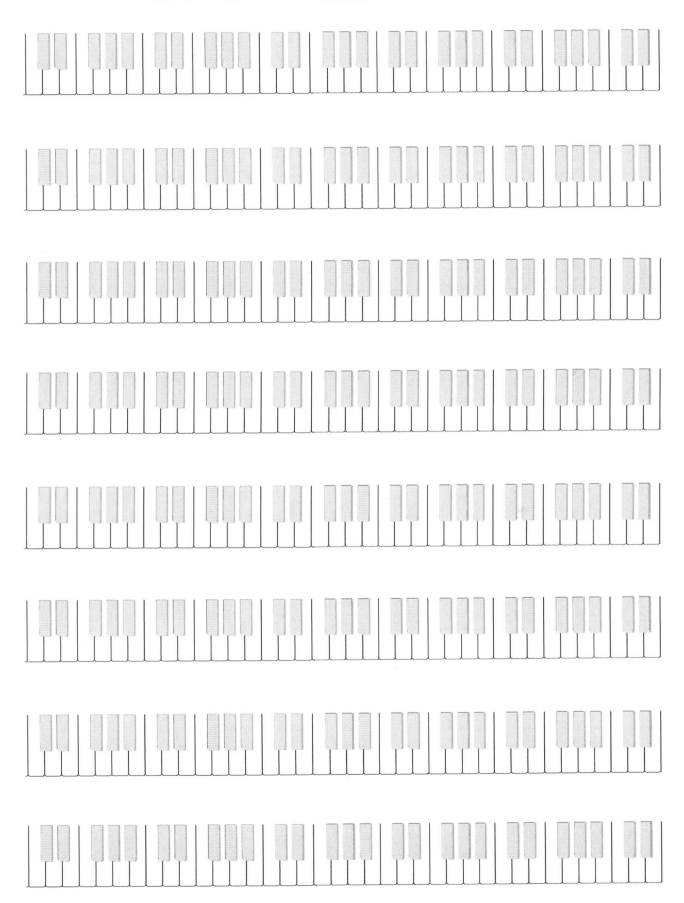

CHEAT SHEET FOR _____

NOTE-READING TOOLS

1. Use the note finder on page T-21 to find the name and keyboard location of any note on the staff.

2. Learn to see the *c*'s.
Conceptually, middle *c* stands at the center of the grand staff. Its satellite *c*'s orbit on lines and spaces around it, making all the *c*'s symmetric around middle *c*. Since the *c*'s are symmetric, any *c* you learn gives you the other clef's *c* for free!

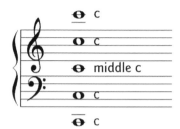

Actually, on the grand staff, you see pulled-apart staves and two middle *c*'s. This allows you to know which hand should play middle *c* or its neighboring notes. For this positive, we pianists put up with the discrepancies that arise when middle *c* appears to be two *c*'s some distance apart.

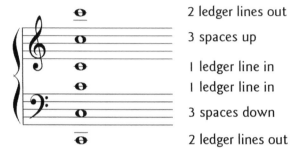

2 ledger lines out

3 spaces up

1 ledger line in

1 ledger line in

3 spaces down

2 ledger lines out

3. Learn the treble *g*'s and bass *f*'s.
Originally, the clef signs were letters.

- On the **G-clef**, the second line up is ***g***.

- On the **F-clef**, the second line down is ***f***.

Use the *c*'s, *g*'s and *f*'s as guide tones for identifying nearby notes.

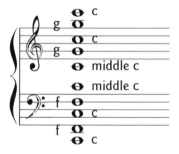

The *c*'s are symmetric.

The treble clef *g*'s and the bass clef *f*'s mirror each other.

4. Identify notes relative to the guide tones.
Learn the musical alphabet going:

- Up   = *c d e f g a b c . . .*

- Down = *c b a g f e d c . . .*

To identify a note, ask:

- Which guide tone is it near?
- Up or down?
- How far?
- What is it?

5. Learn to recognize notes and intervals on the treble and bass clefs.
Use flash cards to drill one or two *c*'s, *f*'s and/or *g*'s with their nearby notes. Gradually go on to more guide tones and their nearby notes. Also, learn the principles for seeing and feeling intervals on pages 5-1 to 5-4, then practice sight-reading both relatively and absolutely.

NOTE FINDER

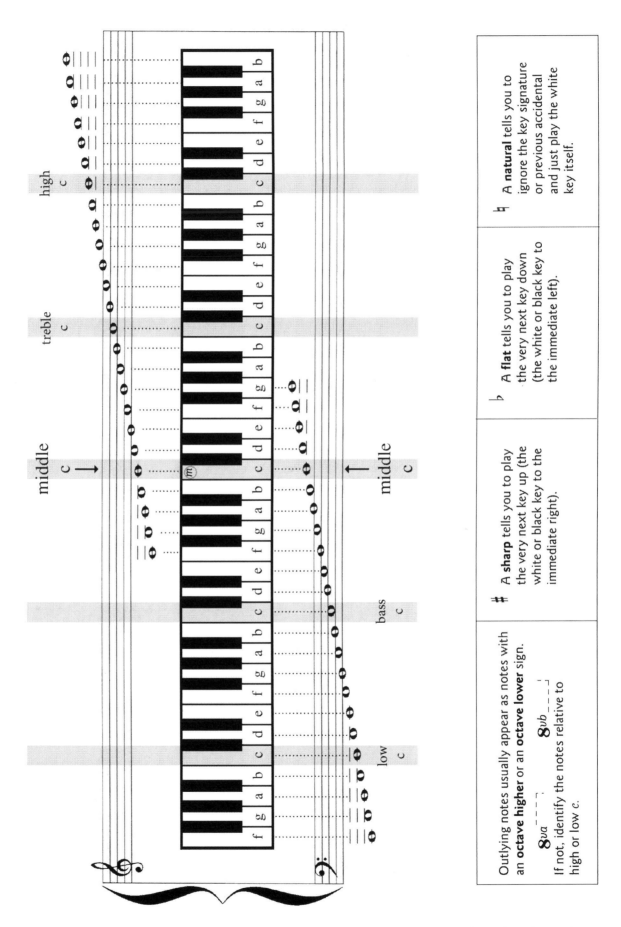

Outlying notes usually appear as notes with an **octave higher** or an **octave lower** sign.

8va ⌐ ‑ ‑ ⌐ 8vb ⌐ ‑ ‑ ⌐

If not, identify the notes relative to high or low *c*.

♯♯ A **sharp** tells you to play the very next key up (the white or black key to the immediate right).

♭ A **flat** tells you to play the very next key down (the white or black key to the immediate left).

♮ A **natural** tells you to ignore the key signature or previous accidental and just play the white key itself.

SCALE-BUILDING TOOLS

To understand how the twelve major scales relate to one another, look at the *circle of fifths* on the facing page. Following the directions below, play some or all of the major scales. Then, gradually over time, discover the many harmonic truths encoded in this amazing musical mandala.

- **At the bottom**, C major has no sharps or flats.
- **Going up by fifths** (counterclockwise) from C, each successive scale **adds a sharp**.
- **Going down by fifths** (clockwise) from C, each successive scale **adds a flat**.
- **At the top**, the three scales have double identities—one *enharmonic* spelling with sharps and the other with flats (B = C♭, F♯ =G♭ and C♯ = D♭).

Up by 5ths (counterclockwise): C G D A E B F♯ = G♭ D♭ A♭ E♭ B♭ F C

1. **Play the C scale.** Put your pinkies on *c*'s an octave apart. Not using your thumbs, play a whole-whole-half tetrachord in each hand: *c d e f / g a b c.*

2. **Play the G scale.** Replace your right hand with your left and play *g a b c*. Then, a whole-step above that, play another whole-whole-half tetrachord with your right hand: *d e f♯ g.*

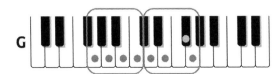

3. **Play each successive scale.** Replacing your right hand with your left, play the lower tetrachord. Then, a whole-step above it, play another whole-whole-half tetrachord with your right hand. For each new scale, keep the previous scale's sharps (or flats), but sharp the seventh scale tone.

Down by 5ths (clockwise): C F B♭ E♭ A♭ D♭ G♭ = F♯ B E A D G C

4. **Play the C scale.** Repeat step 1.

5. **Play the F scale.** Replace your left hand with your right, then move your left hand an octave down from the right hand's top note (*f*). With both pinkies on *f*'s, play a whole-whole-half tetrachord in each hand: *f g a b♭ / c d e f.*

6. **Play each successive scale.** Replace your left hand with your right, then move it an octave down from the right's top note. Play a whole-whole-half tetrachord in each hand. For every new scale, keep the previous scale's flats (or sharps), but flat the fourth scale tone.

THE CIRCLE OF FIFTHS

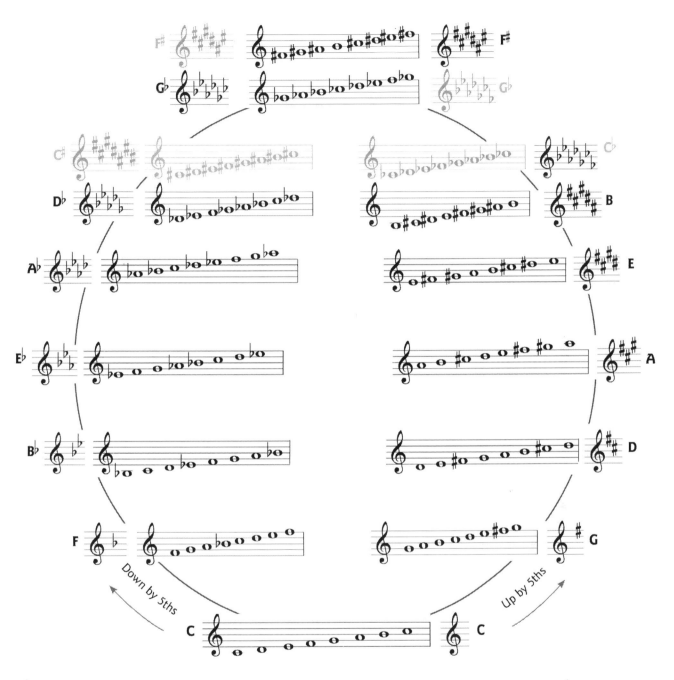

Down by 5ths

Up by 5ths

♭'s	Major	Minor
0	C	Am
1	F	Dm
2	B♭	Gm
3	E♭	Cm
4	A♭	Fm
5	D♭	B♭m
6	G♭	E♭m
7	C♭	A♭m

Major keys with sharps: From the last sharp, go up a half-step.

Major keys with flats: From the last flat, go back a flat (except for the key with just one flat—F major).

Relative minor: From the major key's tonal center, go down three half-steps.

#'s	Major	Minor
0	C	Am
1	G	Em
2	D	Bm
3	A	F#m
4	E	C#m
5	B	G#m
6	F#	D#m
7	C#	A#m

EAR-TRAINING TOOLS

Develop your relative pitch using the solfege syllables.

- **Sing songs using solfege syllables.**

  Popularized by Hungarian composer Zoltan Kodaly (1882-1967), solfege helps you hear the scale tones in relationship to the tonal center *(do)*. When you change keys, the names of the notes change, but the relationships stay the same! Once you learn a solfege pattern, use it as a memory peg for seeing (or singing) that pattern in any key. First, learn the sound of the seven diatonic tones on page 5-8, then add the five remaining double-named chromatic intervals. How does each interval sound to you?

- **Play what you sing.**

  As you play the notes *c, d* and *e*, sing their solfege syllables *(do-re-mi)*. Then, scramble the notes *(do-mi-re)* and sing them. Keep practicing until you can sing each note before striking its key. Finally, as your confidence grows, silently touch each key as you sing, only playing a note if you want to check it. Like the letters in a game of Scrabble, some notes of the scale occur more frequently than others. Once you feel comfortable with three notes, add more notes starting with the following:

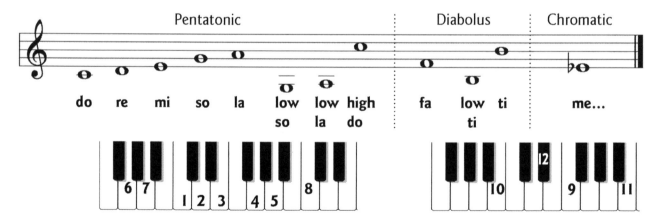

- **Systematically train your ear.**

  To practice interval recognition, melodic dictation and chord identification, seek out ear-training software, books, classes and music buddies.

Perfect Unison *do – do* *c – c*		
Minor 2nd *do – ra* *c – d♭*		
Major 2nd *do – re* *c – d*		
Minor 3rd *do – me* *c – e♭*		
Major 3rd *do – mi* *c – e*		
Perfect 4th *do – fa* *c – f*		
Diminished 5th **Augmented 4th** *do – se* or *fi* *c – g♭* or *f♯*		
Perfect 5th *do – so* *c – g*		
Minor 6th *do – le* *c – a♭*		
Major 6th *do – la* *c – a*		
Minor 7th *do – te* *c – b♭*		
Major 7th *do – ti* *c – b*		
Perfect Octave *do – do* *c – c*		

CHORD-FINDING TOOLS

THE FOUR TYPES OF TRIADS

Every triad contains a pair of 3rds—**four** half-step major 3rds and/or **three** half-step minor 3rds. Play each type of triad on *c*, learn its formula, then build it on other roots.

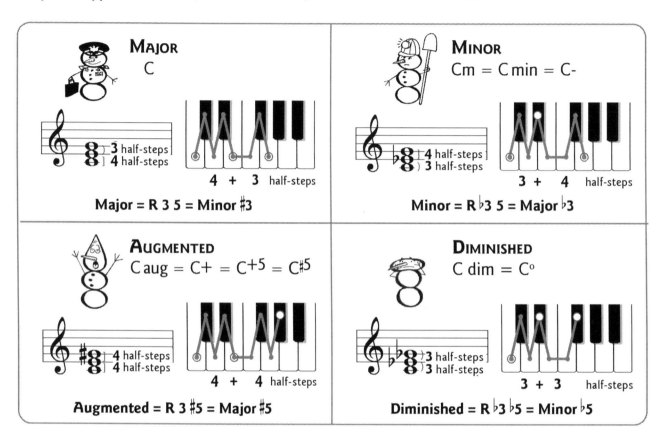

MAJOR
C

3 half-steps
4 half-steps

4 + 3 half-steps

Major = R 3 5 = Minor ♯3

MINOR
Cm = C min = C-

4 half-steps
3 half-steps

3 + 4 half-steps

Minor = R ♭3 5 = Major ♭3

AUGMENTED
C aug = C+ = C+5 = C♯5

4 half-steps
4 half-steps

4 + 4 half-steps

Augmented = R 3 ♯5 = Major ♯5

DIMINISHED
C dim = C°

3 half-steps
3 half-steps

3 + 3 half-steps

Diminished = R ♭3 ♭5 = Minor ♭5

THE TWO TYPES OF SUS CHORDS

Instead of a pair of 3rds, a *sus* (suspended) chord contains one 4th (**five** half-steps) and one 2nd (**two** half-steps). Sus chords sound open and slightly dissonant, as if suspended in aural limbo. Play each type of sus chord on *c*, learn its formula, then build it on other roots.

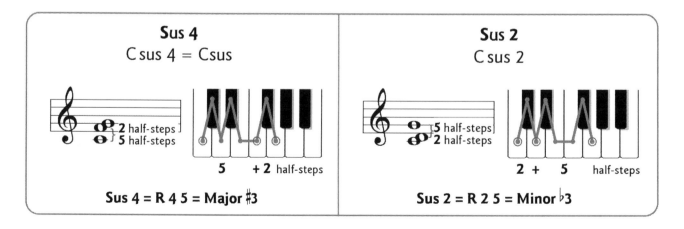

Sus 4
C sus 4 = Csus

2 half-steps
5 half-steps

5 + 2 half-steps

Sus 4 = R 4 5 = Major ♯3

Sus 2
C sus 2

5 half-steps
2 half-steps

2 + 5 half-steps

Sus 2 = R 2 5 = Minor ♭3

c e g

C	= c	e	g
Cm	= c	e♭	g
C♭	= c♭	e♭	g♭
C♭m	= c♭	e♭♭	g♭
C♯	= c♯	e♯	g♯
C♯m	= c♯	e	g♯

ceg
pronounced
"keg"

d f a

D	= d	f♯	a
Dm	= d	f	a
D♭	= d♭	f	a♭
D♭m	= d♭	f♭	a♭
D♯	= d♯	f✕	a♯
D♯m	= d♯	f♯	a♯

doctor **fa**

e g b

E	= e	g♯	b
Em	= e	g	b
E♭	= e♭	g	b♭
E♭m	= e♭	g♭	b♭

egbert

f a c

F	= f	a	c
Fm	= f	a♭	c
F♯	= f♯	a♯	c♯
F♯m	= f♯	a	c♯

face

g b d

G	= g	b	d
Gm	= g	b♭	d
G♭	= g♭	b♭	d♭
G♭m	= g♭	b♭♭	d♭
G♯	= g♯	b♯	d♯
G♯m	= g♯	b	d♯

gee bee dee

a c e

A	= a	c♯	e
Am	= a	c	e
A♭	= a♭	c	e♭
A♭m	= a♭	c♭	e♭
A♯	= a♯	c✕	e♯
A♯m	= a♯	c♯	e♯

ace

b d f "**b**irds **d**o **f**ly"

B	= b	d♯	f♯
Bm	= b	d	f♯
B♭	= b♭	d	f
B♭m	= b♭	d♭	f

Learn More Major and Minor Triads by Group

- All the majors and minors are symmetric, except the **b**irds **d**o **f**ly chords (like B = b d♯ f♯).

C-F-G and Am-Dm-Em	**A-D-E and Cm-Fm-Gm**	**B**	**Bm**
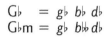	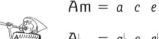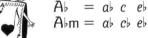	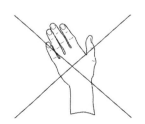	
F♯ = G♭ & D♯m = E♭m	**A♭ - D♭ - E♭ & C♯m - F♯m - G♯m**	**B♭**	**B♭m**

- Learn the all-whites and "sandwiches" (Chapters 6 and 7), then the other groups (pages T-28, 29).
- From triad to flatted or sharped triad, flat (or sharp) every note. Learn **b**irds **d**o **f**ly chords (B - B♭ & Bm - B♭m), "oreos" (A♭ - D♭ - E♭ & C♯m - F♯m - G♯m) and all-blacks (F♯ = G♭ & D♯m = E♭m) as needed.

Alignment alert!

Don't twist your hand to reach the black key(s). Instead, move into the black keys so your pinkie stays lined up with your wrist and arm. Asking your puny little pinkie to play without the support of your arm is asking for trouble.

Cool Frosty Gingerale

C · F · G
All-white majors

Look: All white
Feel: Pitchfork
Sound: Major

C

c e g

F

f a c

G

g b d

lemonADE

A · D · E
Sandwich majors

Look:
Feel: Mountain
Sound: Major

A

a c# e

D

d f# a

E

e g# b

A♭ · D♭ · E♭
Oreo majors

Look:
Feel: Valley
Sound: Major

A♭

a♭ c e♭

D♭ = C#

d♭ f a♭
c# e# g#

E♭

e♭ g b♭

birds do fly

birds do fly majors

B

Look: Root (*b* or *b♭*) is opposite color
Feel: Steep uphill or downhill tilt
Sound: Major

B♭

B = C♭

b d# f#
c♭ e♭ g♭

B♭

b♭ d f

Filthy Gingerale

F# = G♭
All-black majors

Look: All black
Feel: Pitchfork
Sound: Major

F#

G♭

f# a# c#
g♭ b♭ d♭

THE TWELVE MINOR TRIADS BY GROUP

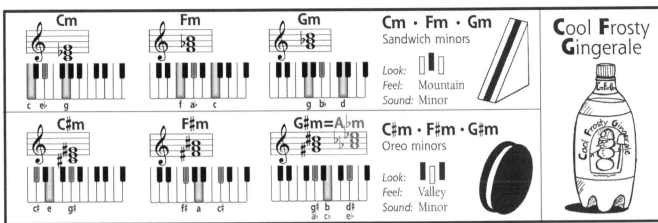

Cm · Fm · Gm
Sandwich minors

Look: ▯▮▯
Feel: Mountain
Sound: Minor

C#m · F#m · G#m
Oreo minors

Look: ▮▯▮
Feel: Valley
Sound: Minor

Cool Frosty Gingerale

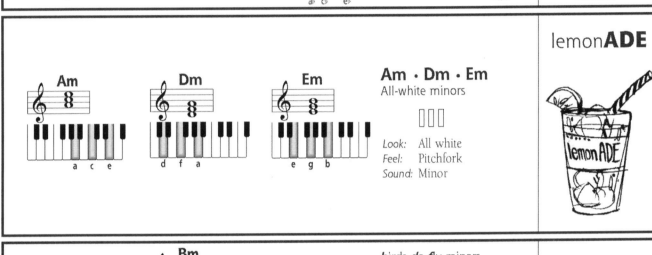

Am · Dm · Em
All-white minors

▯▯▯

Look: All white
Feel: Pitchfork
Sound: Minor

lemonADE

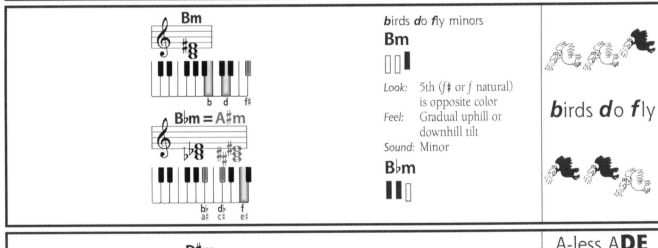

*b*irds *d*o *f*ly minors

Bm

▯▯▮

Look: 5th (*f*# or *f* natural) is opposite color
Feel: Gradual uphill or downhill tilt
Sound: Minor

B♭m

▮▮▯

A-less ADE

Cm · Fm · Gm

*b*irds *d*o *f*ly

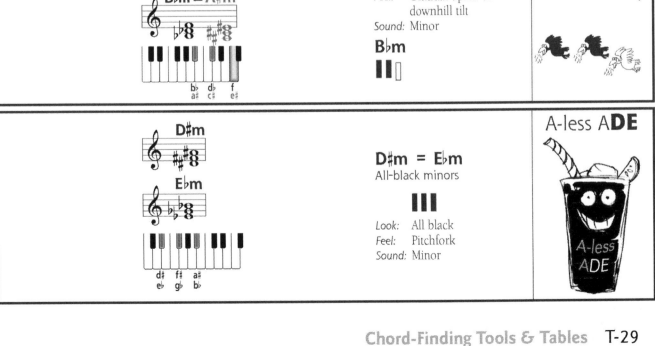

D#m = E♭m
All-black minors

▮▮▮

Look: All black
Feel: Pitchfork
Sound: Minor

FIVE TYPES OF SEVENTH CHORDS

Play these seventh chords in order, savoring each one's distinctive sound. Color code them by triad type + size of 7th, and fill in your own aural memory pegs. To find any 7th on any root, memorize the formulas. To quickly grab 7ths, drill them, starting with the most common—dominant sevenths.

Major 7th CM7	Dominant 7th C7	Minor 7th Cm7	Half-Diminished 7th Cm7♭5 or CØ7	Diminished 7th Cdim7 or C°7
Major triad	Major triad	Minor triad	Diminished triad	Diminished triad
+ half-step down from root	+ whole-step down from root	+ whole-step down from root	+ whole-step down from root	+ 3 half-steps down from root
Mr. Sandman (Intro)	"ev'ry lock that ain't ..." *(King of the Road)*			Bad guy's coming; or "... *Wave* is on its way ..."

THE TWELVE DOMINANT SEVENTHS

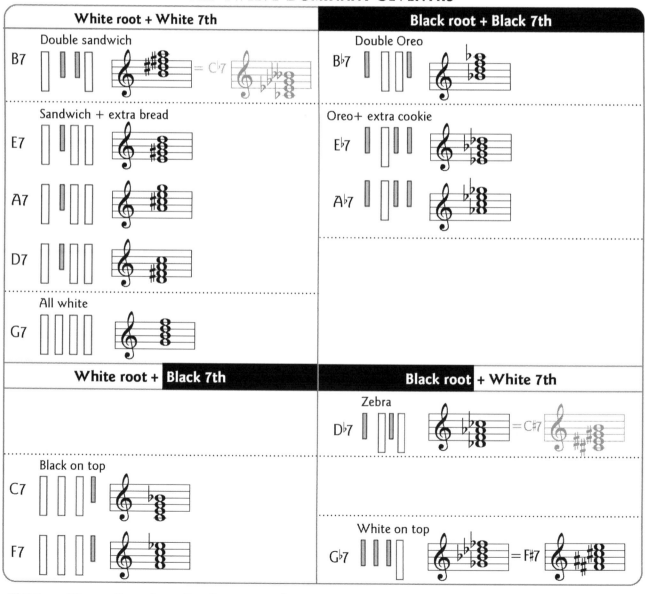

SPELLING THE COMMON CHORDS: Triads, Dominant 7ths and sus

C	c	e	g		C♯	c♯	e♯(f)	g♯	
Cm	c	e♭	g		C♯m	c♯	e	g♯	
C7	c	e	g	b♭	C♯7	c♯	e♯(f)	g♯	b
C+ or aug	c	e	g♯		C♯+ or aug	c♯	e♯(f)	g×(a)	
Co or dim	c	e♭	g♭		C♯o or dim	c♯	e	g	
Csus	c	f	g		C♯sus	c♯	f♯	g♯	

D♭	d♭	f	a♭		D	d	f♯	a	
D♭m	d♭	f♭(e)	a♭		Dm	d	f	a	
D♭7	d♭	f	a♭	c♭(b)	D7	d	f♯	a	c
D♭+ or aug	d♭	f	a		D+ or aug	d	f♯	a♯	
D♭o or dim	d♭	f♭(e)	a♭♭(g)		Do or dim	d	f	a♭	
D♭sus	d♭	g♭	a♭		Dsus	d	g	a	

E♭	e♭	g	b♭		E	e	g♯	b	
E♭m	e♭	g♭	b♭		Em	e	g	b	
E♭7	e♭	g	b♭	d♭	E7	e	g♯	b	d
E♭+ or aug	e♭	g	b		E+ or aug	e	g♯	b♯(c)	
E♭o or dim	e♭	g♭	b♭♭(a)		Eo or dim	e	g	b♭	
E♭sus	e♭	a♭	b♭		Esus	e	a	b	

F	f	a	c		F♯	f♯	a♯	c♯	
Fm	f	a♭	c		F♯m	f♯	a	c♯	
F7	f	a	c	e♭	F♯7	f♯	a♯	c♯	e
F+ or aug	f	a	c♯		F♯+ or aug	f♯	a♯	c×(d)	
Fo or dim	f	a♭	c♭(b)		F♯o or dim	f♯	a	c	
Fsus	f	b♭	c		F♯sus	f♯	b	c♯	

G♭	g♭	b♭	d♭		G	g	b	d	
G♭m	g♭	b♭♭(a)	d♭		Gm	g	b♭	d	
G♭7	g♭	b♭	d♭	f♭(e)	G7	g	b	d	f
G♭+ or aug	g♭	b♭	d		G+ or aug	g	b	d♯	
G♭o or dim	g♭	b♭♭(a)	d♭♭(c)		Go or dim	g	b♭	d♭	
G♭sus	g♭	c♭(b)	d♭		Gsus	g	c	d	

A♭	a♭	c	e♭		A	a	c♯	e	
A♭m	a♭	c♭(b)	e♭		Am	a	c	e	
A♭7	a♭	c	e♭	g♭	A7	a	c♯	e	g
A♭+ or aug	a♭	c	e		A+ or aug	a	c♯	e♯(f)	
A♭o or dim	a♭	c♭(b)	e♭♭(d)		Ao or dim	a	c	e♭	
A♭sus	a♭	d♭	e♭		Asus	a	d	e	

B♭	b♭	d	f		B	b	d♯	f♯	
B♭m	b♭	d♭	f		Bm	b	d	f♯	
B♭7	b♭	d	f	a♭	B7	b	d♯	f♯	a
B♭+ or aug	b♭	d	f♯		B+ or aug	b	d♯	f×(g)	
B♭o or dim	b♭	d♭	f♭(e)		Bo or dim	b	d	f	
B♭sus	b♭	e♭	f		Bsus	b	e	f♯	

DECIPHERING COMPLEX CHORD SYMBOLS

Play the root, then add the 3rd, 5th and specified notes from the root's major scale. Split big chords between your hands. Drop chord tones that don't sound essential (often the 5th). For slash chords, make the lower note (**C/E**) the lowest note in the bass, and voice the upper chord (**C/E**) however you like: C/e *[in Piano Freedom]*= *e g c*; C/E = *e c e g, e e g c* or ... ; C/D = *d c e g, d g c e* or ...

Symbol	Chord		Spelling					Simplification				
Includes:	**dim, ○, ø, ♭5 or –5**											
dim	dim	or ○	R ♭3	♭5				} Diminished	= R	♭3	♭5	
aug	dim7	or ○7	R ♭3	♭5	6							
sus	m7♭5	or ø7	R ♭3	♭5	♭7							
♭**5** or –**5**	7♭5	or 7-5	R 3	♭5	♭7			Dominant 7th♭5 = R	3	♭5	♭7	
♯**5** or +**5**	**aug, +, ♯5 or +5**											
○ or ø	aug (+) or +5 or ♯5		R 3	♯5				} Augmented	= R	3	♯5	
	aug 7+ or 7+ or 7+5		R 3	♯5	♭7							
	sus											
	sus	or sus 4	R 4	5				} Suspended 4th	= R	4	5	
	sus 7	or 7sus 4	R 4	5	♭7							
	sus 2		R 2	5				Suspended 2nd = R	2	5		

Symbol	Chord		Spelling					Simplification				
Does not include:	**M, Maj, 6 or add**											
	M7	or maj7	R 3	5	7							
dim	M9	or maj9	R 3	5	7	9						
aug	M7♯11	or maj7♯11	R 3	5	7	9	♯11	Major	= R	3	5	
sus	6		R 3	5	6							
♭**5** or –**5**	6/9		R 3	5	6	9						
♯**5** or +**5**	add 9	or add 2	R 3	5	9							
○ or ø	**7, 9, 11, or 13 which must include the ♭7**											
	7		R 3	5	♭7			Dominant 7th = R	3		♭7	
	9		R 3	5	♭7	9		Dominant 7th = R			♭7	
	11		R 3	5	♭7	9	11					
	13		R 3	5	♭7	9	13	or				
	7♭9		R 3	5	♭7	♭9						
	7♯9		R 3	5	♭7	♯9		Major = R	3	5		
	7♯11		R 3	5	♭7	9	♯11	Major = R	3			
	7♭13		R 3	5	♭7	9	♭13					
	m, min, or –											
	m6	or –6	R ♭3	5	6							
	m7	or –7	R ♭3	5	♭7			Minor = R	♭3	5		
	m9	or –9	R ♭3	5	♭7	9						
	m11	or –11	R ♭3	5	♭7	9	11					

Answers to Exercises

CHAPTER 1

p. 1-9 **Review**

1. Pentatonic

2. *b*

3. *b* and *d* are true; *c* and *e* are false;
   a is true or false—however you hear it.

4. *c*

5. *a, c* and *e*.

CHAPTER 2

p. 2-16 **Review**

1. *a, d* and *e*

2. ½ 2. W 3. W 4. W 5. ½

3. W – W – ½ – W – W – W – ½

4. *b, d* and *e* are true. C. P. E. Bach's piece is called
   Solfeggio (Italian for the French word *solfege)* or
   Solfeggietto (Italian for "little *solfege*").

5. *a* and *d*

6. Fourth and seventh scale tones

7. *c d e g a*

8. *b* and *d*

9. *c*

CHAPTER 3

p. 3-15 **Review**

1. *c* and *e* are true, while *a* is true if you think it is.

2. First, third and fifth scale tones.

3. Three line notes or three space notes.

4. *a, b* and *d* are true.

5. Left: *5 3 1*; right: *1 3 5*

6.
 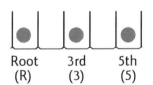

CHAPTER 4

p. 4-6 **Do you understand compound meters?**

#3. In 6/8, it looks like there are **six** beats (**6/8**) per measure and each ♪ (**1/8**) gets the beat.
   However, it feels like there are **two** beats (**2** × 3/8) per measure and each ♩. (**3/8**) gets the beat.

#5. In 12/8, it looks like there are **twelve** beats per measure and each ♪ (**1/8**) gets the beat,
   However, it feels like there are **four** (**4** × 3/8) beats per measure and each ♩. (**4** × **3/8**) gets the beat.

    1. *a* and *b*   3. *a* and *e*   5. b. *St. James Infirmary* (I went **down**)

    2. *b* and *d*   4. *b* and *d*   d. *Farmer in the Dell* (The **far**mer)

                                                       e. *Auld Lang Syne*   (Should **auld**)

CHAPTER 5

p. 5-4 **Can you name these tunes?** *Frère Jacques (Are You Sleeping?), Mulberry Bush* and *Bingo*

p. 5-16 **Review**

    1. Interval

    2. a. 4th b. 5th c. 7th d. 6th e. 8th f. 7th g. 8th h. 3rd

    3. a. 5th b. 6th c. 3rd d. 8th e. 2nd f. 7th g. 3rd h. 7th

    4. *Ten Little Indians*

       Give My Regards to Broadway

    5. *b* and *d*

CHAPTER 6

p. 6-21 **Can you find the closest position voicings for C→F→C & C→G→C** starting in all three positions?

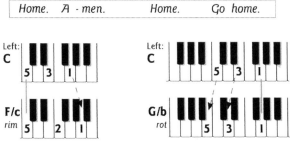

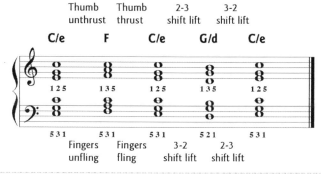
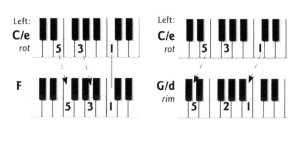

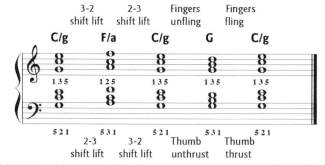
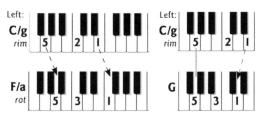

p. 6-41 **Review**

    1. C = **c e g**   F = **f a c**   G = **g b d**

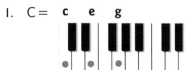
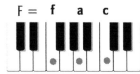
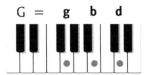

2. Am = **a c e**   Dm = **d f a**   Em = **e g b**   3. B dim = **b d f**

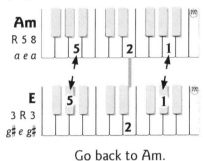

4. *a* and *d*   5. *b, c* and *e*   6. *d* (G major five-finger)

7. a. Am/c, *rot*	b. C/g, *rim*	c. F	d. Dm/f, *rot*	e. C/g, *rim*	f. G	g. F/a, *rot*	h. Em/g, *rot*
i. C/g, *rim*	j. Am/e, *rim*	k. B dim	l. Em	m. G/b, *rot*	n. F/a, *rot*	o. G	p. Dm/a, *rim*

8. *b* and *d*   9. RH `1` `3` `5`   `1` `2` `5`   `1` `3` `5`   10 and 11. See
                 LH `5` `3` `1`   `5` `3` `1`   `5` `2` `1`   page T-34, Chapter 6, for the answers.

CHAPTER 7

p. 7-2 **Can you identify the key?**

Key of C maj—*We Shall Overcome*, traditional   Key of G maj—*Jingle Bells* by John Pierpont, 1857
Key of A min—*Joshua Fit the Battle of Jericho*, trad.   Key of E min—*Sixteen Tons* by Merle Travis, 1947

p. 7-28 **To simplify.**

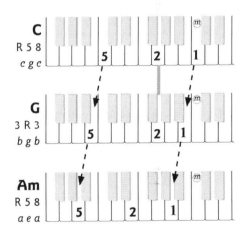

Play R58.

Anchor on finger 2, then swing fingers 5 and *1* down a half-step.

Go back to Am.

On the staff, pencil in the substituted notes.

Lift 5 and *1* down a whole-step, then put 2 on *e*.

p. 7-44 **Review**

1. To convert a minor triad to a major triad, **sharp the 3rd (or raise the 3rd a half-step).**

2.   A =   **a   c♯ e**   D = **d   f♯   a**   E = **e   g♯ b**

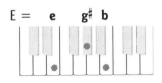

3. To convert a major triad to a minor triad, **flat the 3rd (or lower the 3rd a half-step).**

4. Cm = **c   e♭   g**   Fm =   **f   a♭   c**   Gm =   **g   b♭   d**

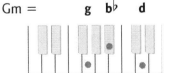

5. The key of C's relative minor is **A minor.**
   The most common type of minor scale, **harmonic** minor, sharps the **seventh** scale tone.

6. a. Aeolian   d. Harmonic   f. Melodic   g. Dorian   i. Natural (current name for Aeolian)

7. Key of A minor—*La Cumparasita* (the world's most famous tango) by Gerardo Rodriguez, 1916

    Key of G major—*St. Louis Blues* by W. C. Handy in its original key (with terrific fills), 1914

    Key of E minor—*The Anniversary Song* by Al Jolson and Saul Chaplin, with music by Ivanovici, 1946; (*Waves of the Danube* by Ion Ivanovici, 1880)

    Key of C major—*On the Sunny Side of the Street* by Jimmy McHugh and Dorothy Fields, 1930

8. *b, d,* (*e,* if it makes you smile) and *f.*

9. The closest position voicings of A minor and D minor:

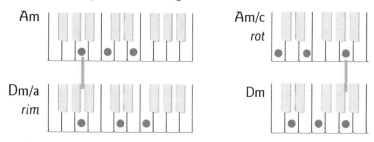

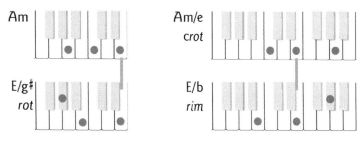

10. The closest position voicings of A minor and E:

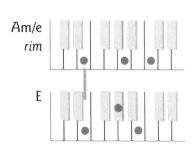

11. *a* and *c* are true, while *d* is true, if the image rings true for you.

12. G7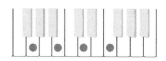

13. b. Interlinked fifths whose roots are the fifths of the next chord

    c. In the Key of C: B dim → Em → Am → Dm → G → C → F

p. 8-8 **CODA Review**

1.   Play an 8-fingered major **scale** with LH **5 4 3 2** and RH **2 3 4 5**, so you see the whole palette. Then, install default fingerings by practicing the major **scale** in each hand. Gradually learn all **1 2**.

2.   Play majors on the **first**, **fourth** and **fifth** (I, IV and V) scale tones.
Play minors on the **second**, **third** and **sixth** (ii, iii and vi) scale tones.
Play diminished on the **seventh** (vii) scale tone.

3.   Play primary chords, **I**, **IV** and **V** in closest position. Start with I in root position, then play the other chords in their most convenient **inversions**, with the root either on **top** or in the **middle**.

4.   Play dia**tonic** sevenths on each scale tone. Expect a dominant seventh on the **fifth** scale tone, for example, key of C, <u>G7</u> = **g b d f**, and key of G, <u>D7</u> = **d f♯ a c**.

5.   Inchworm closest position dia**tonic** sevenths around the **circle** of **fifths**. Expect no acci**dentals** as you simply alternate **root** position and root-in-**middle** position seventh shapes.

6.   From a major key's tonal **center**, go down **three** half-steps to find its relative **minor**. To play the harmonic minor's scale and primary chords, follow the **key** signature, but sharp the **seventh** scale tone.

BIBLIOGRAPHY

Learning Styles

Adams, Noah. *Piano Lessons: Music, Love & True Adventures* (New York: Delacorte Press, 1996).

Bruser, Madeline. *The Art of Practicing: A Guide to Making Music from the Heart* (New York: Bell Tower, 1997).

Burge, David L. *Perfect Pitch: Color Hearing for Expanded Musical Awareness* (Presque Isle, MI: American Educational Music Publications, 1983).

Mathieu, W. A. *The Listening Book: Discovering Your Own Music* (Massachusetts: Shambhala, 2011).

Ristad, Eloise. *A Soprano on her Head: Right-Side-Up Reflections on Life and Other Performances* (Moab, Utah: Real People Press, 1982).

Werner, Kenny. *Effortless Mastery: Liberating the Master Musician Within* (New Albany, IN: Jamey Aebersold Jazz, Inc., 1996).

Wilson, Frank. *Tone Deaf and All Thumbs: An Invitation to Music-Making for Late Bloomers & Non-Prodigies* (New York: Viking, 1986).

YouTube.com. Search by song for performances, instructional videos and piano lessons. If you'd like to play along, click the gearshift icon (⚙) at the bottom right of the screen and select a slower tempo.

Folk, Pop, Blues & Jazz

Aebersold, Jamey. *How to Play Jazz and Improvise, Vol. 1*, book + CD (New Albany, IN: Jamey Aebersold Jazz,Inc, 2015). Most volumes include lead sheets and play-along CDs of jazz, Latin, blues & standards for C, B♭, E♭ and bass clef instruments; a few provide transcriptions of piano comping arrangements.

Blood, Peter & Patterson, Annie, editors. *Rise Up Singing: The Group-Singing Song Book* (Bethlehem, PA: Sing Out Corporation, 2005). For ear players—the words, chords & sources (but no melodies) for 1200 songs.

Cannel, Ward & Marx, Fred. *How to Play the Piano Despite Years of Lessons: What Music Is and How to Make It* (New York: Crown & Bridge Publishers, 1976).

Citron, Alexander, arranger. *Your First Fake Book: Over 100 Songs in the Key of "C" for Keyboard, Vocal, Guitar and all "C" Instruments* (Milwaukee, WI: Hal Leonard Corporation, 1998). Many other fake books.

Collins, Ann. *Lead Lines and Chord Changes: A Practical How-To Approach for Keyboardists* (Van Nuys, CA: Alfred Music Publishing Co., 1988). Available in paperback and on Kindle.

Harrison, Mark. *The Pop Piano Book: A Complete Method for Playing Piano and Keyboards in Contemporary Styles* (Milwaukee, WI: Hal Leonard Corporation, 1998).

Kriss, Eric. *Beginning Blues Piano: Everything You Need to Know to Become an Accomplished Performer of Blues Piano* (New York, NY: Acorn Music Press, 1992). Available in paperback and on Kindle.

Musicnotes.com. Find a song you want to play, buy it in any available key and print it.

Neely, Blake. *How to Play from a Fake Book: Faking Your Own Arrangements from Melodies and Chords* (Milwaukee, WI: Hal Leonard Corporation, 1999). Available in paperback and on Kindle.

The Real Book, Vol. 1: C Edition (Milwaukee, WI: Hal Leonard Corp., 2004). Most jazz players use this fake book to study, jam and perform jazz classics & the American songbook. Created anonymously in 1975, it is now available in multiple keys, with and without lyrics, in both book and e-book form.

Classical Music

Agay, Dene, editor. *Easy Classics to Moderns: Music for Millions, Vol. 17* (New York, NY: Consolidated Music Publishers, 1991). Many volumes of graded collections are available in paperback and on Kindle.

Apel, Willi. *Harvard Dictionary of Music* (Cambridge, MA: Belknap, 1972).

Bachus, Nancy, editor. *The Classical Spirit. Books 1 and 2* + CD. (Van Nuys, CA: Alfred Publishing Co., 2001). Books include information on composers, history, styles & musical trends along with historical paintings & quotes. Pairs of graded books + CDs are also available for the *Baroque, Romantic & 20th Century* eras.

Palmer, Willard, editor. *Chopin: An Introduction to his Piano Works* + CD. (Van Nuys, CA: Alfred Publishing Co., Inc, 2004). Includes information on Chopin's style, ornamentation and pedaling, as well the editor's suggested fingering & ornamentation in gray. Part of the vast, expertly edited Alfred Masterwork Library.

SheetMusicPlus.com. Order songbooks or download sheet music you want to play.

Wachter, Claire. *The Virtual Piano Pedagogue: Online Video Master Courses* (2017). *The Art of the Phrase* and lessons on Beethoven, Chopin, Scriabin, Schumann & Russian composers at virtualpianopedagogue.com.

Wikipedia.org. The web-based, free-content encyclopedia provides many articles on musical concepts, composers, performers, songs, sonatas and lots more.

Technique & Sight Reading

Bates, Barry & Spangler, Linda. *Off-Keyboard Exercise Guide*, (Eugene, Oregon: University of Oregon Senior Citizens Piano Project, 1989). Available for free download at pianofreedom.com.

Clark, Francis, Goss, Louise & Holland, Sam. *Musical Fingers, Books 1 to 4* (Miami: Summy-Birchard Music, 1995). Exercises for both facility and musicality include: finger independence, keyboard topography, impulses, play-prepare and contrasting touch. Available in paperback and on Kindle.

Guhl, Louise. *Sight Read Successfully, Books 1-3* (San Diego: KJOS, 1991). For beginners.

Shanaphy, Edward, Isacoff, Stuart & Jordans, Julie. *Speed-Reading at the Keyboard, Vols. 1 to 3* (Katonah, New York: Ekay Music, 1987). For intermediates.

The Sound of Silence, Harmonics and the Secret Power of Music

Amaro, Ajahn. *Inner Listening: Meditation on the Sound of Silence* (Hemel Hempstead, Hertfordshire, UK: Amaravati Buddhist Monastery, 2012). Available for free download at amaravati.org.

Mathieu, W. A. *Harmonic Experience: Tonal Harmony from Its Natural Origins to Its Modern Expression* (Rochester, Vermont: Inner Traditions, 1997).

Sumedho, Ajahn. *The Sound of Silence: Selected Teachings* (Somerville, MA: Wisdom Publications, 2007). Reprinted for free distribution as *The Ajahn Sumedho Anthology, Vol. 4: The Sound of Silence* (Hemel Hempstead, Hertfordshire, UK: Amaravati Buddhist Monastery, 2014). Available at amaravati.org.

Sullivan, Anita. *The Seventh Dragon: The Riddle of Equal Temperament* (Bloomington, IN: Unlimited Publishing LLC, 2nd edition, 2005).

Tame, David. *The Secret Power of Music* (New York: Destiny Books, 1984).

accent (>): Add emphasis to that note or chord.

accidentals: Signs used to make chromatic alterations. A sharp (♯) raises the note a half-step; a flat (♭) lowers the note a half-step; a natural (♮) cancels the previous accidental. Key signature alterations affect the whole piece, while an accidental in front of a specific note only applies to that note in that measure.

adagio [Italian]: A slow, leisurely tempo.

Aeolian [Greek]: The ancient *mode* (now called natural minor) that begins on the relative major scale's 6th scale tone, such as: *a b c d e f g a*.

allegretto marcato [Italian]: Moderately fast, with distinctness and emphasis.

allegro [Italian]: A fast, cheerful tempo.

allegro con brio [Italian]: A fast, cheerful tempo with fire and spirit.

allegro moderato e marcato [Italian]: A moderately fast tempo with distinct accents.

alternate bass: Instead of always playing the root of the chord in the bass, alternate between the root and another chord tone. For instance, for a C chord, alternate between *c* and *g* (root & 5th).

andante [Italian]: A moderately slow, easy walking tempo. *A con moto:* . . . with motion or energy.

arpeggio [Italian for *harp-like*]: The notes of a chord played one at a time in succession, in any order.

articulation: The extent to which notes are separated (staccato) or connected (legato).

augmented triad: A triad with four half-steps on both the bottom and the top, *i.e., c e g♯*.

bar: A common name for a measure, i.e. an eight-bar phrase has eight measures.

bar line (|): The vertical lines that separate music into measures (or bars).

bass clef (𝄢): The "F" clef sign written at the beginning of the staff means that the pitch of the second line down from middle *c* is *f*.

bass run: Connecting two chords by moving stepwise or chordwise between their roots or other chord tones.

beam: (♩♩): The horizontal line that joins two or more 8th notes; the double line that joins 16th notes together (♪♪); etc.

beat: The unit of time in a composition that feels like the song's heartbeat. It's often set by a conductor's up and down hand movements.

binary form: A common two-part form, AABB, where the first section is played twice, then the second section is played twice.

block: To play the notes of a chord simultaneously.

blues: A genre of late 19th century African-American origin that uses *blue* notes (flatted 3rds, 5ths and 7ths) and/or the twelve bar *blues* form.

break: To play the notes of a chord in two pieces such as *c* then *e* and *g* together.

broadside: A one-sided printing on inexpensive paper used from the 16th to 19th centuries for ballads, news, ads and proclamations.

cantando [Italian]: A smooth, flowing singing tone.

cheat sheet: A page on which you write down whatever helps you remember a song.

chord: Three or more notes played at the same time or played one at a time.

chord tone: Any of the notes of a chord, i.e., the root, 3rd or 5th of a triad. For instance, C major's chord tones are *c*, *e* and *g*.

chromatically: Ascending or descending by half-steps. For instance, *c, c♯, d, d♯, e* . . .

chunk: To divide and conquer a piece, learn a small amount at a time—a measure, two measures, a phrase, a section, or whatever works for you.

circle of fifths: A circle used since the 18th century to visualize the relationship between the twelve major (and/or minor) keys and key signatures.

clef (𝄞𝄢) [French for *key*]: A sign at the beginning of a staff that designates the pitch of one note, hence all the notes. In piano music, the *treble clef* (or G-clef) labels the second line up as *g*; the *bass clef* (or F-clef) labels the second line down as *f*.

closest position voicing: Keeping the common tone(s) in the same position (bottom, middle, or top), add the missing chord tones. For instance, go from C = *c e **g*** to G = *b d **g***.

coda (⊕) [Italian for *tail*]: A section that is tagged on to the end of a piece for the sake of finality.

color tones: Notes added to a chord for extra color. To majors, you can add the 2nd or 6th, i.e., to C major, add *d* or *a*.

common time (𝄴): The most common time signature, 4/4, is called "common time."

comp: To ac*comp*any singers and other musicians, play two-handed chords rhythmically.

consecutive positions: Going from a root position triad through its two inverted positions to the root position in the next octave, or vice versa. For instance, *c e g* - *e g c* - *g c e* - *c e g*.

consonance: The agreeable effect produced by pleasing combinations of tones.

contrary motion: Two voices that move in opposite directions, one going up, the other down.

country lick: Adding the 2nd to a chord, either as a grace note (play *d* before the C chord) or as a pull-off (play *d* on the beat with the C chord, then pull it off while still holding C).

crescendo (<) [Italian]: Gradually get louder.

crossover: Move up or down the keyboard by playing one hand, crossing over with the other, then pulling the first hand under to start again.

crush: Play neighboring notes together. For instance, over a C chord, play both *e♭* and *e*.

cut time (𝄵): Music that looks like 4/4 (the quarter note gets the beat and there are four beats per measure) but feels like 2/2 (the half note gets the beat and there are two beats per measure).

da capo al fine [Italian], abbrev. **D.C. al fine**: Tells you to repeat from the beginning and end at the word, "*Fine*."

dal segno al fine [Italian] abbrev. **D.S. al fine**: Tells you to repeat from the *segno* (𝄋) and play up to the word, "*Fine*."

damper pedal: Depressing the right pedal raises the dampers, allowing the strings to vibrate freely and harmonics to ring out.

D.C. al fine [Italian]: abbreviation for **da capo al fine**.

decrescendo (>): [Italian] abbrev. **decresc**: Gradually get softer. Same as *diminuendo*.

diabolus in musica [Latin for *devil in music*]: A medieval name for the interval with six half-steps, which has two names and spellings: diminished 5th (*c* − *g♭*) = augmented fourth (*c* − *f♯*).

diatonic [Greek for *through the tones*]: A scale that uses just whole-steps and half-steps, such as a major scale (*c* to *c* on the white keys) or any of its modes (*a* to *a* or *d* to *d*, on the white keys).

diminished seventh (°7 or **dim7**): A four-note stack of minor thirds: three half-steps + three half-steps + three half-steps. For instance, B°7 = B dim7 = *b d f a♭*.

diminished triad (° or **dim**): A triad that has three half-steps on the bottom and three half-steps on top. For instance, B° = B dim = *b d f*.

diminuendo [Italian], abbrev. **dim** or **dimin**: Gradually get softer. Same as *decrescendo*.

dissonance: The disagreeable effect produced by a combination of tones that requires resolution.

dolce [Italian]: Sweetly, softly.

dominant seventh: A major triad plus a minor 3rd, (the flatted 7th scale tone), such as C7 = *c e g b♭*.

Dorian [Greek]: A *mode* of a scale that begins on a major scale's second scale tone, for instance, the all-white scale from *d* to *d*.

double bar (𝄁): Two vertical lines signifying the end of a piece or section.

doubles: When two voices in a chord sound the same note in any octave. For instance, C = ***c*** *e g **c***.

downbeat: The accented first beat of each measure.

D.S. al fine [Italian], abbrev. for **dal segno al fine**.

drone: A long sustained note in the bass that repeats over and over.

dynamics: The varying degrees of loudness and intensity in music, such as *piano* (soft), *forte* (loud) and *crescendo* (get louder).

enharmonic: Two names for the same note, scale or key. For instance, *d♭* = *c♯* or D♭ major = C♯ major.

f : The abbreviation for **forte**.

fake book: A collection of songs that show melodies with lyrics and chord symbols (rather than grand staff notation).

fanfare [French for *to blow trumpets*]: A short tune for brass instruments used for ceremonial, hunting and military purposes.

fifth+octave: The 5 R 3 5 chord voicing. For instance, C fifth+triad = *g c e g*.

fine [Italian]: End, close. A sign that tells you where to end a piece, often appearing as **D.C. al fine** or **D.S. al fine**.

fingers fling [*Piano Freedom*]: Moving from a root position chord, anchor on the thumb, fling the fingers a step away, then play *5 3 1* or *1 3 5*. For example, left C (*c e g*) to root-on-top G (*b d g*).

first inversion: A chord that's been rearranged so that the root is on the top (3rd-5th-**root**). For example, C = *e g c*. In *Piano Freedom*, these are called **root-on-top** (abbreviated as ***rot***).

five-finger pattern (abbrev. as **5fp**): The first five notes of a major or minor scale. (C five-finger = *c d e f g*; Am five-finger pattern = *a b c d e*)

five-finger position: Having a hand's five fingers poised over any five neighboring keys. For instance: *c d e f g, a b c d e, f g a b c*...

flag: A curlicue on a stem's right that indicates an eighth note (♪), sixteenth (♬) or shorter note.

flat (♭): Lower a note a *half-step* (g to g♭, or f to e).

forte [Italian], abbrev. **f**: Loud, strong.

frequency: The number of vibrations or cycles per second made by a string or column of air.

fundamental: The lowest tone produced by a vibrating string that generates *overtones*.

gavotte: A lively French peasant dance in moderate 4/4 that originated in the 17th century.

grace note (♪): An ornamental note printed in small type that tells you to subtract the time of the note from that of the adjacent note.

grand staff: A combination staff that includes a treble staff (higher notes) and a bass staff (lower notes) connected by a curved brace.

guide tones: The use of treble clef *c*'s and *g*'s as well as bass clef *c*'s and *f*'s to identify nearby notes.

guitar chords: The chord symbols for a song, either shown alone or above the song's lyrics.

half-diminished seventh (**m7♭5** or **⌀7**): A seventh chord with 3 half-steps + 3 half-steps + 4 half-steps. For instance, Bm7♭5 = *b d f a*.

half-step: From one key to the very next key, white or black, with no keys in-between. For instance, *e* to *f*, *c* to *c♯*, *d♭* to *c*.

harmonic minor: The common type of minor scale keeps the key signature of the relative major (three half-steps up), but sharps its seventh scale tone (such as *a b c d e, f g♯ a*).

harmony: The combination of two or more tones to form chords, either consonant or dissonant; also, the structure of chords in a piece of music.

inchworm: [*Piano Freedom*]: Playing closest position sevenths around the circle of 5ths.

interval: The distance in pitch between two tones, either sounded at the same time (harmonic interval) or sounded one at a time (melodic interval). For instance, 2nds, 3rds, 4ths and 5ths.

inversion: Instead of a root position chord (*c e g*), rearrange the notes of the chord, so that either the 3rd or 5th is on the bottom (*e g c* or *g c e*).

Ionian [Greek]: The ancient *mode* of a scale (now called major), for instance, the all-white scale from *c* to *c*.

Key of C: In the Key of C, the basic palette of notes is *c d e f g a b*, and the note *c* is the tonal center that feels like home.

key signature: The sharps or flats that appear after the clef sign at the beginning of each staff to indicate the key of the piece. For instance, 𝄞♯ =G major or E minor; 𝄞♭ =F maj or D min.

lead sheet (or **lead line**): The melody line, lyrics and chord symbols for a song.

ledger lines (or **leger**): Little lines added below or above the five-line clef to show middle *c*, the notes around it and very low or high notes.

legato (♩♩)[Italian]: To play notes smoothly and connected, with no break in between them.

legato pedal (‿ ˄ ‿): As you play the first chord, depress the right pedal. Still holding down the pedal, lift your fingers and play the next chord.

legerement [French]: Lightly, briskly.

lick: A short repeated melodic pattern in a pop, rock or jazz solo.

Locrian [Greek]: A *mode* of a scale that begins on the major scale's seventh scale tone, for instance, the all-white scale from *b* to *b*.

Lydian [Greek]: A *mode* of a scale that begins on the major scale's fourth scale tone, for instance, the all-white scale from *f* to *f*.

major 3rd: A four half-step 3rd, such as, the bottom interval of a major triad (*c e g*) or the top interval of a minor triad (*d f a*).

major five-finger pattern: The first five notes of a major scale played by fingers *1 2 3 4* and *5.*

major scale: A diatonic scale that steps up in the following order: whole, whole, half, whole, whole, whole, half. For instance, *c d e f g a b c.*

major seventh: A major triad plus a major 3rd, (the 7th scale tone), such as CM7 = *c e g b.*

major triad: A triad with a four half-step 3rd on the bottom and a three half-step 3rd on top (for instance, C = *c e g*).

measure: In written music, the notes are divided into box-like units called measures. In each complete measure, the first note is normally played louder than the others (accented).

melody: A succession of musical tones.

meter: The basic grouping of regularly occurring accents as determined by the time signature (for instance, 3/4 or 4/4).

mezzo [Italian]: Half. *Mezzo forte* (abbrev. *mf*) half loud, moderately *forte. Mezzo piano* (abbrev. *mp*), medium soft, moderately *piano.* In order of increasing loudness: *p* —< *mp* —< *mf* —< *f.*

mf [Italian], abbrev. for **mezzo forte:** Medium loud.

middle *c*: The *c* that's exactly in the middle of the grand staff and near the middle of the piano.

minor 3rd: A three half-step 3rd. For instance, the bottom interval of a minor triad (*d f a*) and the top interval of a major triad (*c e g*).

minor five-finger pattern: The first five notes of a minor scale played by fingers *1 2 3 4* and *5.*

minor scale: A scale whose third note is a minor 3rd (three half-steps) away from its starting note, such as A natural minor (*a b c d e f g a*). A harmonic minor raises the natural minor's seventh scale tone (*a b c d e f g♯ a*). A melodic minor scale raises the sixth and seventh scale tones ascending, then reverts to the natural minor descending (*a b c d e f♯ g♯ a g f e d c b a*).

minor seventh: A minor triad plus a minor 3rd (the flatted 7th scale tone, for instance Cm7 = *c e♭ g b♭*).

minor triad: A triad that has a three half-step 3rd on the bottom and a four half-step 3rd on top, such as Dm = *d f a.*

mitten shape [*Piano Freedom*]: Play an inverted triad (C/g = *g c e*) with a stretch between your thumb and pointer as if you were wearing a mitten.

Mixolydian [Greek]: A mode of a scale that begins on the major scale's fifth scale tone, for instance, play the notes of the all-white C scale from *g* to *g.*

mode: A diatonic scale used in ancient Greece that starts and ends on any of a major scale's notes. For example, the all-white modes are: C Ionian, D Dorian, E Phyrgian, F Lydian, G Mixolydian, A Aeolian and B Locrian.

moto [Italian]: With motion, speed, movement or energy.

mp [Italian], abbreviation for **mezzo piano:** Medium soft (louder than *piano* but softer than *forte*).

ms.: Abbreviation for measure.

mysterioso: Play the song mysteriously.

natural (♮): The sign placed to the left of a note that cancels a previous accidental; a note that is neither sharped nor flatted.

natural minor: Previously known as Aeolian, this minor scale keeps the key signature of its relative major (three half-steps up). Am = *a b c d e f g*

note finder [*Piano Freedom*, page T-21]: A chart that shows the name and keyboard location of any note on the staff.

note palette [*Piano Freedom*]: All the notes in a particular song.

octave: The interval from one note to the eighth tone of its major scale, like *c* to the next *c.*

oom-pah-pah [*Piano Freedom*]: The loud-soft-soft rhythmic pattern of a song in 3/4 time.

open voicings: Voicings of a chord that leave out one or more consecutive chord tones, and sound open and spacious. For instance, C = *c g c'* or *c g e'*.

ostinato [Italian *obstinate* means *persistent*]: A short phrase, usually in the bass, that repeats persistently at the same pitch, in the same voice.

overtone: When a string or column of air vibrates, it produces a variety of tones: its lowest tone (the *fundamental*) plus higher tones (*overtones*).

p [Italian], abbreviation for **piano**: Soft.

parallel 3rds: A series of notes that remain a 3rd apart. For instance, *c e*, *d f*, *e g* . . .

parallel motion: When two or more notes move in the same direction, by the same pattern of intervals, for instance, LH *c g a* with RH *g d e*.

parallel triads: A series of same-shaped triads.

pedal: The right pedal, the **damper pedal**, lifts the dampers off the strings, allowing the notes to keep sounding and overtones to ring out sympathetically.

pentatonic scale: A five-tone scale that contains no half-steps, such as, *c d e g a* or any five consecutive black keys.

pesante [Italian]: Heavy, ponderous, firm.

phrase: The musical equivalent of a sentence or clause.

Phyrgian [Greek]: A mode of a scale that begins on the major scale's third scale tone, for instance, the all-white scale from *e* to *e*.

pianissimo [Italian], abbrev. **pp**: Very soft.

piano [Italian]: 1. Soft (abbrev. **p**). 2. *Pianoforte*, "Soft-loud," the full name for the keyboard instrument that uses hammers to strike strings.

pitchfork shape [*Piano Freedom*]: The look and feel of the hand when grabbing a root position triad. For instance, shaping C major (*c e g*) with the thumb, middle finger and pinkie.

play-prepare [*Musical Fingers* by Clark, Goss & Holland]: Use the energy of playing the first gesture to prepare for the next gesture.

polyphony: Like a round or fugue, a musical texture in which all of the voice parts are equally important.

power chord: The R 5 8 chord voicing. For instance, C power chord = *c g c*.

pp [Italian], abbreviation for **pianissimo**: Very soft.

prelude: Originally, an introductory movement of a piece. In the 19th century, Chopin began to write preludes as stand-alone character pieces.

primo: In a duet, the person on piano right, who usually plays the melody.

progression: A series of chords that make up the harmony of a phrase, section or song.

pull off: Pull off or relase a note from a chord while the other notes continue to sound.

relative major: The major key three half-steps up from a minor, that shares its key signature, *e.g*, the relative major of A minor is C major.

relative minor: The minor key three half-steps down from a major, that shares its key signature, *i.e*, the relative minor of C major is A minor.

repeat sign: The left-facing sign (𝄇) tells you to return to the previous right-facing sign (𝄆) and repeat that section; or, if no right-facing repeat sign appears, to return to the beginning and repeat from there.

rest (𝄻 𝄼 𝄽 𝄾 𝄿): A pause or interval of silence between two notes and any of the signs denoting that silence.

rhythm grid [*Piano Freedom*]: A manipulative aid to use when figuring out how to count rhythms. (See pages T-7 to 8.)

rhythmic pedal: (└────┘) Depressing the right foot pedal and simultaneously playing the chord. Used for rhythmic, dancelike pieces.

rim [*Piano Freedom*]: An abbreviation for root-in-**m**iddle (second inversion), e.g. C *rim* = *g **c** e*.

ritard [Italian]: Slow down.

root (R): The fundamental note of a chord, regardless of its voicing. For instance, *c* is the root of any voicing of the C major chord (*c e g*, *e g **c***, *g **c** e*).

root-in-middle position [*Piano Freedom*], (abbrev. *rim*): The second inversion of a root position triad, which has the root in the middle. For instance, C *rim* = *g **c** e*.

root-on-top position [*Piano Freedom*], (abbrev. *rot*): The first inversion of a root position triad, with the root on top, for instance, C *rot* = *e g **c***.

root position: The chord's root is on the bottom of a stack of 3rds, for instance, C = *c e g*.

rot [*Piano Freedom*]: An abbreviation for root-on-top, a triad in its first inversion, for instance, C *rot* = *e g **c***.

scale [Latin for *stairs* or *ladder*]: A series of notes that ascend or descend in a fixed order, for instance, C major (*c d e f g a b c*) or C major pentatonic scale (*c d e g a*).

scherzando [Italian]: Playful.

second inversion: A chord that has been rearranged, so that the root is in the middle (5th **root** 3rd), for instance, C = *g **c** e*. In *Piano Freedom*, second inversion triads are referred to as **root-in-middle** (abbreviated *rim*).

secondo: In duet music, the part that accompanies the melody. At the piano, the person on piano left usually plays the secondo.

sequence: A repetition of a pattern of intervals, but starting on a different note, such as, *c d e, d e f, g a b*.

seventh chord: A four-note chord that includes a scale's first, third, fifth and seventh degrees, for instance, C major 7th = *c e g b*. On the white keys, three side-by-side skips; on the staff, four consecutive line notes or four space notes.

sforzando [Italian], abbrev. **sfz**: Perform the note(s) with a special stress or sudden emphasis.

sharp (♯): Raise a note a half-step.

skip: The melodic interval of a 3rd, for instance, play *c*, then *skip* over the neighboring white key to play *e* or *e♭*. On the staff, *skip* from one line note to the next line note, or from one space note the to next space note.

slash notation: A way to indicate both the basic chord (on the left of the slash—**C**/e or **C**/E) and the lowest note in the bass (on the right of the slash—C/**e** or C/**E**). This includes inversions (C/e or C/E = *e g c*) and chords with non-chord tones in the bass (C/D = *d c e g* or *d g c e*).

solfege [French, from Italian *solfeggio*]: The use of so(l)-fa syllables to learn scales and melodies.

solo: A piece played by one performer, or a passage in which one performer stands out.

staccato (♩̣ ♩̇) [Italian]: A dot over or under a note tells you to play the note in a shortened, detached manner.

stay: Repeat the same note, staying on the same pitch for the repetition (*d – d*).

step: The melodic interval of a 2nd. For instance, play *c*, then *step* to the neighboring white or black key (*c* to *c♯*—a *half-step*) or the next white key (*c* to *d*—a *whole-step*). On the staff, *step* from a line note to the nearest space note, or a space note to the nearest line note.

straight eighths (♩ ♩): Playing each pair of eighth notes as two notes of equal duration. Used in classical music, rock and ragtime.

suspended (sus): A chord without a 3rd, that has either a 4th (Csus4 = Csus = *c f g*) or a 2nd (Csus2 = *c d g*). Sus chords sound open and slightly dissonant, as if suspended in aural limbo.

swung eighths (♩♩ = ♩ ♪): Playing each pair of eighth notes unevenly, the first one long and the second one shorter, as if you were skipping rather than walking. Used in jazz, blues and swing music.

syncopated, syncopation: Rhythmically exciting music that doesn't put the accents where you expect them. You might rest on a normally accented beat, or stress normally unaccented beats or parts of beats.

tempo: The rate or speed at which you play a piece.

tenuto (♩̱ ♩̄), [Italian]: A dash over or under a note tells you to hold the note for its full time value.

tetrachord [Greek for *four strings*]: A four-note scale pattern, for instance, the major scale has two whole-whole-half tetrachords: *c d e f* and *g a b c*.

thumb thrust [*Piano Freedom*]: A choreography for moving between chords. For instance, from left hand C=*c e g* with *5 3 1*, thrust your thumb a step up to play F=*c f a* with *5 2 1*.

time signature ($\frac{3}{4}$ $\frac{4}{4}$): The numbers at the beginning of a piece that indicate the meter. The lower number indicates the kind of note that gets the beat ($^1/_4$ = quarter note), and the upper number indicates how many beats per measure (**3** in $^3/_4$ or **4** in $^4/_4$).

tonal center [shown as ✱ in *Piano Freedom*]: The main tone or home base, where a melody sometimes starts, often returns and almost always ends.

treble clef (𝄞): The "*G*" clef sign, written at the beginning of the staff, tells you that the second line up from middle *c* is *g*. Usually, the right hand plays treble clef notes.

triad [German for *three tones*]: A three-note chord that includes a scale's first, third and fifth tones, for instance, C = *c e g*. On the white keys, side-by-side skips; on the staff, three consecutive line notes or space notes.

triad+octave: The R 3 5 8 chord voicing. For instance, C triad+octave = *c e g c*.

trill (*tr*) [German *Triller;* Italian *trillo*]: The rapid alternation of two notes a whole- or half-step apart. In the 16th century, these notes were either written out or improvised. Since the 17th century, a symbol tells us to play the ornament, but leaves the exact number and rhythm of the repetitions up to the performer.

twelve bar blues: A common chord progression used in popular music since the early 1900s.

The oldest of the many variants is:

C	C	C	C
F	F	C	C
G	G	C	C

upbeat: One (or several) unaccented notes of a melody that come before the first bar line, for instance:

vamp: A short chord progression that an accompanist repeats until a singer (or instrumentalist) begins to sing (or play).

vivace [Italian]: A fast, lively tempo.

voicing: How the tones of a particular chord are arranged, for instance, C major triad as: *c e g, c e g c, e g c,* or a spacious "open voicing," like *c g e* or *c g c*.

walking bass: Left hand accompaniment style that often walks stepwise from one chord's root to the next chord's root (for instance, C to G as *c c b a | g* ...). More complex variants can start on any chord tone, then move stepwise or chordwise to land on any chord tone of the next chord.

waltz: A $^3/_4$ time dance popular since about 1800, and the music written for it.

wheel of fifths [*Piano Freedom*, pages 8-5 and 8-6]: A wheel that shows a key's seven diatonic chords, their "positions" in the key (I, ii, iii . . .) and common chord travel in that key.

whole-step: An interval made up of two half-steps, for instance, two notes with one black key between them (*c* to *d*), or two notes with one white key between them (*c♯* to *d♯* or *b* to *c♯*).

WIGGLES AND SQUIGGLES

Notes	o	d.	d	♩	♪	♬
	whole 4 beats	dotted half 3 beats	half 2 beats	quarter 1 beat	eighth 1/2 beat	sixteenth 1/4 beat
Rests	▬	▬·	▬	𝄽	𝄾	𝄿

dot (·): Add half again as much   **beam**: ♪♪ = 1 beat = ♬♬

𝄞 𝄢	**clef signs:**	Identify one pitch of the staff, hence all pitches.

treble clef — G-clef   bass clef — F-clef

4/4 3/4 2/4	**time signatures:**	**4** beats per measure / 1/4 (♩) gets the beat **3** or **2** beats per measure / 1/4 (♩) gets the beat

C ¢	**common time:** **cut time:**	Another name for 4/4 time (four ♩'s per measure). Looks like 4/4 (**C**), feels cut in half (**¢**), like 2/2 (two ♩'s per measure).

♯ ♭ ♮	**sharp** or **flat:** **natural:**	Raise or lower the note a half-step. Cancel the previous accidental sign.

𝄪 𝄫	**double sharp** or **double flat:**	Raise or lower the note a whole-step.

✳ ⓜ ○ →	**tonal center** (✳), **middle c** (ⓜ), **first note** (○) or **falling 5th** (→): *Piano Freedom* symbols	

⌢	**slur:** Play two or more different notes in a smooth, connected (legato) manner. **tie:** For two notes at the same pitch, hold the note for the sum of their time values.	

♩·	**staccato:**	Play the note in a very short, bouncy, detached manner.

♩‾	**tenuto:**	Hold the note for its full time value.

♩>	**accent:**	Play the note with extra emphasis.

♩♩ = ♩·♪	**swung eighths:**	Play the first eighth note of each pair longer than the second one, as if you were skipping rather than walking.

< >	**crescendo:** **decrescendo:**	Get louder (open up the sound). Get softer (close down the sound).

𝄆 𝄇	**repeat signs:**	When you reach the left-facing repeat sign, repeat the section starting at the right-facing repeat sign or at the beginning.

⌐1. ⌐2.	**first ending:** **second ending:**	Play up to the 𝄇, then repeat from the beginning or the 𝄆. This time, skip the first ending and jump to the second ending.

𝄋	**segno:**	When you see *D.S. al fine* (*dal segno al fine*) at the end of a piece, go back to the 𝄋 sign and play up to the word "*fine*."

⟅	**rolled chord:**	Play the notes consecutively from bottom to top, as an arpeggio.

Intervals	Unison 2nd 3rd 4th 5th 6th 7th Octave

INDEX OF KEY CONCEPTS

INDEX OF WAYS TO PLAY

INDEX OF WAYS TO PLAY (continued)

INDEX OF SONGS

DRILLS CHECKLIST

_____ 1. **Pentatonic Crossovers**, 1-4

_____ 2. **C Major Scale**, 2-8

_____ 3. **Triad Crossovers**, 3-6

4. **Triad + Octave Voicings**

   _____ A. Triad + Octave (R 3 5 8), 4-10

   _____ B. Power Chord (R 5 8), 4-11

   _____ C. Fifth + Triad (5 R 3 5), 4-12

_____ 5. **Intervals of the Major Scale**, 5-10

6. **All-White Triads**

   _____ A. All-White Triads, 6-12

   _____ B. Left Hand C→F→C and C→G→C Jumping, 6-14

   _____ C. Five-Finger Patterns for C, F & G and Am, Dm & Em, 6-16

   _____ D1. All-White Root-on-Top Triads _(rot)_, 6-18

   _____ D2. All-White Root-in-Middle Triads _(rim)_, 6-19

   _____ E. Closest Position Voicings for C→F→C and C→G→C, 6-20

   _____ F. Consecutive Positions of All-White Triads, 6-22

   _____ G. Adding Pedal Power, 6-23

7. **Sandwich Majors and Minors**

   _____ A. Sandwich Triads, 7-8

   _____ B. Left Hand Sandwich Jumping, 7-9

   _____ C. Major and Minor Five-Finger Patterns for C, F & G and A, D & E, 7-10

   _____ D1. Sandwich Root-on-Top Triads _(rot)_, 7-12

   _____ D2. Sandwich Root-in-Middle Triads _(rim)_, 7-13

   _____ E. Dominant Seventh Crossovers, 7-14

   _____ F1. Magic Formula: Closest Position of C→F→G7, 7-16

   _____ G. Inchworm: Closest Position Diatonic Sevenths Falling by Fifths, 7-17

To turn anything else you want to learn into a memory peg, just drill it in.

Find music you love, apply the drills and skills you've learned,
and experience the joy of piano freedom.
For more ways to live out your piano dreams,
including free lessons, videos, printables, and more,
visit us online:

www.pianofreedom.com

Made in the USA
Columbia, SC
14 November 2022